D1264978

PETER STERRY
PLATONIST AND PURITAN
1613–1672

*A Biographical and Critical Study with
passages selected from his Writings*

BY

VIVIAN DE SOLA PINTO

GREENWOOD PRESS, PUBLISHERS
NEW YORK   1968

First published, 1934,
by Cambridge University Press

Reprinted with the permission of
Cambridge University Press

First Greenwood reprinting, 1968

Library of Congress catalogue card number: 69-10146

Printed in the United States of America

PATRI DILECTISSIMO
HUNC LIBRUM
DEDICO

It is long since I heard much of the name and fame of Mr *Peter Sterry*, long chaplain to *Robert* Lord *Brook*, and after to *Oliver Cromwel* when he was *Protector* (as then called). His common fame was, that his Preaching was such as none or few could understand: which incensed my desire to have heard him, of which I still mist, though I oft attempted it. But now since his death, while my Book is in the Press unfinished, a posthumous tractate of his cometh forth of *Free-will*: upon perusal of which I find in him the same notions (for so far as he meddleth with the same subjects) as in Sr *H. Vane*; and somewhat of what Dr *Gibbon* seemeth to deliver in his Scheme; but all handled with much more *strength* of *parts* and *raptures* of highest *devotion*, and great *candour* towards all others, than I expected. His Preface is a most excellent Perswasive to Universal Charity: Love was never more extolled than throughout his Book. Doubtless his head was strong, his wit admirably pregnant, his searching studies hard and sublime, and, I think, his heart replenished with holy Love to God, and great charity, moderation, and peaceableness towards men: In so much that I heartily repent that I so far believed fame as to think somewhat hardlier or less charitably of him and his few adherents than I now hope they did deserve. *Hasty judging*, and *believing fame* is a cause of unspeakable hurt to the world, and injury to our brethren. But I find it is no wonder that he was understood by few, For his sublime and philosophical notions, met not with many Auditors, so well studied in those things as to be capable of understanding them. It is a great inconvenience to men of extraordinary discoveries and sublimity, that they must speak to very few. RICHARD BAXTER

Catholick Theologie...London...1675. The Second Part, p. 107

There was a man in his [Henry More's] time who deserves to be remembered both as a mystic and a very profound thinker; one who had many of the qualities of Tauler and Böhme, and yet who belonged emphatically to his own age...Peter Sterry...is one of those men into whose writings few have looked seriously without carrying away some impressions which they would be very sorry to lose...The Reader may be utterly lost in the wealth of Sterry's thoughts and imaginations; he will seldom have to complain of poverty or barrenness...Sterry is little read...but a better knowledge of him would often throw light upon the work of his contemporaries, and would enable us to prize them more.

F. D. MAURICE
Modern Philosophy, 1862, pp. 350, 351

CONTENTS

PREFACE

Six years ago I was led to begin a study of the writings and of the life of Peter Sterry by reading the essay on him in Mr F. J. Powicke's *The Cambridge Platonists* and the article by Miss Charlotte Fell Smith in the *Dictionary of National Biography*. I was deeply impressed by the beauty of his style, and by the fine quality of his thought, and I was surprised that he had been so completely forgotten. I formed the plan of drawing the attention of modern readers to his work, and, after some consideration, came to the conclusion that the best way of presenting him to a modern audience would be by means of a book consisting of a biography and critical study forming an introduction to a selection of passages from his writings. I have not reprinted any of his sermons *in extenso*, as I considered that their elaborate scholastic structure with its numerous subdivisions would be a stumbling-block to the modern reader, and, as it was merely a traditional form which he had to use in official utterances, would add nothing to a true understanding of his genius. On the other hand, as I was anxious to give an example of a fairly long continuous piece of his prose, I have reprinted the whole of his admirable Preface to *A Discourse of the Freedom of the Will* as the first of my selected passages. An anthology must always reflect personal taste and bear the mark of the age in which it is made, and I admit that I have chosen passages that are likely to appeal to the modern reader. My aim has been to exhibit not so much those aspects of Sterry's work that probably made the greatest impression on his contemporaries as those elements in it which appear to me to have the enduring and universal qualities of great literature, and which, I believe, truly represent what he himself regarded as the very pith of his doctrine. The form of the anthology was suggested to me by Mr L. Pearsall Smith's admirable selections from the sermons of Donne and of Jeremy Taylor, and I gladly take this opportunity of acknowledging my debt to those two golden little volumes. I have also followed Mr Pearsall Smith's example in giving my own titles to the extracts.

I have been unable to find an authentic portrait of Peter Sterry. The only one that exists seems to be a nineteenth-century stained glass window in the chapel of Emmanuel College, Cambridge, and there is every reason to suppose that this is a wholly imaginary representation. I have therefore considered that the best frontispiece for this volume would be a reproduction of a specimen of his handwriting from the Sterry MSS.

I have been fortunate enough to receive most generous help and encouragement from living members of Peter Sterry's family, notably from Mrs E. Poolman of Melbourne, Australia, who has placed at my disposal her valuable collection of her ancestor's manuscripts (described on pp. 44–58 and 223–226) and the Sterry family papers, from Mrs Audrey S. Pacy, through whose courtesy I was able to find the manuscripts and to communicate with their owner, and from Sir Wasey Sterry, Kt., C.B.E., who has taken a most kind interest in my work, has lent me his unique copies of two of Sterry's printed sermons, and has put himself to great trouble in procuring for me valuable biographical and genealogical information.

I wish to make grateful acknowledgment of the fact that the expense of publishing this book has been met partly by the Syndics of the Cambridge University Press, and partly by contributions from the Governing Body of Emmanuel College, Cambridge, from the Research Fund of University College, Southampton, and from Sir Wasey Sterry. I desire to thank the Research Committee of the Senate of University College, Southampton, also for voting several sums of money to defray expenses incidental to my work of research.

I am happy to be able to record my debt to members of my

own family: to the patience and skill of my wife who has typewritten most of the extracts for me and has made the index, and to the generosity of my father, to whom, as an old admirer of Cromwell, I have dedicated this memorial of one of Cromwell's favourite chaplains. Professors Lascelles Abercrombie and Denis Saurat have taken a friendly interest in the undertaking almost from the beginning, and I have been greatly stimulated both by their conversation and their writings. Like all students of Platonism and mysticism I have often had recourse to the works of Dean Inge and Evelyn Underhill, and owe much to their learning and wisdom. My friend Mr E. H. Blakeney has given me valuable assistance in tracing allusions to classical authors, and Mr Herbert Loewe, to whom I was introduced by Dr C. G. Montefiore, has honoured me by presenting me with a learned note on an allusion to Rabbinical teaching to include in my commentary. I have to thank the Rev. F. E. Hutchinson and my colleague Mr J. B. Leishman for reading through the whole work and for making several useful suggestions which I have been glad to incorporate. I beg to acknowledge the kind permission granted to me by Messrs P. J. and A. E. Dobell to quote two stanzas from Thomas Traherne's poem *Hosanna*. Finally it is a pleasure to acknowledge my indebtedness to the staff of the Cambridge University Press for their kindness, their courtesy and their skilful aid.

V. DE SOLA PINTO

University College
Southampton
October 1933

BIOGRAPHICAL AND CRITICAL
STUDY

I

THE MAN

The purpose of this book is to give some account of an English author of the seventeenth century who has hitherto been almost entirely neglected by students of literature, and to place before the public some specimens of his writings. The name of Peter Sterry does not, as far as I know, occur in any history of English literature, or even in any special survey of the literature of the seventeenth century. Yet a glance through the selections in this volume will be sufficient, I hope, to show the reader that he is a writer of an imaginative prose comparable only with that of the greatest masters of that great age of prose poetry. A closer study will also, I believe, lead to the conviction that he is a true poet, "a great and lovely mind", to use the phrase which Coleridge applied to Jeremy Taylor, the spiritual brother of such men as George Herbert, Richard Crashaw and Henry Vaughan, who, though his chosen medium usually happens to be prose, is essentially akin to the religious poets of the age in the intensity of his feeling and the beauty of his utterance. Finally he deserves to be remembered as one who in the words of F. D. Maurice was "a very profound thinker", the teacher of a doctrine which is valuable both for its own lofty vision, and for its interesting affinities with the thought of Milton, of Spinoza, of the Cambridge Platonists, and other ancient and modern systems of philosophy.

It is true, indeed, that Peter Sterry has never been wholly forgotten by students of mysticism and of the history of religious ideas. Richard Baxter, his great contemporary, distrusted his teaching during his lifetime, but paid a noble tribute to him after his death.[1] A small band of disciples appears to have survived him, and to have published some of

---

[1] See passage quoted as an epigraph to this book, and Appendix II below.

his posthumous works at the end of the seventeenth and the
beginning of the eighteenth centuries. John Byrom, the
eighteenth-century poet and mystic (1692–1763), possessed at
least one of his books,[1] and some of his prayers were reprinted in a little volume that appeared in 1785. In the nineteenth century his writings were highly esteemed by such
men as John Sterling,[2] Frederick Denison Maurice[3] and
Archbishop Trench,[4] and one of his sermons was reprinted
in 1831. Tulloch in his study of *Rational Theology in the
Seventeenth Century* (1872) does not allude to him once, but it
is conceivable that he regarded Sterry as a mystic or visionary
whose theology could not properly be called rational. In
more recent times Miss Charlotte Fell Smith contributed an
excellent short life of Sterry to the *Dictionary of National
Biography*, Mr G. Lynn Turner gave valuable biographical
details in his *Original Records of Early Nonconformity*, and Mr
Major Scott in his *Aspects of Christian Mysticism* (1907) and
Mr F. J. Powicke in *The Cambridge Platonists* (1926) have
written interesting essays dealing chiefly with his teaching.
I included some extracts from his works in an anthology
called *The Tree of Life* (Constable, 1928), and in an essay
contributed to *Speculum Religionis* (Oxford University Press,
1929) I endeavoured to draw attention to the beauty of his
style and thought and to the affinity of much of his doctrine
to the ideas of Blake and of Milton. In an article which ap-

---

[1] *The Rise, Race and Royalty of the Kingdom of God in the Soul of
Man...by Peter Sterry...London...*1683, 8vo. Byrom's copy is
now in the Library of the British Museum (4473, g. 22). It is
inscribed "Johan. Byrom T. C. C. Augt 18. 1711".

[2] See *Memorials of a Quiet Life*, by A. J. C. Hare (London,
1872), II, 96.

[3] See his *Modern Philosophy*, London, 1862, pp. 350, 351, and
cf. Stoughton's *History of Religion in England*, London, 1867, II,
348, 349: "He [Sterry] has of late been mentioned with honour in
high literary circles".

[4] *Letters and Memorials of Richard Chenevix Trench*, edited by the
author of *Charles Lowder*, London, 1888, I, 132.

peared in the issue of the *Review of English Studies* for October, 1930, I gave a detailed account of his unpublished writings with a short study of his life and printed works.

The neglect of Peter Sterry may well be compared with that of Thomas Traherne, whom he resembles in many ways. Traherne's best work, indeed, remained in manuscript until the nineteenth century, while, although only a part of Sterry's writings was printed, it was the best part, and quite sufficient to reveal the quality of his style and thought. But Sterry's works were rare. No public library, as far as I know, even at the present time, contains a complete collection of his books and they seldom appear in the catalogues of second-hand booksellers. Moreover, they are cast into forms which are not attractive to the student of literature. They are chiefly sermons, sermon notes and theological treatises which would easily escape notice amid the mass of dead seventeenth-century divinity. The references to him in well-known contemporary works[1] would suggest, too, that he was a mere hare-brained fanatic, "a high flown mystical divine",[2] and finally he was closely identified with religious and political views which were regarded by most of his fellow-countrymen after the Restoration with abhorrence. He was a chaplain and a personal friend of Cromwell and a strong supporter of the Protectorate, and was thus obnoxious both to royalists and to democrats. He was an Independent minister with singular religious opinions, which were very unlike those of most English dissenters and close to the doctrines of the despised sect of the Quakers on the one hand and to those of the Platonists and Latitudinarians in the Church of England on the other, to say nothing of more dangerous affinities to ancient and modern heresies. He had distinguished himself as a strong opponent of Presbyterianism and was reported to be a sycophant and a time-server. In fact he could not be

---

[1] *E.g.* Burnet's *History of His Own Times* and Ludlow's *Memoirs.*   [2] Baker MSS., vi, f. 83 v.

regarded with favour either by the Whig dissenter or the Tory high churchman, for, like Falkland in politics, he really belonged to that party of sweetness and light, which fortunately included men in the ranks of both the great contending factions of the religious and political struggles of the seventeenth century. The literary hero of the English dissenters is Bunyan, Matthew Arnold's "Philistine of Genius", not Sterry, the lover of poetry and painting, the impassioned pleader for toleration, who was friendly with Anglican divines, spoke politely of the Socinians, and ventured to remind his brethren that even a Pope had once "ascended from the *Papal Chair*, to a Throne in Heaven".[1]

Peter Sterry was baptized at St Olave's, Southwark, on 19 September, 1613.[2] He was the son of Anthony Sterry described in the baptismal register as a "cooper", and elsewhere as a "gentleman".[3] This Anthony Sterry appears to have been a son of Peter Sterry and Jane Longe, and was baptized at Ruardean in Gloucestershire on 16 June, 1584. A number of entries relating to the Sterry family in the sixteenth century appear in the Ruardean parish register. Presumably Anthony came to London and prospered in trade. The word "cooper" may mean either a maker and repairer of casks and similar vessels or a "wine cooper" or retailer of wine. In his will dated 17 March, 1631, he bequeaths to his son Peter "all my messuage or tenement wᵗʰ the yard and appurtenances called or knowne by the name of the black beare scituate and being in Horsendowne lane in the parish of St Olave in Southwark

---

[1] *A Discourse of the Freedom of the Will*, Preface, sig. a2v.

[2] Baptismal Register of St Olave's *s.d.* I owe the discovery of this entry to the patience and energy of my father, Mr J. de S. Pinto, who found it after a long search through the registers of South London churches, and to the kindness of the Rev. A. M. Cazalet, D.D., Rector of St Olave's.

[3] Admission Register of Gray's Inn *s.d.* 1658, where Nathaniel Sterry, Peter's brother, is described as "son of Anthony Sterry of Southwark Surrey Gent."

togeather wth all the waynescott perticõns and things there-in".[1] "Horsendowne lane" is the present Horsleydown Lane which formerly led to the old Horse-down or grazing and exercising place for horses. The Black Bear may have been an inn or tavern, but it may also have simply been the sign of a cooper's yard and workshop. Such signs were not confined to inns in the seventeenth century. Anthony Sterry also possessed a house in "Milne Lane in the parish of St Olave", which he bequeathed to his younger son Nathaniel. No record of Peter Sterry's boyhood exists, but it may be noticed that Southwark, where he was probably brought up, was the home of the earliest separatist Church, that of Henry Barrow, at the end of the sixteenth century. His writings show that he was remarkably sensitive to the rhythms of language, and his imagination must have been affected at an early age by the sonorous music of the great English Bible of 1611. Through all his works there runs a tissue of memories of the more poetical parts of the Authorized Version, especially the *Psalms*, the *Book of Job*, the Prophets, the Canticles, the more exalted parts of the Gospels, the Pauline Epistles, the *Epistle to the Hebrews* and the Apocalypse. His prose is that of a man who has heard and read the language of the English Bible every day from his boyhood. A passage from one of his sermons shows the kind of effect which the reading of the psalms had upon his imagination:

Can you cast your eye on the eighteenth *Psalm* and not tremble? when you see there, the Earth Shaking and Trembling: v. 7. a Fire Devouring: v. 8. the Heavens bowing Down-ward: v. 9. Thick Clouds darkning the Sky; Thunders, Lightnings, Hail-stones flying through the Ayre, the Foundations of the world below discover'd: v. 11, 12, 13, 14, 15.[2]

Elsewhere he speaks of the twenty-sixth chapter of *Leviticus* as that "thund'ring Chapter". These are surely the words of

---

[1] Copy of Anthony Sterry's will in the possession of Sir Wasey Sterry.

[2] *The Clouds in which Christ Comes*, London, 1648, pp. 19, 20.

one who has listened as a boy with wonder and rapture to
those tremendous rhythms and has never forgotten the experience. His acquaintance with classical literature and
ancient mythology is almost as much in evidence in his
writings as his knowledge of the Bible. He recurs to images
drawn from the *Aeneid* especially with nearly the same
familiarity as to those drawn from the Old and New Testaments. It is, perhaps, therefore, legitimate to suppose that
the classics as well as the Bible, Virgil and Homer as well as
the Prophets and the Apostles played an important part in
his education, and that his family like that of Milton was not
only a religious and a Puritan family, but a family of humanists
and lovers of literature and learning. There is no record of
his early life until 21 October, 1629, when he entered Emmanuel College, Cambridge, at the age of sixteen. This fact
is sufficient to prove that his family was at least inclined to
Puritan opinions, for Emmanuel was famous since its foundation in 1584 as a Puritan college. But, at the time when
Sterry was admitted, this college was becoming the centre of
a new movement in English religious thought. Benjamin
Whichcote and John Smith, the two brilliant thinkers who
inaugurated "Cambridge Platonism", had both entered
Emmanuel three years before Sterry, while John Worthing-
ton and Ralph Cudworth came up in 1632 and Nathaniel
Culverwel in 1633. The predominating influence at Emmanuel at this time was undoubtedly that of Whichcote, the
possessor of one of the most acute and interesting minds of
the day. He was elected to a fellowship in 1632, when Sterry
was at the impressionable age of nineteen. Unfortunately
few records of the relations between the two men have
survived, but there is enough evidence to show that they
were on terms of intimacy, and that Whichcote had the
greatest admiration for Sterry's character and ability. The
way in which the fresh and vigorous mind of the elder man
brushed aside the barren disputes between Puritans and High
Churchmen and reinterpreted Christianity in the light of

Plato and the Neoplatonists must have been wonderfully inspiring to a youth educated in Puritan surroundings, but with the mind of a poet and a natural bias towards generous and lofty ideas. Whichcote's delight in Sterry's conversation is shown by a pleasant story that on one occasion when they were "discussing some abstruse Points in divinity", Sterry "explain'd himself with such Ease and Clearness, that the Doctor [Whichcote] rising from his Seat and Embracing him, express'd himself in this manner; *Peter thou hast overcome me, thou art all pure intellect*".[1]

Whichcote's teaching, true to the Platonic tradition, combined a lofty rationalism with deep and genuine religious feeling. He could teach his young friend that "to go against *Reason* is to go against *God*" and that "Reason is the *Divine* Governor of Man's Life".[2] He could also make him feel that "The soul of Man to God is as the flower to the sun; it opens at its approach, and shuts when it withdraws"[3] and that "though the spirit of man in this state be joined to a body, and made a member of this material visible world, yet itself doth belong to another country".[4] It was certainly the mystical side of "Cambridge Platonism" which attracted Sterry most strongly, and it is this element in the teaching of Whichcote and Smith that he was to develop chiefly in his own works, but he was also strongly influenced by their liberal outlook, their "latitudinarianism" and their arguments for toleration. According to Burnet,[5] Whichcote "set young students much on reading the ancient philosophers chiefly Plato, Tully and Plotin". Sterry's writings show that while he was at Emmanuel he must have acquired a truly immense learning, which included an acquaintance, not only with the writings of Plato and Plotinus and the Neoplatonists, but

1 *The Appearance of God to Man in the Gospel*, 1710, sig. A 2.
2 *Whichcote's Aphorisms* (ed. W. R. Inge, 1930), no. 76.
3 Whichcote, *Works*, Aberdeen, 1751, III, 104.
4 *Ibid.* IV, 140.
5 *History of His Own Times*, ed. Airy (1897), I, 331.

with the whole range of ancient philosophy, history and poetry as well as with the works of the Greek and Latin Fathers of the Church, the Schoolmen and Mystics of the Middle Ages and the Italian Platonists of the Renascence such as Ficino and Pico della Mirandola. The one fragment of information concerning his university career which has survived shows him as an ardent supporter of the new school of thought. "He & Sadler hereafter mention'd", writes Thomas Baker in his manuscript notes on Emmanuel College, "were the first that were observ'd to make a public Profession of Platonism in the univers. of Cambridge."[1] This Sadler was John Sadler, afterwards Fellow of Emmanuel and Master of Magdalene, and like Sterry destined to become a friend of Cromwell. He was famous as an orientalist, and it is probable that it was in his company that Sterry studied the Rabbinical and other Jewish writings, the influence of which on his thought is second only to that of ancient Greek philosophy.

On 15 April, 1637, Sterry was elected to a fellowship of his college. It is noticeable that his election almost coincides with the death of Dr Sandcroft, the master under whose rule the Platonist and Latitudinarian movements had taken such firm root in the college. Sandcroft was succeeded by Dr Holdsworth, a Fellow of St John's, a strong Churchman, and an enthusiastic loyalist. In different circumstances Sterry might have spent the rest of his life studying and teaching at Cambridge. As it was, the smouldering quarrel between the House of Commons and the Puritans on the one hand and the King and the High Churchmen on the other was just beginning to burst into flame. A couple of months after Sterry's election to his fellowship, Prynne, Burton and Bastwick underwent the barbarous punishment decreed by the Star Chamber. The next winter was to see the struggle over the payment of ship-money, followed by the disastrous "Bishops' War" in Scotland. It is easy to imagine the feelings

[1] Baker MS. vi, f. 83 v. (Br. Mus. MS. Harl. 7033).

with which a young man brought up in Puritan surroundings and nourished on the literature of the Greek city republics regarded these events. At some time between the date of his election and the winter of 1639–40, he appears to have thrown up his fellowship and left Cambridge. It is probable that he felt that he could no longer conform to the official religious teaching of the university. He followed a course which was common enough among the Puritan clergy who were debarred from livings under the primacy of Laud, and became a chaplain to a nobleman who shared his opinions. Sterry's patron was Robert Greville, Lord Brooke, the cousin and adopted son and heir of Fulke Greville, the poet, and friend of Sir Philip Sidney.[1] Lord Brooke was a contemporary of Sterry at Cambridge, where, in the delightful phrase of Anthony à Wood, he "became learned considering his quality". Wood describes him "in his own nature a very civill and well humor'd person" but "unhappily attainted with fanatical and antimonarchial principles by the influence of his near relations and some schismaticall preachers". Sterry was presumably one of the "schismaticall preachers" who turned Lord Brooke's thoughts towards democracy and puritanism. It appears to have been while a member of Lord Brooke's household that he met Frances Asheworth, a London citizen's widow with a small estate and some children.[2] There were difficulties in the way of a marriage between them, due apparently to Sterry's failure to satisfy Mrs Asheworth's guardians concerning his "ability to settle some proporčonable Livelyhood" on her or "bring any present meanes". This obstacle was removed by Lord Brooke who promised to settle an annuity of sixty pounds on Frances

---

[1] The Chancery document cited below states that Sterry was "called from Cambridge by his Lordshipp".

[2] Chancery Proceedings, Series II (Public Record Office), Bundle 462, no. 63. This document does not specify the number of children, but it states that Mrs Asheworth had "a considerable advancement by the death of her former husband".

Asheworth to begin on the day of her marriage with Sterry, which took place in February, 1641. According to a legal document,[1] much of which is mutilated and illegible, Peter Sterry and his wife never received more than ten pounds of this annuity before Lord Brooke's death. A passage in one of Peter Sterry's letters to his son throws some light on the state of his mind when he was courting Frances Asheworth:

meeting some interruptions in my wooing loves to your Mother, after a day spent in prayer, I had a dream at night; A friend held a cup from me, of which I exceedingly desired to drink; but smiled, and said, when the poyson was taken out, which lay at ye bottom, I should drink freely. The poyson was taken out. The cup was filled with pure and heavenly loves of which you are ye first fruits.

We can conjecture that the poison in this symbolic dream was the suspicion that he was influenced in his courtship by thoughts of Mrs Asheworth's estate. It is clear from Sterry's extant letters to his wife that the marriage was a very happy one, and it is noticeable that his teaching attaches very high importance to the beauty and sanctity of marriage.

Lord Brooke published a little philosophical essay on *The Nature of Truth* in 1640 and *A Discourse opening the Nature of Episcopacy* in 1641. In the composition of these works according to Wood he was helped by "some Puritanicall minister", whom we can suppose to have been Peter Sterry, as both their style and matter are not unlike those of Sterry's own writings. At the outbreak of the Civil War Lord Brooke showed himself to be a strong supporter of the Parliament.

---

[1] This is the document cited on p. 11, n. 2. It is a petition from "Peter Sterry Clearke and Frances his wife" "to the Right Honble erle of Manchester and William Lenthall Esqre Speaker of the House of Commons Commissioners for the Great Seal of England". The date is illegible. It seems to be a request for the payment of the annuity promised to Mrs Sterry, and the legacy of a hundred pounds left by Lord Brooke to Peter Sterry in his will. There is no record of the result of the petition.

He took a prominent part in the military operations at the beginning of the war, when as Lord Lieutenant of Warwickshire he mustered a force for the Parliament and defeated the Earl of Northampton at Kineton near Banbury on 3 August, 1642. On 16 September he was appointed Speaker of the House of Lords and General under the Earl of Essex of the associated counties of Warwick, Stafford, Derby and Leicester. He took Stratford on Avon by assault, and advanced to Lichfield at the beginning of March, 1642/3. He is said to have foreseen his death, and to have ordered his chaplain (presumably Peter Sterry) to preach a sermon on the words of Esther, "If I perish, I perish". According to a royalist story "in a prayer of above an hour long which he conceived, before his setting on the close [*i.e.* before attacking Lichfield Close] he was heard to wish that if the cause he was in were not right and just, he might be presently cut off". He was killed by a musket bullet in the assault on the cathedral, and the superstitious observed that the day was that of St Chad the patron of Lichfield.[1] Milton paid a fine tribute to his memory in *Areopagitica*,[2] where he describes him as "a right noble and pious Lord, who had he not now sacrific'd his life and fortunes to the Church and Commonwealth, we had not mist and bewayl'd a worthy and undoubted patron of this argument" (*i.e.* "to know, to utter, and to argue freely according to conscience").

Lord Brooke appears to have left a legacy of one hundred[3] pounds to Peter Sterry, who continued to live with his family and acted as chaplain to Lady Brooke. In the spring of 1643 Sterry was in London and was nominated in May as one of the fourteen divines chosen by the House of Lords for the famous

---

[1] Anthony à Wood, *Athenae Oxonienses*, ed. Bliss, II, 432–4. Wood also mentions that Lord Brooke "did often bragge that 'he should live to see the Millenary fool's Paradise begin in his life'".

[2] Milton, *Areopagitica*, London, 1644, p. 35.

[3] Chancery Proceedings, *loc. cit.*

Assembly set up at Westminster to reorganize the Church on a Puritan basis. The official records of Sterry's activities in the Assembly are unimportant, but Robert Baillie the Scots Commissioner places him among the Independents or the party which opposed the Presbyterian form of Church government. In a letter dated 7 December, 1643, Baillie includes his name in a list of Independents with those of Goodwin, Nye, Burroughs and others, "manie of them", in Baillie's words, "very able men".[1] Although Sterry did not sign the "Apologetical Narration" printed by the "Five Dissenting Brethren", Thomas Goodwin, Nye, Simpson, Burroughs and Bridge, it seems certain that he supported them in the Assembly, and that he was a member of the group of Independent divines whom Milton described in his sonnet, "On the new forcers of Conscience under the long Parliament", as

> Men whose life, learning, faith and pure intent
> Would have been held in high esteem by *Paul*.

It was probably at this time that Sterry became intimate with Sir Henry Vane the younger, who was one of the chief leaders of the Independent party both in the Assembly and in the House of Commons. On 20 January, 1643/4, he was examined by a Committee of the House of Lords concerning a supposed plot of Vane. The King, who was then at Oxford, had attempted to open a negotiation with Vane and his party, probably with a view to detaching them from the Parliamentary cause. But Vane was too shrewd a statesman to be caught in such a trap. He appears to have sent a certain Moses Wall, chaplain to the Earl of Warwick, to Reading to meet Lord Lovelace, the King's representative, but at the same time he laid the whole matter before the Speaker, a Committee of the House of Commons and the Scots Com-

---

[1] Baillie, *Letters and Journals*, ed. Laing (Bannatyne Society), Edinburgh, 1842, II, 110. See also Anthony à Wood's *Athenae Oxonienses*, ed. Bliss, III, 912, where Sterry is classed with Philip Nye as one of the "notorious Independents in the Assembly".

missioners, and it is clear that his true object in communicating with Lord Lovelace was to endeavour to find out something about the enemy's plans. The House of Lords was unfriendly to Vane at this time, because he had objected to its action in receiving back Lord Holland, who had deserted the Parliamentary cause for a time, without any expression of penitence on his part. The Lords seem to have heard of Vane's negotiation with Lord Lovelace, and to have seized upon the news joyfully as a stick to beat the man whom they regarded as an enemy to their privileges. The Earl of Essex even proposed to charge him with high treason.[1] A Committee of the Lords was set up to inquire into the matter, and it examined among others Moses Wall and Peter Sterry, both chaplains to noble families engaged on the Parliamentary side. A long minute of Sterry's evidence is preserved among the House of Lords MSS. This evidence is very full and explicit and no doubt played an important part in clearing Vane of the charge of treason. Sterry, who is described as "Chaplaine to my lady Brooke", affirms that Vane had repeated to him the substance of the letter from Lord Lovelace "in his owne [Vane's] House in the Piazza in presence of Mr Moses Wall", and that it was in his presence that Vane suggested that Wall should go to Reading. Vane told Sterry that he spoke before him in order that he might have a witness of his intentions in sending Wall, and he assured him that he "had acquainted Mr Speaker and Mr Sollicitor with the Letter". He told Sterry that he was really sending Wall "Upon hope" "that thereby Mr Wall might come to gett some further knowledge of the plott, which was newly discovered in London". Sterry also states cautiously that he heard the names of "my lord of Bedford" and "my lord of Holland" mentioned, but he refuses to commit himself concerning "the manner" in which "this was spoke".

---

[1] *Life of Sir Henry Vane the Younger*, by J. Willcock (London, 1913), pp. 133, 134.

A week later Sterry met Wall again in Vane's house and
Wall told him that "he had bin abroade". On "Sunday last"
Sterry "asked Sir Henry Vane what had become of Mr Wall's
Business; and Sir Henry Vane answered to this effect, there is
nothing of it to any purpose". Later Lady Vane told Sterry
"in way of discourse" the details. Lord Lovelace had expressed the King's general desire for peace, "And that the
King thought Sir Henry Vane and his Party in the House
were very honest men, and if they would be for peace, the
King should hope the more easy to effect it". Finally Vane
showed Sterry and Wall a copy of Lovelace's letter and his
own reply "which was a commendačon of Mr Wall to his
Lopp and an expression...of his owne good inclynačon for
to do any thing for the publique good". The records of the
affair show that Sterry was at this time on the most friendly
terms with Vane and his family and that he was highly
esteemed and trusted by them.[1] Baxter in his *Autobiography*
calls Sterry Vane's "intimate" and notices the similarity of
their religious ideas.[2]

The earliest of Sterry's extant printed works is a sermon
preached by him to the House of Commons on 26 November,
1645, which was printed according to the custom of that
period. It is a learned and eloquent discourse called *The
Spirit Convincing of Sinne*, which shows already the chief
qualities of his thought and style. It is especially notable that
in this sermon Sterry definitely separates himself from the
rationalism of his Cambridge friends. He carefully distinguishes "reason" from "spirit" and lays particular stress on
the superiority of "spirit". Reason, indeed, he admits in the
phrase that Whichcote was so fond of quoting from the
Book of Proverbs is "the Candle of the Lord", but "spirit"
is a higher faculty and it is by spirit alone that spiritual things

---

[1] I have been allowed to examine and copy Sterry's evidence
by the kindness of Mr F. W. Lascelles, Librarian to the House of
Lords. It is calendared in the *Hist. MSS. Commission Report.*

[2] *Reliquiae Baxterianae* (1696), 1, 75.

can be apprehended. "Spirit" is a state in which the soul can rise above reason:

The soule shuts up the windowes of sense, when she would have the room fill'd with the light of Reason. Reason's self must first be cast into a deep sleep and die, before she can rise again in the brightnesse of the Spirit.

But the most striking passages in this sermon are those which refer to the Civil War. Here the preacher's mood is not one of exultation, although he is addressing the Long Parliament just after the final defeat of the royalist armies. For him the war is a tragedy, and in the following noble passage he is moved by pity for the sufferings of his fellow-countrymen rather than joy at the victories of the Parliament:

Three Kingdomes stand before you this day, like those three crosses on Mount *Golgotha*, all laden with broken and bleeding carkasses. These three doth your God take, as one Text, that hee may preach sin to your soules from it, that he may convince you of sin by it.

Behold *Scotland* comes with her thousands of slaine men; *England* with her ten thousands; *Ireland* with her millions, besides innumerable multitudes which no man can reckon up, of families, persons, now undone, now famishing. These come crying to every one of us, *Our bloods be upon your heads, if you weep not for us before our God this day whilest we bleed and dye.* Sure your *hearts* doe *break* at the representation of these things, which your selves know to be at this present farre more sad in *Fact*, then they can be made by any *Relation*.[1]

By this time Sterry appears to have become a well-known Independent preacher at Westminster. Thomas Edwards in his *Gangraena* (1646), a bitter attack by a Presbyterian on the "Sectaries", tells a story of a young maid "religiously affected drawn in to affect the Independents". She becomes "a servant in a family of some ranck and place where the master and mistresse were Independents". "On the Lord's day they were very loose in the forenoon[;] they would go to

[1] *The Spirits Conviction of Sinne*, London, 1645, p. 15.

hear Master Sterry at White-Hall (as not living far from thence) but in the afternoon stay at home" and "rail at the Scots" and "some of our own ministers" and at "books written against the sectaries". This passage shows that in 1646 Sterry was a prominent Independent minister, popular with that section of the Parliamentary party which distrusted the Presbyterians and the Scots. It also shows that he was now a regular preacher at Whitehall.[1]

The mystical vein in his character and his preaching which appealed to men like Vane had the opposite effect on some of his contemporaries. Richard Baxter, who indeed never heard him preach, although he earnestly desired to, is said to have satirized his friendship with Vane in a clever punning epigram: "*Vanity* and *Sterility* were never more happily conjoined".[2] "*Sterility*" no doubt refers to the fact that Sterry published nothing until he was thirty-three. Sir Benjamin Rudyerd described his sermons as "too high for this World, and too low for the other".[3] This criticism may have been inspired by such a sermon as *The Clouds in Which Christ Comes*, preached before the House of Commons on 27 October, 1647, one of the grandest and most imaginative of Sterry's sermons, but full of mystical doctrine and lyrical eloquence which must have astonished and puzzled many of the lawyers and squires of the Long Parliament. He pleads with great eloquence in this discourse against the enslavement of religion to "formes", "ordinances" and "peculiar ways of worship", the idols of the Presbyterians.

"'Tis in vain", he cries, "to attempt to shut up Christ in any Thing. Though you kill Him, that you may keep Him safe; though you lay Him in a Grave hewne out of a Rock in a Garden,

---

[1] Peter Sterry's name occurs in the lists of officiating clergy at St Margaret's, Westminster, under the dates, 1645 and 1647. See Walcot's *History of St Margaret's, Westminster* (London, 1847), p. 86.

[2] *Reliquiae Baxterianae* (1696), I, 75.   [3] *Ibid.*

a Frame contriv'd with greatest strength and Beauty; though you set the Seal of Authority upon it, and a guard about it; yet Christ will rise with an Earthquake and appeare to His Disciples."[1]

On 29 March, 1648,[2] Sterry preached another sermon full of lofty idealism and intense feeling called *The Teachings of Christ In The Soule* before the House of Lords in Covent Garden Church. "*Loathe the World, and live in Heaven*" is the tenor of his exhortation to the assembled peers. "Christ teacheth us to seek a *City*, not of *this Creation*, whose *Builder*, Building, and chief Inhabitant is God. He teacheth us to find this *new Hierusalem*, which is *above* us, *within* us, and there to dwell. He *discovers* this City with its Citizens in our Spirits, and *draws* us into it!"[3] This sermon was printed with a notable Epistle Dedicatory which sets forth the author's theological opinions in some detail.

On February 22, 1649, three weeks after the execution of Charles I, an event which Sterry never mentions in his writings, the Westminster Assembly of Divines held its last meeting. The Presbyterian cause in England was lost. Cromwell was now the avowed patron of the Independents and of toleration, and the Independent leaders such as John Goodwin, John Owen, Hugh Peters, and Peter Sterry were marked out for high ecclesiastical office. On 16 February, 1649, Sterry had been appointed a chaplain or "preacher" to the Council of State,[4] and on 19 July this appointment was confirmed, and he was voted a salary of £100 a year.[5] Lodgings were assigned to him in Whitehall Palace, and he took the place of John Owen, who went to Ireland as Cromwell's

---

[1] *The Clouds in Which Christ Comes*, London, 1648, pp. 48, 49.

[2] A sermon preached by Sterry to the House of Commons on 5 November, 1647, called *England Saved* appears to have been printed, but no copy has survived. See Bibliography, p. 228.

[3] *The Teachings of Christ In the Soule*, London, 1648, p. 42.

[4] Order Book of Council of State, quoted by Masson, *Life of Milton*, IV, 145.

[5] Cal. S. P. Dom. 1649/50, p. 177.

chaplain. On 1 November he preached a sermon to the Parliament entitled *The Comings forth of Christ in the Power of his Death,* in which he gave thanks for Cromwell's victories in Ireland. On 2 November John Goodwin was appointed joint chaplain with him to the Council and their salaries were fixed at £200 a year. On 8 March, 1650, Sterry was re-appointed chaplain in conjunction with John Owen with the same salary, Goodwin having been promoted to the Master-ship of Magdalen College, Oxford. He had now entered on the duties which he was to continue to discharge until the end of the Protectorate. His position was not unlike that of a court chaplain under the monarchy, though his functions and influence were probably wider. He seems, indeed, to have acted as a general adviser to the government in matters connected with religion and scholarship. He belonged, in fact, to the group of Independent divines who really became the leaders of the Church under the Protectorate. At first his position was that of "preacher to the Council of State". When Cromwell assumed the office of Lord Protector, Sterry appears to have become one of his personal chaplains. His colleagues at Whitehall were men of great intellectual dis-tinction. They included the learned and acute John Owen, John and Thomas Goodwin, famous for their massive scholarship and original theological opinions, the subtle and brilliant Philip Nye, Joseph Caryl, author of the great *Com-mentary on the Book of Job,* the vigorous and sometimes violent Welshman, Hugh Peters and, later, the handsome and courteous John Howe, a divine who resembles Sterry in many ways, like him a pupil of Whichcote and a product of "Cambridge Platonism", though he has not Sterry's gift of poetic eloquence. With these men John Milton, now Latin Secretary to the Council and resident at Whitehall from 19 November, 1650,[1] was closely associated. In a minute of the Council dated 14 August, 1650, he is appointed with Sterry, Nye, Thomas Goodwin and others "to view and inventory

[1] Masson, *Life of Milton,* IV, 153.

all the records, writings and papers belonging to the assembly of the Synod [presumably the Westminster Assembly] so that they may not be embezzled and may be forthcoming for the use of the Commonwealth".[1] We can be sure that Milton found Sterry a thoroughly congenial companion. They had much in common, in spite of the contrast between Sterry's "enthusiasm" and other-worldliness and Milton's clear hard logical mind. Both were students of Hebrew, Greek, Latin, Italian and English literature, both were fervent admirers of Homer and Virgil among ancient poets and Tasso and Spenser among the moderns.[2] Both believed in the direct inspiration of great works of art; both were champions of toleration and strong opponents of Presbyterianism. It is a pity that more records of their association have not been preserved. Sterry's philosophic and religious doctrines were, as we shall see, very close to Milton's in many ways and we can hardly doubt that they often held debate on such subjects. Milton is never mentioned in Sterry's extant correspondence, but in one of his manuscript books there is a transcript of the opening lines of *At a Solemn Musick*, a fact which is, perhaps, sufficient to prove that he admired Milton's early poems. Whitehall under Cromwell's rule is generally regarded as a home of austere Puritanism, devoid of all interest in culture or the humanities. Yet we can suppose that there was as much true culture and more genuine appreciation of art and poetry in a court that included such men as John Milton, Peter Sterry and Andrew Marvell, as among the small poets and dilettanti of the Whitehall of Charles II. It is interesting also to notice that Sterry's works abound in allusions to painting and painters and that the two masters whom he singles out for especial praise are Titian and Van Dyck. We can be sure that while he lived at Whitehall he used some of his leisure to study the noble collections of paintings in that Palace and at Hampton Court. There he could admire Van Dyck's great portraits of the royal family and his beautiful "Madone aux Perdrix",

[1] Cal. S. P. Dom. 1650, p. 286. [2] See no. 79 of this selection.

and Titian's splendid "Entombment" and "The Disciples at Emmaus" now at the Louvre.[1]

On 3 September, 1650, Cromwell won his great victory over the Scots at Dunbar and Sterry wrote to congratulate him. His letter has been preserved, and is of some interest for the light that it throws on the relationship between the two men. It is written in that strain of religious exaltation which appealed so strongly to Cromwell. The victory, he writes, "will fill all Spirituall hearts with praises". "The Lord had justified his servants, and ye Worke of his Spirit in theyr hands." "The Lord give to your Excellency, & all his Servants a Spirituall Sight of Himselfe, & his Worke, a Spirituall Understanding of his Counsaile...." The writer ends with a petition on behalf of its bearer a Mr Brettergh who desired to serve in the Army in Scotland.[2]

In September Sterry was left as sole chaplain on the departure of Caryl and Owen to Scotland, but on 17 December, Hugh Peters was appointed by the Council to assist him.[3] A Council minute under this date records that Peters was appointed to preach on Sunday afternoons, so presumably Sterry usually preached at Whitehall on Sunday mornings at this time. The two chaplains are bidden to confer with four members of the Council concerning "their praying every day before the sitting down of the Council, and likewise concerning the reading of some scripture and expounding the same before sermon".

---

[1] The greater part of the collection of Charles I was sold by order of the Parliament. The sale began in 1649 but did not end till 1652 or 1653. Nevertheless Cromwell saved some notable pictures for the adornment of Hampton Court including Mantegna's "The Triumphs of Julius Caesar" and the cartoons of Raphael. See *The Picture Gallery of Charles I*, by Claude Philips, London, 1896 (Portfolio Monographs. Seeley and Co.).

[2] Original letter preserved at the Society of Antiquaries, London. It is printed in Nickolls's *Original Letters and Papers of State*, London, 1743, pp. 18, 19.

[3] Cal. S. P. Dom. 1650, p. 472.

In the following September Charles II and the Scottish Presbyterian army were finally defeated at Worcester, and on 5 November, 1651, Sterry preached one of his most interesting extant sermons to the Parliament at St Margaret's, Westminster, as a thanksgiving for the victory. The title of this discourse is significant: *England's Deliverance from the Northern Presbytery compared with its Deliverance from the Roman Papacy*.[1] A large part of it is devoted to an elaborate comparison between Presbyterianism and Romanism. They are said to agree in setting up "the *Scriptures*, the *Word of God outwardly exprest* as the *Letter* of [the] Law", but without "the *Light of Revelation*" granted to "a Living Member of *Jesus Christ*", and hence as a mere "breathlesse Carkasse, or a Dead Letter". They agree in setting up a human authority as the sole interpreter of scripture, the Pope or a Council in the case of the Romanists, a National or Oecumenical Assembly in the case of the Presbyterians. They agree in "having a very great Jealousy over the *Spirit* of God". Both are suspicious of mystical religion and dismiss it as "*Whimsies, Fancies, Fanatick Furies, Enthusiasmes*". They both maintain "a watchfull Opposition to all Growths of Truth above the pitch, and stature of Opinions commonly received" and are suspicious of all innovations. "They labour, as to hedg in the Wind, to bind up the sweet influences of the *Spirit*." Both lay stress on "*outward Formalities*", "*Ceremonious Observations* of outward Rites". Both make Religion "a *Rise* to *Civil* Pomp and Power", or in other words tend to place ecclesiastical government above civil government and dispose of "*Governments, Nations, Crownes* by vertue of their *Ecclesiastick Censures*". The differences between the two Churches are also noted, and it may be observed that the contrast is not wholly favourable to the Presbyterians. The

---

[1] This sermon was printed both in London and at Leith (see Bibliography, p. 230. Did Cromwell order it to be printed in Scotland for the benefit of the English army, and such Scottish Presbyterians who cared to read it?

Romanists, indeed, "pleased not God", "but yet were agreeable to *men* in their wayes ". "They take, and give a large scope to the *understanding* and *affections* in *generous contemplations*, in *mystical divinity*"; "they entertain the *fancy*, and *senses* with all subjects sutable to them ". This passage shows that Sterry could not help admiring certain aspects of Roman Catholicism, and it makes one suspect that, if his upbringing and education had been in a Catholic instead of a Puritan family, he might have been fairly happy within the pale of the Church of St Teresa and of Crashaw. On the other hand, the Scots "please not *God*, and are contrary to all *men*. These *contemne* the *Spirit*.... At the same time they condemne *humane policy*, as *profane*. They check the delights of *sense* and *fancy*, as *vain*. . . ." It is significant that the preacher hastens here to disclaim any intention of justifying the "*sensualities* of the *Papacy*". Yet he calls both Presbyterianism and Romanism "*the Ghost* of *Judaisme*", but, while Romanism is "the *Ghost* of *Judaisme*[1] cloathed with the *Mantle* which it wore in its life time, appearing in the same *outward pompe*, with the same *delicious pleasures* of *Pictures, Musick, Perfumes*, &c. as of old", Presbyterianism is "*Judaism* undrest, like an *apparition in chaines*, or *Lazarus* when he came forth from the grave with the *grave cloathes* bound about him". It is true that Sterry goes on to point out that the "Scotch Presbytery" is the purest "*outward form*", but he compares it to "a house which the *evill spirit* of *Papacy* had left, a *house* swept *clean* from the filth of profanenesse, *garnished*, with the beautiful things of the *letter*", and he prays that "there be not found the *more divels* in it, besides the re-entry of the *first divel*".[2] In fact the

---

[1] *Loc. cit.* pp. 14, 15. Had Sterry read Hobbes's *Leviathan* (1651), and does he echo consciously or unconsciously his famous description of the Papacy as "the ghost of the deceased Roman Empire sitting crowned upon the grave thereof"? (*Leviathan*, ch. XLVII.)

[2] It is interesting to notice that the references to Presbyterianism and its resemblance to Papacy are cited with approbation by

whole discourse is really based on the thought expressed in
Milton's famous line "New Presbyter is but Old Priest writ
large", and we can imagine that Milton read it with high
approbation. It may be noticed that this sermon contains a
strong element of mysticality and occultism which shows
that in some respects Sterry was essentially a man of his age.
The inspired poet preacher disappears for a while, and gives
place to the typical Puritan "enthusiast", who identifies the
"Laodicea" of the Apocalypse with England, and reckons
that, as the Flood took place 1656 years before Christ, so in
A.D. 1656 there will be another cataclysm preceding the
Day of Judgment. Certain expressions were remembered
because of their daring and almost bizarre use of erotic
imagery. One passage especially in the Epistle Dedicatory to
the High Court of Parliament printed by Sterry with this
sermon gave offence and has been unfairly cited as an
example of Sterry's style and doctrine:

> The Lord Jesus hath his Concubines, his Queenes, his Virgines;
> Saints in Remoter Formes, Saints in higher Formes, Saints un-
> married to any Forme, who keep themselves single for the im-
> mediate imbraces of their Love.[1]

Such erotic imagery, which indeed abounds in Sterry's works,
certainly appears to be in bad taste, in this passage at any
rate, to the modern reader. But it should be remembered that
the reverence in which the letter of the Old Testament was
held, and the accepted contemporary interpretation of the
Song of Solomon justified it in some degree. The works of
Catholic mystics abound in sexual imagery, and it may be
pleaded in defence of Sterry that the doctrine which he is

Bishop Kennet in his "Register" (fol. 1728), pp. 555, 556: "And
in this sermon he doth all along arraign the Presbyterians as
worse and more wicked than the Papists".

[1] England's Deliverance From the Northern Presbytery..., London,
1652 (preached on 5 November, 1651), the Epistle Dedicatory,
sig. A6. It is fair to Sterry to point out that these words do not
seem actually to have been uttered in the sermon itself.

trying to expound by means of the unfortunate metaphor of a celestial harem is really an excellent one. He is pleading for a recognition of the fact that genuine religious feeling can be found among men who differ with regard to rites and forms of religion, and even (a bold doctrine for the seventeenth century) among those who use no rites or forms at all.

A curious incident occurred on 16 July, 1652, when Sterry was preaching in the chapel at Whitehall before a distinguished audience which included "The Chief States of the Land" on the subject of the Resurrection. A naked woman suddenly appeared among the congregation, and cried out that she was the Resurrection. According to his own statement the preacher became aware of a disturbance at the back of the chapel, and saw enough of the woman to perceive that she was "bare to the middle of her back". He did his best to reassure the congregation by telling them that there was no danger, and that it was only a mad woman who caused the disturbance. The woman was removed by the soldiers who were on guard at the door of the chapel. On 8 October a very extraordinary epistle was addressed to Sterry by a certain David Brown from his "great Brick house with the Barn, at the North end of Soho in the fields streight up Hedge lane from Charing Cross", an address that gives an interesting glimpse of the rural surroundings of Whitehall in the time of Cromwell. Brown was so pleased with his performance that he published it on 23 November with a Prologue, a short and sensible answer from Sterry and his own polite rejoinder under the catchpenny title of *The Naked Woman or a Rare Epistle sent to Mʳ Peter Sterry*. The Epistle is a long rambling affair full of irrelevant anecdotes and citations from scripture. It seems to be the work either of a crazy Puritan, or more probably of someone who wished to make Sterry appear ridiculous by aping the worst extravagances of Puritan phrase and sentiment. His chief complaint against Sterry is that he took no action in the matter either at the time of the disturbance or afterwards. Sterry's concise, courteous and business-like reply shows that the complaint was groundless, and forms a striking contrast to Brown's turgid effusion. The most interesting passage in that curious work is the allusion to the closing of the theatres. Brown writes "the Playhouses in London are quite discharged" and also that "the great Timber barn in the Palace of *Whitehall* itself" is "demolished, which was erected for the vile exercises of masks and plays, and those to be alwayes in the night season (even crossing the Ordinance of God, which he hath appointed for people to rest, and in the day to travell)...". This passage makes one suspect that Brown knew that Sterry differed strongly from most Puritans on the subjects of art and poetry, and that he was hoping to make him look ridiculous by provoking a discussion on the subject of dramatic performances. Sterry wisely refused to be drawn into such a controversy. At the same time the appearance of the pamphlet, coming as it did so soon after the sermon against the Presbyterians, cannot have done his reputation much good among the rank and file of the Puritan party.

The opinion of him held by the more extreme and visionary sectaries is illustrated in a book published in 1652 by William Erbury called *A Sword Doubled or A Scourge for the Assyrian*. Erbury mentions Sterry with other Independent ministers as among those who "hold forth Christ in the spirit" and are "neerest Zion, yet are they not come into it". In other words, such men as Erbury enjoyed Sterry's fervid and poetical preaching, but recognized the fact that he was not likely to follow them in their eccentricities.

On 22 June, 1653, we find Sterry in company with Nicholas Lockier called upon "to return thanks and praise to the Lord for his great mercy in giving the late seasonable victory of the fleet of this Commonwealth against the Dutch Fleet". The victory appears to have been the battle in which Monk defeated the Dutch on 3 June.[1] On 6 October Sterry was appointed with Caryl and Owen as one of a small committee

[1] Cal. S. P. Dom. 1652/3, p. 434.

to examine a book which a certain Dr Holmes had submitted
to the Council.[1] This Dr Holmes was apparently Nathaniel
Holmes or Homes, D.D., a well-known Independent divine
and scholar who acted as minister of St Matthew's, Friday
Street, under the Commonwealth and Protectorate.[2] According to Anthony à Wood the book was "ΑΠΟΚΑΛΥΨΙΣ
ΑΝΑΣΤΑΣΕΩΣ, *The Resurrection Revealed or the Dawning of
the Day-star About to Rise and Radiate a Visible Incomparable
Glory*, etc.", London, 1653.

"This piece", writes Wood, "is looked upon by some to be
learnedly written, who take the author to be a perfect Chiliast or
Millenarian, as Mr Jos. Mede, Dr Hen. More and many other
orthodox, as well as heterodox divines. Peter Sterry that high
flown blasphemer, and Joseph Caryl perused this book, and gave
their judgments thereof, and the last of them gave an imprimatur
to the title. Whence 'tis very easy and proper to observe how ready
and extreamely forward the last pretended reformers were, not
only to countenance but patronize the many generally exploded
opinions (in matter of religion) of their brethren however heterodox, erroneous and groundless: in so much that divines by public
appointment were ordered to peruse their books, and after a
transient cursory view of, to represent them to the world, in
extravagant lavish characters of their extraordinary worth and
excellency. As for the author Holmes, tho' he was accounted a
Millenarian, yet he doth not contend for a carnal, sensual and
gross liberty, and worldly to be enjoyed before the general
resurrection by the saints, but spiritual, purified and refin'd
freedom from the dominion and enslaving vassalage of sin and
corruption to be exercised in holiness and sanctity."[3]

This passage is, of course, coloured by the prejudice of a
strong royalist and the phrase "high flown blasphemer"
casually applied to Sterry is due to the gossip concerning his
behaviour at the time of Cromwell's death.[4] Holmes's book
is a small but stout folio of 563 pages crammed with theological and biblical learning bearing on the subject of the

---

[1] Cal. S. P. Dom. 1653/4, p. 189.
[2] *D.N.B.* s.v. art. Holmes or Homes, Nathaniel.
[3] Wood, *Ath. Ox.* ed. Bliss, III, 1170.   [4] See p. 38.

Resurrection. His doctrine is not unlike Sterry's own, but he has no literary gift. It is noticeable that, like Sterry in his sermon against the Presbyterians, he refers to the belief that the Messiah would come "in the year 1656 or thereabouts".[1] On 31 October Caryl and Sterry seem to have reported favourably concerning the book and a warrant was issued to pay Holmes £50 to enable him to print it.[2]

In the autumn of 1653 Cromwell found use for Sterry's powers as an orator and a logician in a conference with a certain Mr Feake, an Anabaptist minister,[3] and others of the same sect who were giving trouble to the government. We are told that Cromwell on this occasion used Sterry "and two or three more of his ministers to oppose spirit to spirit, and to advise Feake and the rest to obedience, as the most necessary way to bring in the kingdom of Christ".[4] We may well believe that Sterry's eloquence and his immense theological learning were useful weapons for a government which had to deal with a heterogeneous multitude of sectaries whose heads were filled with religious "enthusiasm" and half-digested scriptural knowledge. On the 22nd of the following March he is found testifying to the good conduct of Stephen Sayers, a porter at Whitehall who was applying for arrears of wages and other moneys due to him.[5]

Cromwell's attempt to organize a national church on a comprehensive basis in the spring of 1654 gave Sterry new employment. On 20 March he was selected as a member of the Board of Commissioners or "Triers"[6] "for approbation

---

[1] ΑΠΟΚΑΛΥΨΙΣ ΑΝΑΣΤΑΣΕΩΣ, 1653, p. 548.

[2] Cal. S. P. Dom. 1653, p. 225.

[3] It may be remembered that Tabitha, the Puritan girl in Cowley's *Cutter of Coleman Street*, was "o' the Fifth Monarchy Faith" and used to go "every *Sunday* afoot over the Bridge to hear Mr *Feak*, when he was Prisoner in Lambeth House".

[4] Thurloe State Papers, I, 621. Intercepted letter dated 2 December [1653]. [5] Cal. S. P. Dom. 1654, p. 45.

[6] *Acts and Ordinances of the Interregnum*, II, 856.

of Publique preachers" along with Francis Rous, Thomas Goodwin, John Owen, his old Cambridge friend John Sadler, and other prominent Independent divines and scholars. This appointment is certainly a sign of the high esteem in which he was held, for the scheme of a Broad National Church was a darling one of the Protector, who was particularly proud of the integrity and learning of his board of "Triers". As a member of this body Sterry is recorded in the State Papers for the years 1654 and 1655 to have dealt with the cases of several "sequestrated ministers" (*i.e.* episcopalian and other clergymen ejected by the authorities) and to have reported to the Council concerning their "submission to the present government and fitness to preach the Gospel".[1] His name is again found among the Commissioners appointed on 28 August for the county of Surrey "to eject scandalous, Ignorant and Insufficient Ministers and Schoolmasters".[2]

On 21 September, 1654,[3] he was appointed "to preach every fortnight on Thursday at the Chapel at Whitehall in the forenoon", and on 23 January, 1654/5, he was called upon by the Protector and his Council to help them in the "seeking of God".[4] On 24 July the Council appoints "Mr Sterry to preach once on the Lord's Day at Whitehall or Hampton Court as shall be ordered".[5]

In the autumn of 1655 Cromwell was petitioned by Manasseh Ben Israel to readmit the Jews to England, and he seems to have considered a project for granting English citizenship to them. A conference on the subject was held on 13 November between the Council of State and twenty-eight other persons, who were chiefly divines. Its consultations led to no decision, and on 11 December the Protector added Hugh Peters, Peter Sterry and a certain Mr Bulkely to

---

[1] Cal. S. P. Dom. 1654, pp. 369, 373; 1655, pp. 34, 50.
[2] *Acts and Ordinances of the Interregnum*, II, 983.
[3] Cal. S. P. Dom. 1654, p. 370.
[4] Masson, *Life of Milton*, v, 31; Cal. S. P. Dom. 1654/5, p. 21.
[5] Cal. S. P. Dom. 1655, p. 256.

the clerical part of the conference,[1] apparently in order to strengthen the body of opinion in favour of the proposals. Although no record survives of Sterry's activities at this conference, we can be sure that with his advanced views on the subject of toleration and his deep reverence for Jewish thought and learning he gave his full support to Cromwell's proposals. When we remember the numerous references to Rabbinical teaching in his works, we may well suppose that he may have been in touch with some of the Jews who came to London to press the claims of their nation on the government.

It is pleasant to find that when Sterry was holding this influential position as chaplain to the Protector and member of the Board of "Triers", he exerted his influence on at least one occasion in favour of a distressed royalist. Robert Mossom, a schoolmaster of Richmond and a clergyman of the Church of England,[2] petitioned the Protector in January, 1655/6, against an injunction which restrained him from teaching. He had been sequestered from a living in 1650 "for reading the book of common prayer and for no other delinquency". He attached to his petition certificates testifying to his good conduct from Richard Graves of Lincoln's Inn and Peter Sterry whose original note is preserved at the Public Record Office.[3]

By experience I can testify to this before, having had severall children with Mr Mossom, & can ad this; y^t he hath had more peculiar distinguishing kindness to ye children of parents best affected to, & most engaged for this cause, & gouvernement.

From this note it would appear that Sterry's children had been at Mossom's school at Richmond. It would appear from his correspondence that there were at least five of them,

---

[1] Masson, *Life of Milton*, v, 71; Lucien Wolf, *Manasseh Ben Israel's Mission to Oliver Cromwell*, p. 50; Cal. S. P. Dom. 1655–6, p. 52.

[2] He became Bishop of Derry after the Restoration. See article on him in the *D.N.B.*

[3] Cal. S. P. Dom. 1655/6, p. 134.

Peter, Christopher, Joseph Lee, Frances and Gratiana. We know that the family was living at West Sheen at the time of the Restoration, and it would appear from this scrap of information that Peter Sterry already had a house there in 1655. This conjecture is supported by the record quoted above of his appointment to the special Board of "Triers" for the county of Surrey.[1]

We are reminded of his association with Milton by his appointment on 4 January, 1656, to the committee for collecting money for the distressed Protestants in Piedmont, the Waldenses on behalf of whom Milton wrote his great sonnet *On the late Massacre in Piedmont*.[2] A minute of 12 June records an ordinance appointing him with Owen and Caryl to undertake the work of reading the catalogue of the books in the library of the famous Dr Ussher, Archbishop of Armagh, "and to report what manuscripts and other books should be bought by the State".[3]

There are various records of quarterly and half-yearly payments of his salary under the Protectorate, but there appear to have been arrears. On 26 June, 1656, he petitioned the Protector for four years' arrears and asks to be "paid out of a debt of £2000 owing to the late King or other discoveries". An order was made that he should be paid £425[4] and a further sum "in lieu of his stipend". He does not appear to have received the money, for he had to petition again on 17 February, 1656/7, and the petition was referred this time by Cromwell himself in his own hand to the Council. The Protector's personal intervention had the desired effect, and Sterry actually seems to have received £475 on 18 February "and the allowance in future till the provision ordered by Parliament is made to him".[5]

---

[1] See p. 30.   [2] Cal. S. P. Dom. 1655/6, p. 100.
[3] *Ibid.* p. 370.   [4] *Ibid.* p. 389.
[5] *Ibid.* 1656/7, pp. 280, 285. See also Bodl. Rawl. MS. A62, Thurloe Papers, pp. 5, 6, where payments to Sterry amounting to £200 in all are recorded.

He preached another Guy Fawkes Day sermon to Cromwell's second Parliament on 5 November, 1656, this time to celebrate Captain Stayner's victory over the Spanish West India Fleet.[1] The discourse was published under the title of *The Way of God with his People in these Nations*. Besides thanksgiving for the victory it contains a strong plea for toleration, which must have made it particularly acceptable to Cromwell.

It is just possible that in the following year Sterry was acting as assistant to Milton, now partly incapacitated by his blindness, in the work of the Latin Secretaryship to the Council of State. Philip Meadows had been appointed to this post in October, 1653, when he was chosen in preference to Andrew Marvell, who also was an applicant. In February, 1657, Meadows was sent as an envoy from Cromwell to Frederick III, King of Denmark, and Marvell was appointed joint secretary with Milton. Curiously enough, Marvell does not, as one would expect, seem to have been appointed in place of Meadows. The work of the office appears to have grown so much that both a joint secretary and an assistant secretary were now considered necessary, and in addition to Marvell, on 8 September, 1657, "Mr Sterry" is ordered "by and with the advice of the Council" to "officiate in the employment of Mr Meadows" with a salary of "200 merks" or £66. 13s. 4d. per annum.[2] It is possible that this "Mr Sterry" may have been Peter, although it would seem rather strange that he should have been appointed to undertake a third set of duties in addition to these which he performed as chaplain and "Trier". His scholarship and his close sympathy with Milton's views on the other hand would have fitted him very well for the post. It may be, however, that this "Mr Sterry" is not Peter, but his brother Nathaniel,[3] also at this

---

[1] See Firth, *The Last Years of the Protectorate*, I, 52, 53.
[2] Cal. S. P. Dom. 1657/8, p. 89; Masson, *Life of Milton*, v, 71.
[3] Pepys met a Mr Sterry on 8 March, 1659/60. He calls him "secretary to the plenipotentiary in Denmark" and says that he

time an Independent divine, but later a conformist.[1] Even if the assistant secretary were Nathaniel and not Peter Sterry the appointment would be significant in connection with Peter Sterry's career. A beautiful extant letter[2] shows that the brothers were on intimate and affectionate terms, and the fact that Nathaniel was assistant to Milton and Marvell would probably mean that both the brothers were well acquainted with the two poets.

Cromwell died on 3 September, 1658, and with other chaplains Sterry seems to have been in attendance on him during his last illness. There is a great deal of gossip concerning Cromwell's death, and the events connected with it, much of which is probably apocryphal. Sterry's reputation has suffered considerably from these stories. He was, no doubt, genuinely attached to Cromwell and probably, like Marvell, he felt his death keenly. We can well imagine that his fervid imagination may have led him to use some extravagant language on such an occasion, and that certain imprudent expressions were misunderstood or misrepresented by his hearers. Like the passage in the sermon against the Presbyterians, such expressions would be dangerous weapons in the hands of men who desired to blacken the reputation of a friend of Cromwell. The best known story of Sterry's con-

---

had just returned to England. This was certainly Nathaniel. In the Domestic State Papers there is a record of £30 granted to him "towards Charge of his journey to the Sound" (Cal. S. P. Dom. Chas. II, 1659/60, p. 595).

[1] Nathaniel Sterry was a Fellow of Merton College, Oxford. He became Dean of Bocking in 1665, according to Anthony à Wood "by favour of Archbishop Sheldon". There are many references to him in Anthony à Wood's Diary. See also below, p. 49. The Thurloe Papers in the Bodleian (Rawl. MS. A62, p. 38) record a payment of £100 on 31 August, 1658, "to Mr Peter Sterry for ye use of his brother Nathaniel Sterry being for soe much due for his attendance one half year on ye publique Service".

[2] See No. 64, p. 178.

duct on this occasion is that of Burnet, and, as it is the only allusion to him in his *History of His Own Times*, it is probable that the neglect of Sterry's writings and his reputation as a mere Cromwellian fanatic are largely due to it. Burnet professes to have his information from John Tillotson, afterwards Archbishop of Canterbury. Tillotson's story, according to Burnet, is that he came into the presence chamber at Whitehall a week after Cromwell's death on a fast day.

On the one side of the table Richard [Cromwell] with the rest of Cromwell's family were placed, and six of the preachers were on the other side: Thomas Goodwin, Owen, Caril and Sterry, were of the number. There he heard a great deal of strange stuff, enough to disgust a man for ever of that enthusiastic boldness.

He reports that "Sterry, praying for Richard, used those indecent words next to blasphemy, *Make him the brightness of the father's glory, and the express image of his person*".[1] The text from the *Epistle to the Hebrews* was a favourite one of Sterry's. It occurs several times in his printed works and it is not improbable that Tillotson heard it from his lips on this occasion. If he applied it to Richard Cromwell, he was only using the same kind of language that scores of royalist divines before and after applied to far less worthy rulers. We must also remember that such an expression would not seem in the least blasphemous to one who, like Peter Sterry, considered that every human soul is potentially a true "image" or "manifestation" of God in the fullest sense of the words.[2] He would probably have applied it not only to Richard Cromwell but to any man or woman. But such high doctrine is very liable to be misunderstood and it is the common fate of the mystic to be mistaken for a blasphemer.

The other story is that he definitely asserted that Cromwell

---

[1] Burnet, *History of His Own Times*, ed. Airy, II, 148. The reference is to Heb. 1, 3.

[2] Cf. "Every man in his Natural state is a divine Spirit, an Immortal Soul, an Image of God, a Son of God in a deep Sleep." *The Rise, Race and Royalty, etc.*, 1683, p. 497.

was in heaven, and actually prayed that he might act as a mediator to intercede for England. Robert Baillie the Scottish Presbyterian, who detested the Independents, wrote that "Mr Sterrie in the Chapell after his [Cromwell's] death prayed! 'O Lord thy late servant here is now at thy right hand making intercession for the sins of England'".[1] Ludlow's version is that "Mr Sterry stood up and desired them not to be troubled 'For,' said he, 'this is good news; because if he was of great use to the people of God when he was amongst us, now he will be much more so, being ascended to heaven to sit at the right hand of Jesus Christ, there to intercede for us, and to be mindful of us on all occasions'".[2]

A still more elaborate account of Sterry's alleged prayer is given in a republican pamphlet called *A Second Narrative of the late Parliament* (*so-called*), published in April, 1659, where Sterry is described as "that cringing Court-chaplain *Peter Sterry* that also bows to what ever is uppermost".[3] The same tale was apparently known to Samuel Butler who used it as the basis of an amusing passage in the third part of *Hudibras*, where the poet implies that Sterry, when he spoke of the Protector in heaven, mistook the true heaven for the tavern called "Heaven" at the end of Westminster Hall.

> Toss'd in a furious *Hurricane*,
> Did *Oliver* give up his *Reign*:
> And was believ'd as well by Saints,
> As Moral Men and Miscreants,
> To Founder in the Stygian Ferry:
> Until he was retriev'd by *Sterry*,

---

[1] Baillie, *Letters and Journals* (Bannatyne Society), III, 425.

[2] Ludlow, *Memoirs*, ed. Firth, Oxford, 1894, II, 45.

[3] *A Second Narrative of the late Parliament* (*so-called*)...*Printed in the Fifth Year of Englands slavery under its New Monarchy*, 1658, p. 42. A copy of the Pamphlet is in the Thomason Collection in the British Museum (E. 977). The "8" of 1658 on the title-page is changed to 9 and the date "April 29" added in a seventeenth-century hand, possibly that of George Thomason himself.

Who in a false erroneous Dream,
Mistook the *New Jerusalem*
Profanely for th' *Apocryphal*,
False Heaven at the *End o' th' Hall*.[1]

The story, it may be noticed, emanates entirely from hostile sources, and it is pleasant to be able to pronounce it definitely to be a calumny. Sterry himself, as no biography has hitherto observed, categorically denies it in the following passage in the dedicatory epistle "To the Christian Reader" prefaced to his Sermon entitled *The True Way of Uniting the People of God in these Nations*:

> *The little pleasure which I take in, as also the little profit, which for the most part redounds from* Verbal Apologies *have made me long silent, while thou mayest perhaps have read, or heard reported words, as having proceeded from me in a publick Sermon, which were absolutely untrue both for the form of Expression, and the Sense. It seems not unfit upon this occasion of appearing in Print, nor improper for my present subject, to give thee this Account of my self.*
>
> First, *It appears to me a very* vain *thing for any person in this world to determine with an infallible Assurance the state of any person in the next world without a particular, infallible, and extraordinary Revelation from Heaven in the case, which I never pretended to.* Secondly, *According to my poor measure of Understanding in the* Gospel, *nothing can more fundamentally subvert the whole Mystery of* Christ *together with all Evangelical, Spiritual Principles, and Truths; nothing can more directly oppose the Supream Design of the Father, the Peace and Comfort of all his Children; than to joyn any Creature with our Lord* Jesus *in the Great Work of his* Mediation, *a principal part whereof his* Intercession *is, the value, and Vertue of which Part, as of the whol Mediation, consists in this, That our* Lord Jesus, *our only and ever blessed Mediator, and Intercessor is the only true, Eternal God, of one undivided Essence with the* Father, *and in all things* equal *to Him.*
>
> *I humbly intreat thee,* Christian Reader, *to judg of me according to these* Maxims, *and to believe that I never did, and through Grace hope, that I never shall express any thing unsuitable to them.*

Sterry concludes with a few words to his calumniators which are inspired by a noble charity and humility.

[1] *Hudibras*, Pt. III, ii, 215–24 (ed. 1678).

But it is good for us to say to all in all Cases, as St Paul *saith to the* Galatians: You have not injured me: I am as you are: be you as I am. *I am as you are; I set my soul in your soul's stead. Be you as I am, in the fellowship of the same Grace, and Love of the Father;*[1] . . .

There can be no doubt that these words refer to the story told by Baillie, Ludlow and the author of the *Second Narrative*, and after reading them no one can suppose that there was the slightest foundation for this foolish tale. Unfortunately it seems to have been well known, and the name of "high flown blasphemer" bestowed casually on Sterry by Anthony à Wood in the *Athenae Oxonienses*[2] is certainly due to its currency among the royalists.

Sterry's name appears in the list of persons to whom mourning was granted for Cromwell along with his colleagues Lockier and Peters, the Latin secretaries Milton, Marvell and Sir Philip Meadows,[3] and other official persons connected with the government and Cromwell's household. He is said to have been out of favour as a "court parasite"[4] after Cromwell's death. There is no support for this statement except the bare word of Baillie, whose allegations concerning the Independents must always be received with caution. The last payment to Sterry as chaplain to the Council of State recorded in the State Papers is dated 2 November, 1658.[5] He was certainly still preaching in London on the eve of the Restoration, for the last of the sermons printed in his lifetime is stated on the title-page to have been "Preached in White-Hall Chappel on the Lords Day in the afternoon, January 1, 1659" (*i.e.*, according to modern reckoning, 1660). The title of the sermon is significant. It is *The True Way of Uniting the*

---

[1] *The True Way of Uniting the People of God in these Nations*, London, 1660, Dedicatory Epistle "To the Christian Reader", sig. B1v, B2, B2v.

[2] See p. 28 above.

[3] Cal. S. P. Dom. 1658, 1659, p. 131.

[4] Baillie, *Letters and Journals* (Bannatyne Society), III, 425.

[5] *Ibid.* p. 585.

People of God in these Nations and the sermon is an impassioned plea for reconciliation and peace.

"We are to weep", he says, "for having been *Actors* in our *Divisions*. Who can wash his hands in Innocency, and say, that, he hath not been in some kind an *Accessory* in the Guilt of our confusions, although he hath been no *Principal?* Hast thou not contributed to them by advising, abetting, encouraging, countenancing of them; at least by withdrawing that Barr, which thou mightest have put in their way by thy Counsel, Assistance, and Interest?"[1]

England, however, was in no mood to listen to Sterry any more than to Milton's *Ready and Easy Way to establish a Free Commonwealth*. Soon Monk was in London, the Long Parliament restored, the Presbyterians and royalists triumphant, and Independency in the dust. Maidstone, the steward of Cromwell's household, who must have been well known to Sterry, wrote a letter to John Winthrop which shows how difficult the position of an Independent minister must have been in those days:

...eminent professors of it [religion], having achieved formerly great victories in the war, and thereby great power in the army, made use of it to make variety of changes in the government, and every one of those changes hazardous and pernicious....They were all charged upon the principles of the authors who being Congregational men [*i.e.* Independents], have not only made men of that persuasion cheap, but rendered them odious to the generality of the nation.[2]

A passage in one of Sterry's later writings suggests that he may have stood in the crowd and watched the entry of Charles II into London. He compares the "approaching Day" of union with Christ to "the entrance of Kings" when "Streets, Walls, and Tops of Houses are hung with rich Tapestry, and Embroidery".[3] For an idealist philosopher and a visionary like

[1] *The True Way of Uniting the People of God in these Nations*, London, 1660, p. 15.
[2] Quoted in Firth's *Cromwell* (ed. 1900), p. 449.
[3] See No. 84, p. 186.

PETER STERRY

Sterry such changes would have little enough significance. He would regard them, as he regarded all the appearances of this world, as fleeting and evanescent shadows passing over the face of Eternity.

Nevertheless his position as an intimate friend of Cromwell, and a severe critic of the Presbyterians must have been a very uncomfortable one. His old friend Vane, and his colleague Hugh Peters, were imprisoned and executed, and Milton is said to have been in danger. Baillie writes exultantly on 31 January, 1662:

It was the justice of God that brought Peters, Harrison, and others to a shameful death; to hing up the bones of Oliver, Bradshaw, Ireton, Pride, on the gibbet at Tiburne, to disgrace the two Goodwins, blind Milton, Owen, Sterrie, Lockiers and others of that maleficent crew.[1]

Sterry was no regicide, and probably no republican. The only definite political ideas expressed in his writings are those of peace and reconciliation. The government of Charles II had many weaknesses, but it was not likely to punish a man merely because he had been a friend and admirer of Cromwell. Sterry seems also to have had the good fortune to find a pleasant retreat from London and a kindly and cultured patron. We have already seen that as early as 1656 he had a house at West Sheen near Richmond. At some time after the death of Cromwell he became chaplain to Philip Sidney, Viscount Lisle, eldest son of the Earl of Leicester. This nobleman had been a member of the Council of State of the Commonwealth in 1648, and a member of Cromwell's Council since 1653. He was granted a pardon by Charles II soon after the Restoration, and he lived at Sheen Priory, the ancient monastic estate at Richmond, which belonged to the Crown, and was apparently given to him by Cromwell. He obtained a lease of it on 8 August, 1660, from the new government. The old monastery had disappeared and, according to Evelyn

[1] Baillie, *Letters and Journals* (Bannatyne Society), III, 443.

(writing on 27 July, 1678)[1] "Within this ample enclosure" were "several pretty villas and fine gardens of the most excellent fruits, especially Sir William Temple's (late Ambassador into Holland), and Lord Lisle's, son to the Earl of Leicester, who has divers rare pictures, above all, that of Sir Brian Tuke, by Holbein". It is significant that Sterry's first patron was a Greville and his second a Sidney, both families traditionally inclined to Platonism and to the arts. According to Collins, the historian of the Sidney family, Lord Lisle "entertained himself with some of the greatest Wits of the Age...". "I have heard it well attested", he adds, "that he set apart one day in the week for entertainment of men of letters."[2] It is a pity that Collins does not give the names of Lord Lisle's literary friends or details concerning these gatherings at his house. It is not unlikely, when we remember that Sterry was his Chaplain, that they included Milton and Marvell. In his correspondence with Sir William Temple, Cowley, Waller and Denham are all mentioned familiarly. A man of Sterry's tastes must have been happy in this pleasant Surrey retreat amid such congenial society, and what Sir William Temple in describing the place calls "the Pleasures of the Air, and the Earth, and the Water"[3] and Sterry himself "the Springing Life, the ffreshness, & flourishing Lustre, the solemnity, the Quiet...the Mixtures of light and shade, ...the murmurings of windes, the clearnes & course of Rivers". Accounts of the Restoration have given a general impression that the majority of the nation indulged in a carnival of wild debauchery, while a minority of sullen

---

[1] *Evelyn's Diary*, ed. Austin Dobson, III, 18.

[2] Arthur Collins, "Memoirs of the lives and Actions of the Sidneys", etc., in *Letters and Memorials of State...*, London, fol. 1746, I, 149.

[3] Sir William Temple, *Letters*, etc....*Published by Jonathan Swift...London...MDCC.* I, 69. Letter to Lord Lisle dated, Brussels, August 1666. Cf. also letter of Lord Lisle dated Brussels, August 1667, on pp. 115–19.

Puritans looked on in disgust from their hiding-places. It is pleasant to learn that there were persons who were neither narrow-minded Puritans nor debauched cavaliers, and that there were places where life was as sweet and rational and comely as it had been at any time in English history.

Sterry was not one of the persons excepted by name in the Act of Indemnity of August, 1660, from the general pardon granted by Charles II, nor when the lists of exceptions were drawn up does his name, like Milton's, appear to have been considered by the Commons. However, John Goodwin and Philip Nye were among the twenty delinquents other than the actual regicides excepted by name, and Hugh Peters was classed as an actual regicide. As Sterry had been closely associated with all these men under the Protectorate, his situation must have been for a time at any rate exceedingly precarious. Like other adherents of the former government he took the precaution of obtaining a special pardon from the King, which was granted on 9 November, 1660. He is described in it as "Peter Sterrie in our county of Surrey Clerk or by whatever other name or surname of office or of place the same Peter Sterrie may be described called or named or lately was described called or named". It is couched in the usual comprehensive terms and covers a variety of actions in support of the previous government committed up till 10 June, 1660. Passages that may have a particular significance in Sterry's case are those that contain a pardon[1] for "scratching erasure and interlineation of any Rolls Records writs warrants recognitions or other memoranda in any Court or Courts" and which release him from "all and singular suits and causes of suits before the said tenth day of June of which the examinations may exist at the Ecclesiastical Court...or before any Ecclesiastical Judge or Ecclesiastical

---

[1] The original pardon is now in the possession of Mrs E. Poolman, who has kindly furnished me with a copy of the Latin original and a contemporary English translation, which I quote.

Commissioners whatsoever within our Kingdom of England".

Sterry was certainly lucky to obtain the protection of this comprehensive pardon immediately after the Restoration. It is pleasant to conjecture that it may have been due to the clemency which he exercised towards royalists and episcopal clergy when he was a powerful member of the household of the Protector. In some ways, however, the security that he had obtained may not have helped his reputation, and it may have lent colour to the story that he was a kind of Vicar of Bray ready to change his allegiance with every change of government. Anthony à Wood in his *Life* of Robert d'Evreux Earl of Essex, who had been a member of Cromwell's Council, describes him as "changing with every change, and keeping still (like his father-in-law William Earl of Salisbury and Peter Sterry the minister) on that side which had proved trump".[1] Such a writer as Wood was, of course, incapable of appreciating the philosophic indifference of a man like Sterry to changes of government. Incidentally Wood omits to state that Sterry did not conform to the restored episcopal Church. His brother Nathaniel, who had also been an Independent minister, took this course and became Dean of Bocking. Peter Sterry, however, remained a minister of what was now to become the proscribed and persecuted sect of Independents till his death. We may be sure that he was not prevented from rejoining the Church by any pedantic scruples concerning rites or ceremonies or outward forms of religion, which, like his old friend and master Whichcote, he regarded as things indifferent. His motive in

---

[1] Wood, *Athenae Oxonienses*, ed. Bliss, III, 197. Wood seems to have borrowed from the pamphlet (quoted above, p. 36) called *A Second Narrative of the late Parliament (so-called)* (London, 1659), p. 15, where in a list of Cromwell's peers, Lord Viscount Lisle is described as "having learned so much by changing with every Change and keeping still (like his Father-in-law the Earl of Salisbury, and *Peter Sterry*) on that side which hath proved trump".

remaining an Independent minister must have been simply loyalty to his brethren and to the memory of the men of the Protectorate.

A good deal of light on his life immediately before and after the Restoration is thrown by the valuable collection of his manuscripts which I have been able to use through the generosity of his descendant Mrs E. Poolman of Melbourne, Australia. These manuscripts include transcripts of a considerable number of his letters. Four of them are addressed to his wife and of these four two are dated, one "4 May 1657" and the other "Chelsey Novr 25th 1662". They show that a relationship of singular beauty and tenderness existed between Peter and Frances Sterry. The language is that of the most exalted spiritual love, the love of the *Vita Nuova* and *Epipsychidion*, and from them we learn that Sterry realized in some measure that great dream of a perfect marriage of true minds for which Milton yearned all his life.

Frances Sterry is addressed as "My Dearest love, and most truly sweetest of all Earthly sweets".

"As you come into my minde", Peter writes, "when is it in ye day or in ye night, y^t you come not into my minde? a sweet Spring presenteth it self to me, with A new heaven, and a new Earth, in which at once all things, sing, shine, send forth their sweetest odours together, flowers, Birds, ye Sun, ye holy Angells...."

He has a vision of "Two heavenly lovers, in whose face a perpetuall Youth flourisheth, in whose Bosomes ye fountain of eternal love openeth itself, and sendeth forth continually fresh streams of pure sweetnesses, and perfect joyes into each others breasts, where they mingle, become one". "Thus my Dear you & I every Day, or Night, yea every minnute in the hour fly into ye Imbraces of each other." "You may see", he writes, "by this Letter y^t Nothing can divide you from mee, y^t you are ever my pleasant Garden....In ye contemplation of you, with an Eye of Love, have I written these Lines, and found y^t true of Plato; y^t Love is a pleasant Birth, in a

beautifull Subject."[1] He refers constantly to his belief that
human loves were due to the union of all good spirits in
Christ, or to the fact that they all partook of that spirit which
formed the body of the "Heavenly Man". By a quaint and
beautiful simile he links this belief to his love for his wife and
daughter: "Say to your Darling Daughter, y^t wee three are
one heart diamond, each of us a Corner in y^t pretious stone,
while our Jesus is ye whole Diamond".[2] It is a pity that we
do not know more of the woman who inspired these letters.
In a note among the transcripts from her brother-in-law
Nathaniel Sterry to his nephew Peter Sterry the younger he
describes her as "one of ye tenderest, one of ye best, and
wisest y^t I know".

Thirty-three of the letters are addressed to a daughter,
apparently a second Frances Sterry, who married a Mr Webb.
A number of them are dated, two were written at Whitehall
as early as 1 and 13 April, 1658, when Peter Sterry was still
chaplain to Cromwell, others at "West Shene" on various
dates between 1660 and 1665. These letters are full of mystical
religion and also of a great love and tenderness.

"O my Daughter", he exclaims in one passage, "wrap your
selfe up in your Jesus, as a sun like garment reaching downe to
your Feete; Crowne your self with ye Starres of ye Fathers highest
Glorys."

Elsewhere he bids her to "Bee ever a Pure, Princely Princesse
offering up sweete odour in ye temple".

In one curious letter dated 24 January, 1660, he describes
to his daughter a morning walk taken by her father and

---

[1] Cf. Plato, *Symposium*, 206 D.

[2] By a "heart diamond" Sterry seems to mean a diamond cut
in the shape of a heart. The *O.E.D.* does not give the compound.
Jewels in the shape of hearts were not uncommon in the sixteenth and seventeenth centuries. Shakespeare mentions one in
2 *Henry VI*, III, ii, 107. Judging from other passages (see below,
p. 74), I believe that Sterry had a fairly intimate knowledge
of the jeweller's art.

mother at Sheen and gives an account of their conversation in dialogue form.

"Not long since", he writes, "I walked forth in ye morning to meditate, as you know my manner to bee. Your Mother some time after followes & overtake[s] me in my Lords part of ye Parke." The last words suggest that the Sterrys occupied a house close to Lord Lisle's, and were allowed to use his grounds. Then husband and wife walk together "towards Richmond Hill". Their conversation is mainly of religion, but there are some pleasant human touches too. "Here on this Hill", Mrs Sterry says, "about a month hence wee shall have our pretty sweete violets." "While wee thus Walke, & Talke", the writer continues, "wee say one to another now we have all y^t wee could wish, if wee had our Daughter with us to Pertake of these pleasures."

There are many affectionate messages to Frances and her husband and children.

The time seemes long to your Mother, & mee, since wee had ye comfort of your presence, and conversation with us, thorrow wch there breaths forth upon us a refreshing Spirit of so much Child like respect, & sweetnes, of so much saint like heavenlyness, & Divinity.

Remember my true Love to your Husband, & your little boy. I write this letter partely to comfort you if he should continue ill.

Our dearest Respects and Loves to your Husband, selfe, & sweete Children, Brother John, & all with you.

Your Mother & I beleive, wee meete you often and see your face shining.

Give Rowland 2 Kisses from us. Remember our kinde loves to your Husband.

This Rowland appears to have been the son of Frances Sterry. There was a granddaughter too, a third Frances, and in one charming passage Peter Sterry bids his daughter "Like a good Shephardesse take care of my two Lambs ffr. & Ro: that I may find them lovely & prosperous when I see them."

In an undated letter he tells his daughter that "Alarmes

come from all parts", and we can suppose that the words refer to the anxious times after the death of Cromwell.

The largest and perhaps the most interesting part of the correspondence consists of sixty letters addressed to Peter Sterry the younger, who appears to have been the eldest child of Peter and Frances Sterry.[1] Few of these letters, unfortunately, are dated. The earliest date which occurs is 1 September, 1658. Others are "7 November, 1660", "Aug. 26, 1661", "Oct. 31, 1662", and "November ye 13 1665". If we take these dates in connection with the contents of the letters, it would seem probable that they cover a period extending from several years before the Restoration till some time between 1665 and Peter Sterry's death in 1672. These letters are again mainly religious in character, and the amount of mystical theology and biblical allusion which they contain seems to a modern reader very strange in letters from a father to a son who must have been a mere child when many of them were written. Sometimes, indeed, they rise into prose poetry of a beauty comparable to the best passages in Sterry's sermons and other published works.[2] There are, however, more intimate and mundane touches here and there, which give us a picture of a touching and beautiful relationship between the father and son, and a tenderness similar to that shown in the letters to the younger Frances.

The earlier letters in the collection are addressed to the younger Peter at Eton. He was probably sent to school there because the Provost appointed by the Parliament was Francis Rous, an Independent divine with mystical tendencies akin to those of the elder Sterry, now chiefly remembered as the author of the metrical version of the Psalms.

It appears that Sterry took a great interest in his son, and visited him every fortnight at Eton. The younger Peter fell

---

[1] See above, p. 32. Sir Wasey Sterry prints one of these letters in his *Annals of The King's College of Our Lady of Eton Beside Windsor*, London, 1898, pp. 132, 133.

[2] See, for instance, Nos. 54, 56, 57, 58, 65, 75 in this selection.

into bad ways at school, and caused his father much anxiety and pain. He is reproved for "Sensuality, Tiplings sinfull compliances with vaine persons, associating with evil & unsuitable companions". In one letter, obviously written with deep feeling, the father is doubtful whether he will even trouble to read what has been written, and he calls him "dead in ye worst sense, dead in sin". We hear of his "Love of Carnall Pleasures, associating with evill Company, haunting of Tavernes", and still worse "Lies to cover shame with, deceit of Trust, falsehood in mony-matters, cozenages, pilfring". His father was particularly grieved because he associated with unworthy companions. There is a curious mixture of the aristocratic fastidiousness of the scholar and the gentleman with the moral condemnation of the Puritan minister in his words when he writes that "There is nothing, which I should grieve for & hate more in any Child, then to haunt common houses, to have a Tipling humor, to love the converse of meane, worthles, ordnary Persons"; "bee as scrupulous", he writes in another letter, "in choosing your company, as in distinguishing brasse from silver". These are words that make us realize the gulf that lies between such men as Sterry and Vane and Milton and the good-humoured, free-living, pleasure-loving England of the cavaliers.

We hear of the younger Sterry's "late Night Walkes with those of whome I wrote to you, wch you so assured mee to be false", and of his "wanton wand'rings in y^t dangerous Wildernes of Lust with the Strange woman, and your sinfull expences on her, out of your Master's Estate". It appears in fact that he had not only fallen into vicious habits, but had deceived his father and his tutor in money matters. The father advises him to lead a more careful life in future.

Keepe your Bed, & Bed fellow, Keepe ye Colledge, and goe not into Towne. Keepe with your selfe, & bee with no Company, especially in all private places. Never be in the Company of any woman Kinde. Be very free to y^r Mr Speake often with him, acquaint him with all your Temptations, & dangers, and troubles;

be perfectly advised, and governed by him. Goe to your M^r for w^t ever you want, pens, Inck, or paper, or any other thing for your selfe, or brother, he will supply you; write to me on munday next...; & give me an exact account how everything stands with you in your spirit in all respects, your debts, your company, & brother.

It appears from this passage that a second son was also at Eton at this time. There is a charming reference to him in another letter to the younger Peter: "be Kinde to your brother. Doe Nothing with him but w^t you can do in Love. Never rate him, nor by any means strike him. That will Spoile his Spirit, & your owne".

The temptations of Eton proved too much for the younger Peter Sterry. "If you finde ye temptations of y^t place still to strong for you", his father wrote, "I am resolved to remove you." It is clear from the correspondence that he was removed. It seems that he had no aptitude for scholarship and his father sent him to sea. There is a short note from Nathaniel Sterry, his uncle, among the transcripts, addressed to the younger Peter, which seems to refer to this event. It is in this note that the description of Mrs Sterry which I have already quoted occurs. It begins with the words "Dr Coz.", and it is signed "N.S.".

"The designe of this", writes Nathaniel, "is to let you know....This voyage is ye great Hinge of y^r Life which will turne it one way, or other." He advises his nephew not to "Governe" himself "by a present Humour" but "by setled principles of work & wisdome".[1] "Dear Cousin," he continues, "I know you so well as to be assured y^t you will

---

[1] Nathaniel Sterry was a man of sense and apparently an excellent tutor. Among the Tanner MSS. in the Bodleian there is a copy of an interesting "direction for a good & profitable proceeding in study by Mr N. Sterry E. C." In this document he advised undergraduates to "read Spencer & Daniels poems for the furnishing of yor English tongue, for what good will all learning doe you if you cannot make use of it in the mother tongue? wch excellency few looke after, wch is an extraordinary folly".

preserve alwayes your affection to your Mother & follow her advise, she is as one of yᵉ tenderest, one of yᵉ best, and wisest yᵗ I know. And for Captain Williams, [referring apparently to the commander of Peter's ship] I would in every thing so comply with him as might rather shew my prudence in Considering my intrest, than my spirit in reflecting on my Condition." These words suggest that the young man was difficult to deal with and had rather too high an opinion of his "Condition". His troubles do not seem to have ended with his departure from Eton. It appears that he still had debts which he concealed from his father, although the elder Sterry had pressed him often (his own expression) to reveal them, and had offered to pay them and pardon it all. At sea he seems to have fallen into vicious and extravagant ways again. We hear of a debt of four pounds contracted after he has been a short time at sea.

"Is it fit", asks his father, "for you to ly ashoare constantly at bed; & at board with Passengers who are their own men, perhaps men of estates, or dissolute persons? How unreasonable is it for you to spend 2l a day for your dyet, wⁿ you may have it in yᵉ ship & cost nothing, wᵗ will this amount to; how many ports may you be forced to put in at? how long to ly in a place, wᵗ will yᵉ charge be at this rate? Besides I know well, & who Knows not what places of Temptation Ports are, & how dangerous to young men in all respects to ly Ashoare? It is proper, fit, & necessary for you to keepe yᵉ ship for Meales, & Bed, there to employ yoʳ leysure times in Religion, Learning, & Navigation; and if [you] come on Shoar for your recreation to let it be as seldome as may bee. I am much troubled to see you still unchanged in these 2 great points of evill, & danger, Love of company, & sensuall pleasures, vaine idle; & prodigall expence of money. I expect now that your place shall maintaine you, and to see you a wary husband, watchfull over every penny, & carefull to preserve and improve your adventure? After this rate you will soon consume your Stocke and render mee uncapable of supplying you."

The last words suggest that Peter Sterry had bought for his son a share in the ship on which he was serving.

Later the younger Sterry seems to have been placed in business, and we hear of him as an apprentice. "The sooner you are entered into business the better," his father writes. "Your brother U kept ye Cash ye first day of his service. The great rule wch you must never faile in, is still to write before you pay or deliver out any money." The "brother U" mentioned here is difficult to identify. I am inclined to think that "brother" stands for "brother-in-law" and the reference is to Mr Webb, the husband of Frances Sterry. The passage is a curious one to come upon amid the mystical religion which is the chief theme of the letters. It reminds us that Peter Sterry was the son of a merchant, and shows that there was a curious strain of commercial probity mingled with his lofty religious and philosophic speculations. He warns his son against the dangers of drinking and gaming while he is a "prentice": "Take heed of wine from which I warne you not out of Jealousie, because excesses of wine are so frequent among Merchants." "Gaming" is also to be avoided and he is charged never to "take dice, or card" into his hand while he is "a prentice", but this prohibition does not extend to playing for "a very small matter" with "neere relatives" "if they should require it of you". Peter Sterry's master is away, and he is bidden to be "exactly honest, & true in word, and deede. Let your Faithfulnesse & diligence, double now in your M^r's absence, bee very punctuall in money matters and every trust."

There is a letter written obviously at the time of the Plague and the father is solicitous for the son's health. "Be carefull of your health this sickly time." The last letters were perhaps written just before Peter Sterry's death. He refers to an illness and to his verse translation of the Canticles which we know that he undertook to amuse himself in his last illness.

It would be a mistake to suppose that the letters are merely the austere reproofs of a Puritan father to a weak and vicious son. They are full of tenderness and affection. The elder

Sterry is always exhorting his son to remember his own dignity as an image of God, and an heir of eternity. He bids him think of himself as "yᵉ Lords Rose tree in his Garden". He tells him to remember that "Sin cutts you off from that Best, & most Blessed Spirit God himselfe, yᵉ onely Roote of all Good, in which you first sprang, & by which you were once sustained, & nourished, as a Deare, & Delightfull Branch in that Tree of Light & Love". He is always encouraging him and warning him against despair. Even in the most melancholy of his letters it is hope and trust in divine goodness that is the burden of his message, instead of the gloomy threats of divine wrath that we usually associate with Puritanism: "Though you be as a Tree twice dead, & pull'd up by the rootes, Hee can make you to live, & to grow, being Himselfe a Roote, and the Power of an Endless Life in you". The father is quick to perceive "ingenuous & gracious expressions" and "buddings of grace" in the son's letters. He encourages him to avoid wickedness on the truly Platonic ground that it is folly: "Bee not wicked over much: cur moriturus es ante tempus; Abandon not your self to evill. But if you fall as a Man, ly not in yoʳ filth as a beast: Defend not evill, give not yoʳself up to a rage in it, to an enmity against the Good, to a despair of ever being better, like a Devill". When the younger Peter shows signs of grace, his joy is unbounded: "O; my Son;" he writes, "every appearance of the Grace of Christ in you, is a Kisse with a Kisse of yᵉ mouth of God himselfe upon my Soule. It comes to me as a pretious answer of my prayers, as a Vision in the Spirit, of heaven opening upon mee, & Jesus descending, & smiling upon mee, & showing you to mee in his bosome".

In order to keep his son from despair and gloom, he even expounds to him his favourite doctrine that sin is a necessary stage in the development of the soul, and that it does not exist "without an Act of Counsaile in God". Profound and beautiful as such a doctrine may be, it was surely hardly a wise one to unfold to a young man like the second Peter

Sterry. The affection of the father for the son is very obvious in the letters. When he is reproaching him with his misdeeds he writes: "My heart aches and breaks when I write these things". He is always longing for letters, and complaining of his son's slowness in writing. "Assure yo^rselfe", he writes, "from your Parents and Friends of all that can be expected fro ye most affec^{te} Relations to the utmost of their power." "No parents can have a more tender affection to a lovely & beloved Childe or more delights in the Society of it, than those which the Love, & esteeme of you breede in the hearts of your Father & Mother." In one of the most beautiful passages in the letters he conceives the earthly relationship of the father to the son as a covering to a divine relationship, comparing it to the staff sent by Brutus to Delphi which was outwardly of wood but contained within a staff of "pure, massy Gold".[1]

He is particularly anxious about the younger Sterry's religious life, and he often recommends exercises in mystical prayer, and meditation.

Ah! if you have stolne times for Evill, so you redeemed time to be locked up in your chamber by day to be alone on your face at ye feete of ye God of love at Midnight.

Retire your selfe, read, meditate, redeeme some hours to be locked up, & lye on your face before your God. Call into your memory w^t you have seene, w^t you have heard, w^t you have felt in ye Word of Life. W^t Joy, w^t sweetnes of heavenly Love, what peace, what security, rest in comunion with God.

Occasionally he also alludes to the religious observances of a more public character. He recommends Peter when he is away from home "Once every weeke [to] heare a lively, spirituall sermon", and he asks him to "Give...an account how constant you are in praying, & reading; how oft you have bin at some good meeting".

He is concerned with the intellectual progress of his son as well as his spiritual condition. He complains once of his

[1] See below no. 65 of this selection.

handwriting: "Your Letter...was written with an un-gracefull hand. I would have you in all things bee carefull to form your Letters, words, Lines, Cleare, even, & beauti-full". He gives much advice concerning reading and study of the Bible is, of course, often enjoined: "Spend your spare time in reading yᵉ Scriptures, some good booke, & some Ingenious Booke; yᵗ may quicken & polish your Parts". The last words are very significant. Sterry, like Milton, was a scholar as well as a Puritan. The parts of the Bible that are specially recommended are *Psalms* (notably nos. 20, 91 and 116), the *Book of Proverbs* and the *Epistle to the Hebrews*. After the Bible he chiefly commends the writings of Robert Bolton, a very popular Puritan divine of the older generation who died in 1631, and left numerous published sermons and other religious works. Once the younger Sterry is bidden also to read "Mʳ Herbert", and it is pleasant to find that the great Anglican and loyalist poet was a favourite of Cromwell's chaplain. Once also the elder Sterry tells his son to

have those verses of Virgill often in your mind where Evander sayes to Aeneas:

> Aude hospes contemnere opes, et te quoque dignum
> Finge deo.

It is notable that several of the letters are written in Latin, and it would appear that the father and son were accustomed to converse in that language.

We learn a little about Peter Sterry's own life and environ-ment from the letters. One is in dialogue form like the letter addressed to Frances Webb described above, and like that letter it gives a pleasant glimpse of the rural life led by the Sterry family in Lord Lisle's park at Richmond. This time the dialogue is between Peter, Frances (Mrs Sterry) and Gratiana, apparently a younger daughter. It is said to be written in order "to communicate to you those pleasures of heaven with wᶜʰ Jesus Christ entertained me, your Mother and Sister, as he walked with us this morning up yᵉ hill from whence I now write".

"Frances" is made to speak some beautiful words, which shows that Peter Sterry's love of nature was shared by his family:

See how delightfull ye bushes and gardens every where coloured with ye fresh green of ye new leaves, and the severall whites of ye sparkeling blossoms. As ye wind ruffles them, and ye birds sing in ye midst of them; you would think ye blossoms, and ye leaves sung to you, and y^t they were as beautifull, as they are Musicall.[1]

The letter is signed "P. ff. G.", *i.e.* Peter, Frances, Gratiana. In another letter he mentions casually to his son that "My Lord Lisle takes up himself very much in his retirement with that ingenious delight of planting trees, setting flowers and seeing them grow".

There are occasional guarded references to the safety of the family. We hear once that "things goe not so ill here as to discourage us". Another rather mysterious passage seems to allude to the Plague and to suggest that the house in which the younger Peter lived in London was suspected of infection and that the elder Sterry feared that if his son came to visit him certain children who were in his care might be exposed to danger:

"I have been watchfull & industrious with my Sister", he writes, "to prevent ye accesse of any persons, which seemed to have been neere any danger for that family sake, & the children intrusted to us. If it should be Knowne what the state of the family is, in wch you are, & you should be seene here, I should be contemned as partiall & unjust, although no evill should arrive. If any thing should happen by any other meanes or the immediate hand of God: a great storme of reproach from all ye country would fall upon mee."

It is clear from this passage and from other indications in the

---

[1] This is the order of the words in the passage as it stands. The transcript is not in Peter Sterry's own hand, and I am inclined to think that he wrote "as Musicall as they are beautifull" and that the copyist has reversed the order of the two adjectives.

manuscripts that Peter Sterry acted as tutor to children after the Restoration. Some very affectionate letters among the transcripts are addressed to a Mr Robert Liddell who seems to have been one of his pupils. One of them begins with the following words:

Deare Mr Robt
You were my first charge in this family, and are still in my heart very deare to mee.

This "Mr Robert" was probably a son of Sir Thomas Liddell of Ravensworth in the county of Durham who married Anna a sister of Sir Henry Vane the younger, Sterry's old friend of the days of the Commonwealth. Pepys saw him on the "Katherine yacht" on 2 June, 1666, with "a very pretty daughter, and in a very pretty travelling dress";[1] who may have been one of Sterry's pupils.

The Calendar of Domestic State Papers records under the date of 7 October, 1662, the granting of a "Pass for Henry & Thomas sons of Sir Thos Liddell Bart of Chelsea & Nath Sterie their governor to go beyond sea for 3 years". Thus it appears that Nathaniel, Peter Sterry's brother, acted as tutor to two of the young Liddells during a "grand tour" on the continent. Besides the manuscript correspondence there are five letters of Peter Sterry printed at the end of the posthumous volume called *The Appearance of God to Man in the Gospel* (1710). They all deal with theological matters and are all addressed to a nobleman who is probably Lord Lisle. The first is dated 30 January, 1668; the others have no date. Two of them are signed with the name Adamas, which also occurs among the manuscripts. It would appear that it was a name given to Sterry by his intimate friends. It is interesting to notice that Adamas is the name of the wise and benevolent druid in *L'Astrée*, the famous French romance of Honoré D'Urfé published in 1607–19. It is strange to find that these

---

[1] *Pepys's Diary*, ed. Wheatley, v, 288.

Puritans were readers of the same high-flown courtly and pastoral romances that were fashionable among the cavaliers. It would seem that there was a point of contact between the "enthusiasm" of mystical religion and the "enthusiasm" of the heroic school of Love and Honour.

We learn a little more about Sterry from notes among the manuscripts. There is a kind of commonplace book among the manuscripts in his own hand, the first entry in which is dated "Novem: 22. 59 Spittle." Other dates which occur are "Decem: 1.", "March 2ᵈ.", "Apr: 2.", and "July 20. die Jovis. 1665. Shene Peste Flagrante". The entries in this book are original meditations and notes on the writer's reading, extracts from ancient authors and translations. Among the authors whose works are cited are Maximus Tyrius, Plutarch, Plato, Plotinus, Ficinus, Behmen, Proclus, Hammond on the New Testament, "Pre-Adamita 1655" and others.

These notes are certainly the records of a hard-working student and of a man of considerable learning. Another very interesting testimony to his culture is a rough list of some books which he had with him at Chelsea, possibly at Sir Thomas Liddell's house, in 1663:

> Bookes at Chelsey Apr: 21. 1663.
> Thom: Aquin: summes. Brother
> fficinus 2 volumes
> Behmen. Myster ffur: Sacr: 3
> ffletch: Shakesp: Endym:
> Litter Hebr: Lex:
> Greene Bible. Hebr. Hagiographa.
> Seneca ffarn:
> Grand Cy: Vol: 1st Cassandra
> Thaulerus Dauen: Arvirag.
> Origen: Philoc: Savonarola
> Sʳ ffr: Bacon Instaur.
> Two bound Paper bookes
> Hammond on new Test.
> Pierius: Map-booke Ovid.
> Simpson. Proclus in Tim: Cusanus. Plotinus.
> Behm: Aurora

I do not profess to understand the meaning of all the items in this list, but it is surely a very remarkable collection to be found in the possession of a Puritan divine, including as it does not only the *Summa Theologica* of St Thomas Aquinas, the works of the Cardinal Nicholas of Cusa, Ficino the Italian Platonist, Savonarola the Florentine reformer, the Neoplatonists Plotinus and Proclus, the philosophers Seneca and Bacon, the German mystic Jacob Behmen or Böhme, and the Greek father Origen, but also the works of Fletcher, Shakespeare and Ovid, as well as the fashionable French romances *Le Grand Cyrus* and *Cassandra*. It is the library of a man of very wide and varied tastes, of one who was quite free from the vulgar Puritan prejudice against profane literature.

The records of the latter part of Sterry's life apart from the manuscripts are few. By good fortune a glimpse of him just after the Plague of 1665 is afforded by a curious manuscript life of a Mrs Mary Carleton, a pious London lady, written by her brother, Samuel Crisp, preserved among the Rawlinson MSS. in the Bodleian Library.[1] Mrs Carleton, according to her brother's account, went to live at Addington just after the Plague, and Samuel Crisp and his wife stayed with her there for seven months.

"We enjoyed many pretious seasons", he writes, "this summer [? 1666] in her house, by the excelent ministry of the worthy servants of God; Doctor Wilkinson; and Mr Sterry; every Lords day in her family; which she exceedingly prized, and would call one Peter, and the other Paul, the doctor laying the conscience open to the Law, and Mr Sterry pouring in the oyle of Joy to heale it by the gosple; not but that the docter preached true gosple doctrine too; her heart was wonderfully ravisht at the sweet sound of the gospel which came from their lips; and sparkled out agayne at her eyes;..."

---

[1] Bodl. MS. Rawl. D. 106, ff. 33b, 34. This Mary Carleton is a very different person from the German swindler who assumed that name, and is described by Pepys under the name of "the German Princess".

The Carletons and Crisps were wealthy London merchants. Ellis Crisp died in 1625 and his son, Sir Nicholas Crisp, was one of Charles I's most loyal supporters in the City. Samuel Crisp and Mrs Carleton would appear to be younger children of Ellis Crisp. Another brother, Tobias, mentioned by Samuel in his Life of his sister, was an antinomian divine whose books were condemned by the Westminster Assembly. "Doctor Wilkinson" is Henry Wilkinson, D.D., an Independent minister who was made a Canon of Christ Church, Oxford, in 1648, and Lady Margaret Professor of Divinity in 1652.[1] We find Sterry in 1668 acting as one of a "combination" of nonconformist ministers who held a "lecture" at Hackney, which was said to include eight of the best preachers in the City. In the "Return of Conventicles" made by Bishop Henchman in that year Peter Sterry's name heads the list, and among his colleagues are other veteran Independents such as Philip Nye, Dr Thomas Goodwin and Dr John Owen.

In the spring of 1672 the famous Declaration of Indulgence suspending the penal laws against dissenters was issued by Charles II, and Sterry was one of the first nonconformist ministers to apply for a licence to preach under the new enactments. His popularity as a preacher is proved by the fact that the licence is desired for no less than three places, the houses of Mr Edward Bushell in Hackney and at Little St Helen's, and the house of Mr John Berry in Filpot Lane. The application is dated 10 May, and it was granted on the 16th. On 22 July another licence was granted to him to preach at Berkhamsted in the house of a certain Richard Pemble.

He did not live to derive much benefit from the new policy of toleration or to see its reversal. He was ill in May and is said to have dictated his essay on "The Mystery of Divine Wrath" on his sick bed on the 23rd of that month.

---

[1] See *D.N.B.* s. v. art. Sir Nicholas Crisp, Tobias Crisp, Henry Wilkinson.

He also amused himself during his illness by making a paraphrase in verse of the Canticles which is preserved among his papers. He died on 19 November. A friend,[1] who was probably Joshua Sprigg, a well-known Independent divine, was with him at the end, and asked him shortly before his death "how his Mind stood". Sterry answered "with much Composure; *That it then pleased God also to give him full assurance of those Truths he had taught others*". It would appear from these words that he had a moment of mystical illumination on his death-bed similar to those which he seems to have experienced at times during his life.

Peter Sterry was buried in the Church of Little St Helen's, Bishopgate, and it seems probable that he died at the house of his friend Mr Edward Bushell in the parish of Little St Helen's where he was accustomed to preach.

Sterry's friend relates that he brought the news of Sterry's death to Whichcote, who was then rector of St Lawrence Jewry. He says that Whichcote expressed "surprize and concern". Well, said he, "*as much as the world thinks me to love Money, I tell thee, I should well be contented to part with half of what I have to obtain only some Hours free Conversation with that great Enlightned Friend of ours, who is now taken from us.*"[2] To "try his affection" Sterry's friend asked Whichcote "*as a farther expression of your Kindness and Esteem for him, to Preach his Funeral Sermon*". "*That I will most readily* reply'd the most Benign Doctor, *in case you* your *self, shall think it proper or advisable at this time of Day.*" The last words suggest that the news reached Whichcote rather late. If he did preach a funeral sermon on Sterry, it has not survived.

---

[1] The editor of the volume of posthumous writings by Sterry called *The Appearance of God to Man in the Gospel*. In a pencil note in my copy of this book he is identified with Sprigg. Baxter in his short account of Sterry in his Autobiography writes, "Mr Sprig is the chief of his more open Disciples" (*Reliquiae Baxterianae*, 1696, I, 75).

[2] *Appearance of God to Man in the Gospel*, etc. A 2 v.

Peter Sterry's widow, Mrs Frances Sterry, survived him and seems to have died in 1682. Her will is extant[1] and was proved on 28 July of that year. It shows that she had an estate of about a thousand pounds, most of which she leaves to her son Peter and to his sons Peter and Francis. There are also small legacies to her other children and grandchildren among which it is pleasant to find a bequest of her "Black Ebony Cabinett" and "Silver Cupp and lidd" to Frances Webb. The impression of the younger Peter Sterry's character gained from his father's letters is confirmed by this will. His mother leaves the money for him in trust with Nathaniel Sterry, Dean of Bocking, his uncle, who is instructed to pay him only the interest and not the capital, while by a first codicil Peter is permitted to draw fifty pounds to pay part of a debt of a hundred pounds which he has contracted, and by a second codicil Nathaniel Sterry is allowed to take a certain amount, if he "shall see it convenient either to purchase a place or otherwise for his [*i.e.* Peter Sterry's] preferment and advantage of future living", provided that "it do not exceed two or three hundred pounds". Peter Sterry the third, son of the improvident Peter the second, married on 8 May, 1699 Miriam de Lillers, daughter of a certain Jacob de Lillers, at St Helen's, Bishopsgate, the church where his grandfather was buried. He died in January 1703/4 and was buried on the third of that month in the Church of St Peter the Poor.

It was probably this Peter Sterry who disposed of a fine library which was sold on 13 March, 1700/1, by William Turner at the *Angel* at Lincoln's Inn Back-Gate under the title of "Bibliotheca Sterriana the Library of Dr Sterry, Deceas'd".[2] This library is almost certainly the library of the first Peter Sterry, who was apparently admitted to the degree of doctor by the bookseller. We must not of course suppose that the list represents all his books. For instance, there is no work of Plato, and it is clear from his writings that he must have

[1] Copy furnished by Sir Wasey Sterry.   [2] Br. Mus. S.C. 240.

possessed a complete Plato; we have also the testimony of the list of 1663 that his books included a Shakespeare and a Fletcher as well as writings by Jacob Behmen. Probably books with specially intimate associations were retained by members of the family.

As it stands the sale catalogue represents a fairly extensive collection. There are many Greek and Roman classics including the poets Homer, Pindar, Euripides, Apollonius Rhodius, Terence, Plautus, Virgil, Horace and Persius; the historians Herodotus, Thucydides, Tacitus, Dio Cassius and Diodorus Siculus; among the philosophers in addition to two complete Aristotles there is, as we should expect, a strong array of Platonists and Alexandrians, Christian and Pagan such as Origen and St Clement, Plutarch, Maximus Tyrius, Plotinus, Iamblichus, Porphyry, Proclus and the Pseudo-Dionysius, as well as the Fathers, Tertullian and Athanasius. There are also the Greek romances of Achilles Tatius and Heliodorus. Modern philosophy is represented by the Jew Maimonides, the Italian Ficino, the Frenchman Descartes and the Englishmen Bacon and Henry More, Renascence scholarship by Scaliger, Lipsius, Casaubon, Vossius and Selden; romance by Barclay's *Argenis* and poetry by Tasso's *Gerusalemme Liberata* and *Aminta*. There is some theology and Church history, a number of philological works and rather a striking collection of old geographical and topographical writings ranging from the geographies of Strabo and Ptolemy to Camden's *Britannia*. Finally, welcome evidence of a sense of humour in Sterry, which appears little enough in his writings, is forthcoming in the presence among his books of a Lucian, the *Virgile Travesty* of Scarron in the illustrated edition of 1653, and the *Epistolae Obscurorum Virorum*.

From the records of his life, his extant correspondence, and his published and manuscript writings Peter Sterry appears as a man of great beauty of character and spiritual charm. He seems to have possessed something of that "secret of Jesus", the lack of which among the English Puritans was deplored by Matthew Arnold. It may be admitted that he was neither a hero nor a martyr, and that he passed his life in pleasant sheltered surroundings, and enjoyed the favour and friendship of eminent men. But there is no reason to suppose that he was a time-server or a sycophant as his enemies suggested, and it does not appear that he ever relinquished or disguised his convictions for the sake of material advancement, though Bunyan would, doubtless, have described him as a Mr By-Ends, for whom religion went "in his silver slippers". But he had exactly the qualities that Puritans like Bunyan lacked, the qualities of intellectual freedom, flexibility of mind, imagination, tolerance and loving-kindness. A contemporary[1] writes of his "great *tenderness*... which throughout his whole Ministry, and in all his other converses, he delighted to be still expressing towards all the *weak* and *little ones*". His works show that he united with this tenderness a wide culture, a true humanist's delight in learning and a love of beauty in all its manifestations. His religion is no dark prison house of the spirit, but a living aspiration towards that divinity which he found within himself, in nature, in works of art, in humanity, and above all in a vision of a harmonious and divinely ordered universe which seems sometimes to have been vouchsafed to him, and which inspires some of the noblest passages in his writings.

[1] Jeremiah White in the Preface to *The Rise, Race and Royalty of the Kingdom of God in the Soul of Man*, London, 1683.

II

THE WRITINGS

Peter Sterry's published writings apart from the seven printed sermons, to which allusion has already been made, are to be found in three posthumous volumes. The earliest is a small folio entitled *A Discourse of the Freedom of the Will*, printed three years after the author's death from an unfinished manuscript, which, according to the "Stationer's Preface to the Reader", he was preparing for publication at the time of his death. It is interesting to notice that this stationer is John Starkey "at the Miter near Temple Bar in Fleet Street", who had published Milton's *Samson Agonistes* four years before. The second of the posthumous works to appear was a stout octavo, the sonorous title of which indicates its contents: *The Rise, Race and Royalty of the Kingdom of God in the Soul of Man opened in several Sermons...as also The Loveliness and Love of Christ set forth in several other Sermons...Together with An Account of the State of a Saint's Soul and Body in Death.* It is in fact a collection of sermons together with a discourse on the immortality of a "Saint". It was published in 1683, and was apparently edited by Jeremiah White, like Sterry an Independent minister and a former chaplain of Cromwell, who writes a long and diffuse Preface, from which we learn much of his own opinions, but very little of Sterry. It was not until 1710 that the third volume appeared. It is entitled *The Appearance of God to Man In the Gospel and the Gospel Change Together with several other Discourses from Scripture To which is added an Explication of The Trinity And a Short Catechism.* The editor of this book was probably Joshua Sprigg, a well-known Independent divine, said by Baxter to have been a disciple of Sterry.[1]

[1] See above, p. 60.

The contents of this volume include a number of sermons, answers to five questions on theological points, a discourse on the subject of the Trinity and the five printed letters on religious topics already mentioned.[1] Sprigg's Preface, unlike that of White, is short and businesslike and contains some valuable information concerning Sterry, which has already been quoted. He states that the book consists of "papers which were scattered into several hands, being carefully collected for the use of private Persons". The title-page announces a Second Part which "will contain Miscellany tracts on several subjects handled Metaphysically. To which may be added a Paraphrase of the *Canticles* in Verse. Together with many excellent Letters to Friends taken from the Original Manuscripts, left by P. S. Late of *Emanuel* College *Cambridge*, and Minister of the Gospel in *London*". Sprigg prints "An Advertizement" at the end of his Preface which runs as follows:

Reader, The Contents of a Second Part is here inserted for thy Information, in which mention is made of what the Curious, and understanding in this kind of Writings, might wish to see; yet the Expectation of the Encouragers to this Part is so little, as puts a Stop to the going on of the Press, till a Trial be made by these of their Reception with the Publick.

It may be easily understood that little support was forthcoming to a work of this kind in the age of Swift and Pope. The Second Part, according to a list of Contents given by Sprigg, was to include several discourses and essays on philosophical and religious subjects, as well as some part of Sterry's correspondence and the paraphrase of the Canticles in verse with which he had amused himself during his last illness. The manuscripts from which the volume was to have been compiled have fortunately been preserved by Sterry's descendants. They are the body of unpublished writings contained in seven bound volumes to which reference has already been made in connection with Sterry's correspond-

[1] See above, p. 56.

ence. A description of these volumes and their contents is given in the bibliography at the end of this book (pp. 223-6). Besides a considerable number of transcripts of letters, they include the discourses mentioned by Sprigg in his list of Contents, some poems, and the personal notes quoted in the first part of this Introduction.

The most impressive of Sterry's works is certainly *A Discourse of the Freedom of the Will*. In the state in which he left it, it is fragmentary and, in parts, chaotic, with a good deal of repetition, while the argument is by no means easy to follow. But if it is a wilderness, it is a wilderness of riches, a maze of splendours which recalls the profusion of Milton's Eden. It is full of subtle and profound thought, and also of noble poetic prose. The Preface, in particular, an impassioned prose hymn to divine love and charity, is perhaps Sterry's most memorable achievement, and not unworthy to rank with the noblest prose of the age. The form of the *Discourse* is curious. It begins as a philosophic treatise in the manner bequeathed to the Renascence by the Schoolmen, an argument proceeding through a chain of reasoning and buttressed at every point by authority. Later, however, Sterry adopts another form favoured especially by Italian thinkers of the Renascence, that of a learned commentary on a poem, like Pico della Mirandola's famous commentary on the *Canzone* of Benivieni. The poem chosen by Sterry is one of the Latin *metra* of Boethius taken from the *De Consolatione Philosophiae*, the work that was so universally admired in the Middle Ages, and which still maintained its reputation at the Renascence. Sterry quotes the Latin and gives also a very free translation of his own, which is an English poem of some merit, and perhaps his best extant work in verse. The theme of the *Discourse* is an attack on the doctrine of Free Will, as commonly understood, on much profounder and more philosophical grounds than those usually advanced by the determinists who followed Calvin. Sterry's reasoning involves a fairly complete statement of his metaphysical and theological opinions, which sometimes appears to carry him away from the main thread of his argument. "How have I wandred", he exclaims pathetically at one point, "and delightfully lost my self by drinking in eagerly this Wine of Angels and glorified Saints,...".[1]

The *Discourse* is a very learned work and the authors cited show an immense range of reading which includes, not only, as we should expect, the Bible, Plato, Plotinus, Porphyry, Iamblichus, Proclus and the Pseudo-Dionysius, but also Homer, Virgil, Horace, Ovid, Aristotle, Boethius, St Thomas Aquinas, Peter Lombard and other Schoolmen, Jews like Leo Hebraeus, medieval thinkers like the Cardinal Nicholas cf Cusa, Renascence philosophers like Ficino and Campanella, and contemporaries such as Cudworth and More.

Apart from the *Discourse*, Sterry's most interesting work is to be found in his sermons, especially those printed between 1645 and 1659 and those which are included in *The Rise, Race and Royalty of the Kingdom of God in the Soul of Man*. There are some noble passages in the third posthumous volume and also among the unpublished writings, but, taken as a whole, these works are inferior in literary quality to the *Discourse*, the early sermons and the collection of 1683.

Sterry's writings will probably appeal to most modern readers less for the doctrines that they teach than for the music and colour of their language and imagery. He deserves the title of poet as much as any English writer who has used prose as his chief medium of expression. Unlike many seventeenth-century divines, he would not have disowned the name, for, as we have seen, he was a student and admirer of both ancient and modern poetry, and, as we shall see, it was part of his philosophy to believe that true poetry was divinely inspired. When I call Sterry a poet, I mean that he is a writer who uses language, not for the purpose of conveying abstract or prosaic meaning, but, to use the phrase of Professor Lascelles Abercrombie, as an "incantation". It is a curious

[1] *Discourse*, p. 76.

fact that in the middle of the seventeenth century prose was so often used in this way, especially by religious writers. Milton, indeed, was a great poet in both harmonies. But Jeremy Taylor, Sir Thomas Browne and Thomas Traherne are commonly true and splendid poets in their prose and rather prosaic writers in their verse. It seems that just at the time when verse was losing its old glory of colour and music, something of the spirit of Elizabethan poetry descended upon English prose, and turned it for a short time into an instrument for imaginative expression which has rarely been equalled in range and magnificence. To the list of the great prose poets of that age we must now add the name of Peter Sterry. At its best his style has that creative quality, that magic which Matthew Arnold pronounced to be the characteristics of true poetry. In Sterry's prose it is a magic which is akin to that which is found in the most notable lines and phrases of the religious poets of the age, that touch of the infinite which is the rarest gift of those poets, felt for instance in Herbert's

> Church-bells, beyond the stars heard; the soul's blood,
> The land of spices; something understood.

Vaughan's

> Dear, beauteous death! the Jewel of the Just,
> Shining no where, but in the dark;

or Traherne's

> The Streets were pav'd with Golden Stones,
> The Boys and Girles were mine,
> Oh how did all their Lovly faces shine!

This is precisely the quality of sentences and phrases scattered all through Sterry's writings, such as the following:

> Death, rubbing the Rust of this Dust from the Body of a Saint leaves it all a shining, rich incorruptible Dust of pure Gold.
> To be encompassed with all the Stars, all the Points of Heaven, as so many sweetly flaming Eyes of Divine love and Glory....
> Thou hast a love-Union, and by this Union, a Communion with

all the Treasures of the God head in the Sun, and in the Moon; in the Heavens above, and in the Deep which lieth below.

To use another phrase of Arnold's, it is genius rather than intelligence which is the presiding deity over most of his writing. In his sentences words are commonly no mere arbitrary symbols for abstract thoughts, but living things that dance and glitter and sing:

The Holy Angels, thine own Servants from thy Court in Heaven attend thee all thy way with Heavenly Provisions and Minister unto thee as is appointed there. Thy resting place every Night is ordered in the Promise. The Blessed Angels go before thee. They take up thy lodging for thee. They make it ready with Heavenly Furniture. They set a Guard about thee for the fear of the night.

The diction here is very simple. There is no simile or metaphor, no unusual word or construction, but there is the magic of true poetry. The words "provisions", "furniture" and "lodging", which in themselves seem to us so prosaic, have become things of beauty in this setting as dull greys or browns can be invested with unexpected charm and dignity in the painting of a great artist. It is not, however, only in this very simple music that Sterry excels. He can build the towering and involved periodic sentence with an amplitude and a majesty that rivals the work of that great verbal architect Jeremy Taylor himself:

All this God doth, that he may eternally display the unsearchable Riches of that Variety which is in himself, that he may swallow up the Understanding of every Creature, Man or Angel, into an admiration and adoration of the incomprehensibleness of his Wayes, his Wisdom, his Blessedness and Glory, who at once bringeth forth these Varieties (which like Morning Stars and Sons of God in the purest unmixt Light and Love, dance and sing together in his Bosom) into such fighting Contrarieties, upon the stage of the earthly and created Image here below, making that the seat of deformity, shame, woe and death, while it figureth out the highest Joys and Glories of eternal Life above, who again *gathers* up all those *jarring* and tumultuous *Contrarieties* into the first state and *supream Unity*, where the Variety is far more vast and boundless in the whole, far more full and distinct in every branch of it, where the whole is all, an eternal Melody, an eternal Beauty, an eternal Joy, unexpressibly Divine, pure and ravishing, where each branch, in its own distinct Form, is a Beauty, a Melody, a Joy, equally pure, perfect and ravishing with the whole, being crowned with the Unity and Eternity, which is the Highest Unity.

Such an intricate texture of sound and meaning is the work of a writer who has the artist's desire to create elaborate beauty as well as the theologian's to convey true doctrine to his readers. Some of the phrases flash like stained glass windows in the sun: "which like Morning Stars and Sons of God in the pure unmixt Light and Love dance and sing together"; "An eternal Melody, an eternal Beauty, an eternal Joy, unexpressibly Divine, pure and ravishing."

The most obvious quality of Sterry's style, as of that of Jeremy Taylor, is the splendour and variety of his imagery. His writings abound in metaphors and similes, which are not merely illustrations of his argument, but poetic images with an independent life and beauty of their own, as well as, in many instances, a peculiarly vital relation to the object with which they are compared. Coleridge's words on himself may well be applied to Sterry:

My illustrations swallow up my thesis. I feel too intensely the omnipresence of all in each, platonically speaking; or psychologically, my brain fibres or the spiritual light which abides in the brain marrow...is of too general an affinity with all things, and though it perceives the *difference* of things, yet is eternally pursuing the likeness or rather that which is common beween them.[1]

The gift of evoking by means of magical phrase images that have something of the vitality of the creations of the great poets is one that Sterry shares with other great prose writers of his age. His images are often as radiant and lovely as those of Taylor, and sometimes as majestic and impressive as those of Milton himself. Like Taylor he is a lover of

[1] *Anima Poetae*, ed. E. H. Coleridge, London, 1895, p. 104.

nature, and like Taylor's his nature poetry is to be found in
an immense number of images drawn from the common
sights of the English countryside. He is extremely sensitive
to light, and his pages are full of sunshine and starlight,
of glittering skies and water and sunlit flowers. Without
troubling ourselves about his philosophy or theology we can
enjoy much of his writing for the sake of those fresh and
lovely pictures. The sky with its changes of light and shade
and colour makes a special appeal to him, and he can paint it
sometimes with the delicacy of a Turner or a Shelley. He can
show us "the sweet colours of a fair summer-morning in the
sky...so made that they fade not, but go on changing still,
until they all vanish into pure light". We can enjoy with him
"the lovely Morning, the Golden Hour of the Day, when
there is no more shades or pure Light, but both are mixt, and
sweetly married into the pleasant Flowers of Saffron or
Roses", or we can contemplate "a morning beam begotten
between a pure sun and a sweet air". We can turn our eyes
upwards and see "the shady blueness in the clear Heavens
above us, which seemeth to terminate our sight". We can
look on "the Sun setting red in a lovely evening, because
being low he shineth with his bright beams thorow the
rising mist" or watch a gorgeous sunset (perhaps from the
top of Richmond Hill) like "a City on Fire or a Sea of blood".
We are made to feel the majesty of the heavens at night by
numerous allusions: "The firmament in which the innumerable stars are set", "innumerable Stars with springing lights
sparkling forth", "the stars in a clear skie in an evening",
"the Evening Star leads forth all the rest of the Stars into the
open Sky". Water too, especially clear water with reflections,
appears frequently. "A man under the *Law*" is said to be
like one "on the Brink of a River" who "looks not up, to
see the glorious *Image* it self of the Skie, but looking down,
sees the *Shadow* of it at the Bottom of the Waters". Sterry
delights in painting the reflection of the sky in streams or
rivers. He shows us "the shapes of the Clouds, or the Face

of Heaven in a clear stream", and he muses on "a silver stream, flowing quietly in a clear channel, where the Image of the Skie and all the Heavenly Bodies figures itself constantly and clearly". The English countryside with its flowers and gardens and meadows is a never-failing source of inspiration. We can "go forth" with him "in a fair Summers day to look upon the green Fields, and clear Skie...a refreshing to our Natural Spirits", which "begetteth a lightsome Joy in us". We can gaze on "the Violets and Roses of the Spring...the sweeter and more beautiful for the winter going before them". We can watch curiously "A Bee in a Garden" that "sitteth upon every flower and plant, sucking the vertue forth from it. This it formeth into One Sweetness in it self, which is Honey. Full of the Honey it flyeth to its Hive, and there layeth up its pleasant Treasures", or we can meditate upon "two lillies or Roses joyned together upon one stalk in a fair Morning or a bright Forenoon", or upon "the *Mary-gold*" that "opens it self only to *this Sun*". We are taken into "a Garden of Flowers by night" where "the Flowers are seen in dusky, and dark forms, while the shades of night lie upon them, as Vails upon their Beauties. When the bright day riseth upon this Garden, the Flowers appear in their naked and shining Beauties, in their proper and lovely figures". "Lillys...Flowers-de-luces, Flowers of Divine light...", "the choicest slips of flowers" flash before our eyes. We find ourselves in "a Meadow with the Trees and Flowers by a Riverside", and at another time we are made to feel "the Joy of Harvest, when the countryman bringeth in the last shocks of ripe Corn out of the Field with Songs and Garlands". Such a writer naturally pictures Grace as "gentle Showers upon the New-mown Grass" and Christ as the good gardener who sets "a *Quick set* hedge" round the faithful, and waters us "with his owne *Foot* walking up and down in the midst of us that our Beds and Plants are *green*".

There is often a charming tenderness in Sterry's references to common natural sights that makes us think of Keats or of those forerunners of Keats, William Browne and Robert Herrick. He speaks with a delightful warmth of feeling of "a lovely summer morning in its first sweetnesses and light", of "a lovely Rose", of "the Heaven, the Air, the Earth, the Waters in a golden calm and serenity", of "the Summer... with its Golden Skies and Sunshine, with its Gardens of Roses, and Fields of Corn", of "the seed of Corn" which "first comes up in the tender blade like a low herb", of "the Flies" that "dance in companies" and "Plants" that "bud and gem in the sweet Spring beams", of birds too, the bird that "spreadeth itself over its Nest to hatch, and cherish its young ones", of "a little Bird ty'd by the Leg with a String", which "often flutters and strives to raise itself".

Another source of Sterry's imagery, which is unusual among seventeenth-century divines, is to be found in the arts. I have already referred to his interest in painting. His writings abound in allusions to that art and illustrations drawn from its processes. He remarks that "The Work of some Excellent Painter is known by this that it is a *finisht piece*. Every part, every point hath its just and full proportions, as from a spring of life opening it self there, as if Nature herself were a vital sense. This gives the life, the beauty, the sweetning to the whole piece, a living form to the Workman". We are told that "the chief skill in pictures consisteth in the evenness and justness of placing the *shades*, that according to the degrees of the declining Light, the shades may gradually increase, until they sink into the deepest obscurity, or be bounded by a new Light springing up out of these shades", and that "a skilful painter is most discerned in laying his shadows. By these he maketh his work softer, sweeter, more full of life, and more taking", and we remember that the seventeenth century was the great age of *chiaroscuro*, a word of which the first use recorded in the *Oxford English Dictionary* is in a work published in 1686. We are reminded, too, of the realism with which painters of the Dutch and Flemish, and also some of the later Italian schools treated biblical subjects, when we are informed that "*Lazarus* with his Rags, his running Sores, and the Dogs licking them, represented to the life in an excellent Picture, done by the hand of *Vandike* or *Titian*, or some great Master is a worthy and most agreeable entertainment for the eye and fancy of any Princess, a rich ornament and rare Jewel for the Chamber or Cabinet of a Prince". Sterry has certainly seen a portrait painted and has observed how "A Painter, who is drawing a Beautiful Person keepeth his Eye ever upon the Life. Whether he lay dark or bright Colours, whether he make Shade, or Light, crooked lines, straight or circular, still he is forming that lovely Face in every stroke and colour". He does not hesitate to compare God Himself to a painter. "The most skillful Painter, sweetning and beautifying his Work in the whole, and in the parts of it, by the mixtures and interchanges of Light and Shade, Grace and Severity, still terminating all in the sweetness and light of the Divine Grace, as the end of all." The art of the jeweller interested Sterry as well as that of the painter. He frequently mentions gold and silver and precious stones, especially diamonds, pearls and rubies. He knows a curious old method of cleansing pearls by thrusting them into a pigeon's crop "where the heat of the pigeon takes off the stain", and uses it very aptly as an illustration. He knows too, that "There are Three Things which commend a *Diamond*: 1. *The* Goodness of the Stone. 2. *The* well-setting. 3. *The* well-cutting of it". In one place he compares the salvation of a Saint to "a rich Piece of fine Enamelling", and he describes the process, with which he is clearly familiar: "First the Ground on which the Enamelling lieth, is Gold. Then you have the rich Enamel upon the Gold. Lastly some beautiful Picture is formed in the Enamel.... All the Work is a curious, close, and fine Enamelling". Music, too, is sometimes mentioned, but less often than the visual arts. The lute, the favourite seventeenth-century instrument in English households, provides illustrations. "Discordant touches on a Lute", we are told "offend the Ear, but in a

Lesson of Musick, they are themselves harmonious, and enrich the Harmony of the whole Lesson." The Angels are "like *Notes* in a Musical Lesson, Diversities in the Harmony".[1] God is compared to a musician as well as a painter, and the universe, as in Dryden's *Ode*, to a universal harmony, "a Divine Musick" which "soundeth through all the parts and changes of the Coelestial and elementary Spheres *charming* those Souls that have *awakened* and *purified senses*", "A Universall musick where the well Measured Motions and Sweet Sounds of all the strings meet in every skilfull touch of every string".

It is natural that much of the imagery of a writer like Sterry should be of literary origin. His reading like Coleridge's must have been "oceanic". It ranges from the Bible, the Fathers of the Church and the Jewish Rabbis through the whole field of classical philosophy, history and poetry to the work of the Renascence poets and thinkers, books of travel and science and apparently even to romances and fairy tales. The Bible, of course, is an almost inexhaustible treasury. Sterry's knowledge of the Authorized Version (as well as of the Greek and Hebrew originals and the Vulgate) is the knowledge of a man who has spent the greater part of a lifetime in such a minute and loving study of every sentence of the Old and New Testaments as could probably be scarcely paralleled even among divines in modern times. Yet in spite of this familiarity, the poetry of the Bible seems to have moved him as intensely as the poetry of his beloved skies and fields and streams, and evokes from him similar felicities of phrase and diction. He loves to retell the great stories of the

[1] *Discourse*, p. 81. Mr J. B. Leishman has drawn my attention to the following remarkable parallel to this image in a poem called *Die Engel* by the German poet Rainer Maria Rilke:

> Fast gleichen sie einander alle,
> In Gottes Garten schweigen sie
> Wie viele viele Intervalle
> In seiner Macht und Melodie.

Old Testament, Noah's Flood, Jacob's Wrestling and his Dream, Rebecca at the Well, the Princes digging with their staves and singing "Spring O Well" in the *Book of Numbers* and many others, and to make them serve as symbols of the life of the spirit. In a similar way he makes splendid use of the gorgeous setting of ancient Hebrew worship, "the Tabernacle of white linnen wrought with all fine and rich colours, one over another upon it of Goats' hair, of Ram's skins died red, of Badger's skins," "the Palms, the Lilies and Cherubims of the Temple, carved first in Cedar, and then covered with massy Gold", the golden mercy-seat and the golden cherubim in the Holy of Holies. There is no puritan austerity in allusions like these, but rather that mixture of aesthetic and religious feeling which is usually associated with Catholicism. Nor is it any one part of the Bible which appeals predominantly to his imagination. His prose is like a glowing fabric shot through and through with memories of every part of the Authorized Version, from the visions of the Hebrew Prophets and the Apocalypse and the glowing poetry of the Canticles to the narratives of the Gospels, the sayings of Christ and the teaching of St Paul. For Sterry the Bible is no mere manual of piety, no collection of the dry bones of doctrine. It is living concrete poetry like the flowers, the stars and the clouds, literally, and not merely in pious metaphor, a well-spring of spiritual life. A chance phrase or allusion in its pages is a spark that can always kindle him to flame. It may be the throne of Solomon with its six steps and its lions and its footstool of gold, the golden candlesticks in the Temple, the silver trumpets of the Sanctuary in the Wilderness, or an Angel descending from Heaven in the Apocalypse, which he sees with the eyes of the spirit, like an old Italian or Flemish painter; "While thou readest", he writes, "let this *heavenly love* be as a *Seraphim* flying down upon its flaming wings from the Throne of Love into thy Bosom, to enlighten thy whole Soul with its beams unto a Divine Candour".

After the Bible comes classical myth and legend. I have already mentioned his affection for Virgil and the *Aeneid*. Christ is the spiritual Aeneas appearing to Dido or the Soul of Man out of a Cloud. Sin, like Cupid in the form of Ascanius, disguises itself as Goodness and Beauty, and breathes "fatal poyson" into the veins. Sterry hopes that his great *Discourse* may, like the two silver doves which led Aeneas to the golden tree, lead the reader to the "heavens of Divine Truth and Goodness". Man on earth is like Aeneas in the underworld, who by the mere brandishing of a sword which is the Spirit of Christ can put to flight "all ye alluring, or affrighting Appearances of this Life, like so many Hellish Hags, & empty shades". Homer, too, is used, though less frequently than Virgil. The golden chain by which the world was attached to the throne of Zeus, and curiously enough too, the unquenchable laughter with which the gods greeted the trapping of Ares and Aphrodite in the net of Hephaistos, serve as apt illustrations of Sterry's doctrine. The myths of Semele, Ixion, Proteus, Orpheus and other pagan tales are employed with the utmost freedom. For Sterry, indeed, they were no relics of "idolatry", but part of a genuine though incomplete revelation of the true religion.[1] The classical historians occasionally furnish a striking image. The story in Herodotus of the dumb son of Croesus, and Tacitus's anecdote of the rescue of Tiberius by Sejanus are examples, and naturally there are a number of allusions to the myths of the ancient philosophers and especially to those of Plato. Plato for Sterry is not merely a "divine philosopher"; he is also the poet of the great myths of the *Phaedo*, the *Phaedrus* and the *Republic*; who had a vision of the world as it might appear from the Sun bathed "in a Sun-like Glory", and of the Soul with its two great golden wings; while to Plotinus he owes the magnificent image of the "First Soul" that "hath its face ever turned to the Face of God". The only modern poets who are mentioned by name are Tasso and Spenser. One

[1] Cf. p. 112 and note.

of his finest images is certainly drawn from *The Faerie
Queene*,[1] and he actually uses Shakespeare's phrase "the gentle
Rain from Heaven",[2] and probably alludes to his works elsewhere. He knows contemporary books of travel and science.
A quaint passage refers to "such a Brute Creature, as is seen
in some parts of Africa by travellers" and to the theory that
explained the gorilla as "the shape of a Man into which no
Rationall, Immortall spirit descends". "Naturalists", we are
informed, "tell us that some Candles may be so made that all
the Persons seen by those lights shall appear as Ghosts one to
another, or the whole place seem full of Snakes, and dreadful
Serpents", and the Spirit of Man is compared to the "Christalline humour in the eye" through which "we are taught by
Natural Philosophy" that "the Images of things are seen".
The lore of the Jewish Rabbis was certainly well known to
Sterry, and some of their fancies are woven into the rich
texture of his prose poetry. Such, for example, are their
notions of a Greater Adam whose head reached the skies, of
the creation of man from precious dust or powder and of the
marriage of soul and body. Finally he seems to owe a considerable number of images to romance and possibly to
romantic drama. In the pages of this grave divine we are
sometimes transported to the region of fairy tales and we
find ourselves unexpectedly

> In a land of clear colours and stories,
> In a region of shadowless hours,

where we hear of "a Royal Bridegroom, which in the habit of
a shepheard, presents and marries himself to the Beloved
Maid in the midst of the Woods", of "a Princely Bridegroom
leading his Royal Bride in his hand through delightful walks,
when Spring is in its prime", or of a magical Palace of Pearl
at the bottom of a fountain.

Sterry's published works are cast into the rigid conven-

---

[1] See no. 1, p. 124 and note *ad loc.*
[2] See no. 94, p. 190 and note.

tional forms of the seventeenth-century sermon or treatise. But these were certainly not the forms in which this genius naturally tended to express itself. His sermons, with the possible exception of *The Clouds in Which Christ Comes*, are not like those of Donne, for instance, remarkable for their structure as complete pieces of organized eloquence, nor can the *Discourse* or his shorter essays (even allowing for the unfinished state of the former) be admired as examples of sustained reasoning or prose architecture on a large scale.[1] The natural form in which his writing tends to crystallize is that of the short prose poem or meditation consisting of a vivid presentation of one or more images followed by an interpretation in a spiritual or religious sense, or conversely the enunciation of a spiritual truth followed by imagery that illustrates and embodies it. The present selection is an attempt to detach a number of these prose poems from cumbrous archaic settings which have little interest for the modern reader, and to arrange them in a sequence that is designed to illustrate the main features of Sterry's doctrine. It will be noticed that the extracts are generally complete in themselves, and can be understood and appreciated without reference to their context. They are simply prose counterparts of the poems of such men as Herbert, Crashaw, Vaughan, and Traherne; and, if they had been cast in verse form, would no doubt have had the same reputation. Sometimes, indeed, Sterry treats almost exactly the same themes as the religious poets, and it may be of interest to place examples side by side. Traherne in his poem, *Hosanna*, has two fine stanzas describing a moment of vision when he saw the whole world transmuted into a heaven of glory:

---

[1] See the remarks on Sterry in Mr W. Fraser Mitchell's recent book on *English Pulpit Oratory from Andrewes to Tillotson* (S.P.C.K. 1932), pp. 298–300. Mr Mitchell's unsympathetic view of Sterry's work is probably due to the fact that he is interested in sermons as "pulpit oratory" rather than as literature.

The Deity, the Deity to me
Doth All things giv, and make me clearly see
   The Moon and Stars, the Air and Sun
      Into my Chamber com:
   The Seas and Rivers hither flow.
Yea, here the Trees of *Eden* grow,
   The Fowls and Fishes stand,
      Kings and their Thrones,
   As 'twere at my Command;
   God's Wealth, His Holy Ones,
And Ages too, and Angels all conspire:
While I, that I the Center am, admire.

No more, No more shall Clouds eclyps my Treasures,
Nor viler Shades obscure my highest Pleasures;
   No more shall earthen Husks confine
      My Blessings which do shine
   Within the Skies, or els *abov*:
Both Worlds one Heven made by Lov,
   In common happy I
      With Angels walk
   And there my Joys espy;
   With God himself I talk;
Wondring with Ravishment all Things to see
Such *Reall* Joys, so truly *Mine*, to be.

In the following passage Sterry describes a similar experience in prose which is surely no less truly poetical than Traherne's verse:

O what a Heaven doth he continually walk in, to whom all Things round about him are hung with these Curtains of *Solomon*, the living Brightnesses of a Divine Light; the Flower of Light springing from the Face of God? In what lovely Images doth this Light, as the Looking-Glass of Eternal Truth and Love, present him to himself, his Company, all Things round about him, to him? In the 68th Psalm v. 17. *The Chariots of the Lord are* said to be *Thousands of Thousands, and God himself in the midst of them, as on Mount Sinai*. While thou first fastnest the eye of thy Spirit on the Majesty of God, and then beholdest all things as they appear in the Light of the Divine Presence; thou indeed art in Heaven. All Things are as the Angels of God, as Divine Emanations, Divine Figures, and Divine Splendors circling thee in on every side, and God himself as a Fountain of Gloryes in the midst of them.

The simplest form of Sterry's prose poetry is one sentence containing a single image or metaphor:

Divine Truth is as a *Rose Tree*, which, as it hath its beautiful perfumed Roses, so it hath *prickels* to guard those Roses from rash and rude hands.

A sentence like this is a complete poem in itself, as perfect in its way as an epigram in verse by Landor or a poet of the Greek Anthology. We are reminded of Shelley's words in *A Defence of Poetry*:

The parts of a composition may be poetical, without the composition as a whole being a poem. A single sentence may be considered as a whole, though it may be found in the midst of a series of unassimilated portions.

One method of elaboration is simply to expand and develop a single image:

This *Manifestation* of Christ was at the first Creation, as a small spring onely, but a living one. From the Fall, to the Giving of the Law, this Spring drives along upon the face of the Earth, thorow all manner of mixtures, a very weak store and strength of Waters. From thence it begins to make a channel to it self, and to run along in a fair stream. At the Incarnation, and Ascencion of Jesus Christ, this Stream enlarged it self into a Broad River. But our Lord shall come the *Second time*, then shall this River become a great, and wide sea, covering the face of the whole Earth.

Sometimes several images are combined as in the following passage on Prayer:

While the Soul is wholly intent upon the Glory of God in Prayer, many sweet Appearances, high Truths shew themselves clearly to the Soul, which were before Unthought of, or very difficult. They now appear, as in their Element, like Stars to him that looks stedfastly on a clear Skie in an Evening. They come forth, as out of their Bride-Chamber, ready Trim'd, prepar'd for the Soul...often they come thick and swarming about the Soul...; like Bees out of a Hive. A Man frequently learns *more* and *better at one Hour's Prayer*, than in the Study of many days.

Here the truths that appear to the man in prayer are likened to stars, to brides, and to bees, without any effect of incongruity. The images are all exquisitely appropriate and harmonious. Sometimes a group of images is used with much the same kind of effect as the recurring rimes in an elaborate stanza:

Thus *God* is round about His own; a *Wall encompassing, enclosing* them around; a *Fire* devouring Outwardly every Evill, that would break in upon them; a *Light* shining inwardly, multiplying upon them all Formes of Life, all Beautifull, Glorious Manifestations; shooting ten Thousand Beames of Joy into their Hearts. Thus the *Lord* hath been a *Wall* to us, a *Sea-wall*, a *Wall* between us and a *Sea* of Blood. The Lord hath been a Fire for us Consuming our Enemies. He hath been a *Light*, standing still over our Heads, like the *Sun* over the head of *Joshua*, while he pursued the *Canaanites*, and made an End of them. He hath been a *Calme*, *Sweet* Light to us in the midst of a Thick Darknesse, and a Tempest.

A favourite method is to open a paragraph with a beautiful and vivid word picture, and to proceed to use it as a vital metaphor for some point of doctrine:

He that in a clear Evening fixeth his eye on the Firmament above him, beholdeth by degrees innumerable Stars with springing lights sparkling forth upon him. If God lift up a little of his Vail, and by the least glimpses of his naked Face enlighten and attract the eye of our Soul to a fixed view of Himself, with what Divine Raptures do we see the eternal Truths of things, in their sweetest Lights, springing and sparkling upon us, besetting us round in that Firmament of the Divine Essence as a Crown of incorruptible Glory?

A passage like this contains something like the strophe and antistrophe of an ode. Not only are alliteration and assonance used with striking effect but the words "lights...springing... sparkling" recur in the second half of the paragraph like recurring colours in a pattern. Many of Sterry's noblest passages are built up from memories of his reading. His mind was stored with images and phrases from an immense range of literature, but he does not, like some seventeenth-century writers, make his works a mere mosaic of quotations. To use the phrase which Sir W. Osler applied to Burton, he is a transmuter rather than a transmitter of the thoughts of other men. Ideas and expressions derived from his reading are fused together by his imagination, transformed into new shapes, and given new shades of meaning. They have gone down, to use the pregnant metaphor of Professor Livingstone Lowes, into the "deep well" of the creative imagination and emerge after their "sea change" as entirely new creations with a fresh beauty and significance. The process may be illustrated by some examples. In one of his sermons his theme is the presence of Christ in the world. He thinks of the *Aeneid*, his favourite poem, and he remembers how in the First Book Aeneas enters Carthage unseen, wrapt in a white cloud by his mother Venus, and hears Dido and his comrades lament his absence and speak of him as lost. Then the cloud is riven as with a flame and the hero stands before them, a divine figure in the sunshine:

> Scindit se nubes et in æthera purgat apertum,
> Restitit Aeneas claraque in luce refulsit
> Os humerosque deo similis.

Here is a magnificent image for the beauty of Christ breaking through the cloud of worldly experience and dawning on the believer. Then the burning words of the Second Isaiah come into Sterry's mind:

> For thou shalt breake forth on the right hand and on the left; and thy seede shall inherite the Gentiles....

Virgil and the Bible have provided the material, but out of these splendid memories, when a new imagination has done its work, there is formed high poetry of an original and transcendent beauty:

> The Prince in the Poet wrapt about in a Thicke and Darke Ayre, entred into Carthage, passed thorow the Court into the presence of the Queene, there stood in the midst of them un-perceived, while they speak of Him, as absent, lament him as

lost; till the Aire purified it selfe to a Clearnesse. So the Great
Prince of Peace and Spirits, as He comes forth, casts a Cloud about
Him; so he comes on upon us; so he encompasseth us, is still in
Motion. Yet still we speak of Him, as far above and beyond the
Starry Sky, and of His Comming, as at a Great Distance. But,
Behold! He is already in the midst of us; He breaks forth on our
Right hand, and on our Left, like a Flame, round about us, and we
perceive Him not.

At another time he is meditating upon the Resurrection, not
the physical resurrection of the body, but the mystical
resurrection of the spirit of the believer, in this life. Two
great texts of the New Testament are in his mind:

And hee shall send his Angels with a great sound of a trumpet,
and they shall gather together his Elect from the foure windes
from one end of heaven to the other.   (*Matt.* xxiv, 31.)

Behold, I shew you a Mysterie: we shall not all sleepe, but wee
shall all be changed, In a moment, in the twinckling of an eye, at
the last trumpet (for the trumpet shall sound, and the dead shall
be raised incorruptible, and we shall be changed).

(1 *Cor.* xv, 52, 53.)

In the following passage these two noble strains of word
music are mingled together and a third, no less noble,[1] is
produced:

Jesus Christ sends forth His Angels to gather His Saints from
the four Winds, at the Resurrection. When the Body of a Saint
crumbles and scatters into Dust; Every Dust lies gatherd up into
the Bosome of some Holy Angel. There all the Single Dusts are
comprehended in one Form of a Glorious Body. In this Form
the Angel brings them forth at the Call of Christ: This is the
Resurrection of the Body. This is as true of each Piece of Life and
Death in our Persons or Affaires while yet we are on Earth. When
our Happinesse, Hopes, and Hearts are ground into the smallest
Dust; They then lie Compact and compleat in their Angelicall
Chamber; on a sudden, as at the Blast of an Angels Trumpet, or
Glance of an Angels eye, can Jesus Christ give our Dead Hopes
a Glorious Resurrection out of their Dust.

---

[1] Cf. Browning's *Abt Vogler*: "That out of three sounds he
frame, not a fourth sound, but a star".

Such a passage is an elaborate work of art as full of examples of technical skill as a sonnet by a great poet. Notice the slow and majestic opening, leading up to the thunder of the central sentence: "This is the Resurrection of the Body". Then comes the spiritual interpretation or application of the image with its partial repetition of the opening theme and its subtle alliterations and assonances, followed by the dramatic crescendo ("on a sudden..."), and the solemn climax, formed by the combination of the three emphatic monosyllables, "Dead Hopes...Dust" with the sonorous music of "glorious Resurrection".

Sterry seems occasionally to have experimented in a prose poem of a still more elaborate kind than the types which I have attempted to describe. This is something like the Platonic Myth, not a mere metaphor or analogy but a sustained and detailed description of visionary objects or events with a spiritual or symbolic significance. The myth of the Souls in *A Discourse of the Freedom of the Will* (no. 43 in this selection) is a striking example, and among the manuscripts there are some pieces (like the *Chariot*, no. 21 in this selection), where he seems to be trying to write such myths as separate compositions without the traditional framework of sermon or treatise. His models would appear to be the visions of the Hebrew prophets and the myths of Plato. If he had spent the latter part of his life in a country and an age more sympathetic to his way of thinking than the England of Charles II, he might have proceeded farther with such experiments and enriched English literature with new literary forms.

His compositions in verse are slight and unimportant. The two most interesting are the imitation of Boethius in *A Discourse of the Freedom of the Will*, already mentioned, and an unfinished lyric among the manuscripts, which shows strong affinities both to Spenser and to Vaughan.[1]

Other pieces in verse among the unpublished papers include the verse paraphrase of *The Canticles* which he wrote

[1] See Appendix 1, Two Poems by Peter Sterry.

during his last illness and a curious series of dialogues in octosyllabic lines. Neither has much value as poetry, though technically they are respectable. If he had practised the art of writing verse as assiduously as some of his contemporaries, he might have been a passable minor poet of the school of Vaughan and Traherne. Perhaps it is fortunate on the whole that he devoted the greater part of his energy to the writing of that magnificent poetic prose which is an instrument with a range of harmonies incomparably superior to those of all kinds of verse except that of the great poets.

III

THE DOCTRINE

In a manuscript treatise preserved in Dr Williams's Library[1] entitled *The State of Souls Moderately Examined*, Richard Baxter describes what he calls "a method of theologie" "lately revived" "by some deep students who are verst in yᵉ Platonike Philosophie, & thinke yᵗ Reason must know more of the Divine Being than Scripture". He characterizes these doctrines as "a mixture of *Platonisme*, Origenisme & Arianisme not having *all* of any of these, but somewhat of *all*". Among such thinkers he places Osiander, Scaliger and "an excellent pious wit Peter Sterry". He is in fact describing a type of religious thought which goes back at least to Clement of Alexandria, which is found at the beginning of the Middle Ages in John Scotus Erigena and at the end in Nicholas of Cusa, and which attracted some of the finest minds both of Renascence Italy and of seventeenth-century England. It is a philosophy of religion which sees in Christianity the natural outcome and true continuation of the best ancient Greek thought, as well as of the religion of the Hebrews, and which, as Baxter rightly says, places Reason (but Reason conceived in the high Platonic sense of νοῦς) above the revelation of scripture. Baxter clearly dislikes and distrusts this type of thought. He perceives that, if its premises are accepted, ancient paganism can no longer be regarded as mere idolatry and a deception of the Devil, but as part of a continuous revelation of the Divine Being to mankind. He takes Sterry as a prominent contemporary example of a teacher of this kind of doctrine, and he objects particularly to his determinism, and to his philosophic conception of Christ as "an Universall Soul" and "a *Top Branch*

---

[1] Baxter MSS. Treatises, IV, ff. 227–55.

in ye Tree of Being". To modern minds free from Baxter's fundamentalism the very qualities that he mentions to condemn will probably serve as a recommendation of Sterry as a thinker, nor will the term "Pagano-Christian", which he applies to his religion, appear particularly alarming any more than his statement that "the doctrine draws a little from Origene, & most from Arius, & more [sic] from Plato, & Averrhois, & most [sic] from over-bold conjecturing Reason". Elsewhere[1] he expresses distrust of Sterry's doctrine because of "the excessive pregnancy of his wit", which "produceth so great a superabundance of Metaphors or Allegories, that they make up almost all his style; so that to any ordinary Reader his matter is not so much *cloathed* in Metaphors, as *drowned*, buried, or *lost*". What Baxter calls Sterry's "pregnant wit" and "pious florid oratory" we should now perhaps call the poetry of a noble imagination. In the seventeenth century few orthodox Christians believed seriously in the inspiration of poetry. But here again Baxter's hard, narrow but penetrating mind has perceived a quality of Sterry's thought that really exists, although Baxter entirely misinterprets it. Sterry's religion and philosophy are essentially the religion and philosophy of a poet, and they anticipate the doctrine of much of the greatest modern English poetry, notably that of Blake, of Wordsworth and of Shelley.[2]

---

[1] *Catholick Theology*, London, 1675, II, 109.

[2] Baxter writes (*loc. cit.*), "I had rather be instructed in the words of the most barbarous Schoolman, adapted to the matter, than be put to save my self from the temptation of equivocations in every sentence which I hear, and to search after that Truth (which is known only naked) under so florid a disguise and paint". Baxter is himself misled by a metaphor here into separating "Truth" from its expression. For a poetic mind like that of Sterry the expression is a part of the "truth". We can compare and contrast Baxter's attitude with that of one of the greatest of modern thinkers: "I find myself now taking more and more as literal fact what I used in my youth to love and admire as poetry". F. H. Bradley, *Essays in Truth and Reality* (Oxford, 1914), p. 468 n.

In Baxter's words Sterry was indeed "deeply verst" in the whole Platonic and mystical tradition. He owes much to Plato, especially to the more poetic and imaginative dialogues such as the *Phaedo*, the *Phaedrus*, the *Symposium*, the *Republic*, and the *Timaeus*, to the Neoplatonism of Plotinus and to the Christian Platonists, Clement of Alexandria, Origen and John Scotus Erigena, something to Jewish and perhaps to Arabian thought, to the German mystics of the later Middle Ages, to the Italian Platonists, Ficino and Campanella, and to the Spanish-Italian Jew Leone Hebreo, all of whom he quotes by name, as well as to the "Teutonic Philosopher" Jacob Böhme, some of whose books he possessed,[1] and a great deal to the fifteenth-century thinker, Cardinal Nicholas of Cusa, whose works appear in the list of books which he had with him at Chelsea in 1663 and whose influence on his theology is very marked indeed.[2] Sterry's doctrine is certainly eclectic, but his eclecticism is a gathering together and reinterpretation of some of the noblest elements in European thought. It may be admitted that he has not the power to weld these elements into a great philosophic system or to add to them any striking original contribution, but it can be claimed that he has left an extremely interesting and highly suggestive synthesis which looks forward to the best modern idealism, the idealism of the great poets and philosophers of the nineteenth century, as well as backward to ancient Greece, Alexandria, the Middle Ages and the Renascence.

Like his masters, Plotinus, Origen and Nicholas of Cusa, Sterry is a strict monist. He believes that all Being is one

---

[1] See list of books on p. 57.

[2] *Ibid.* See also notes to nos. 3 and 8. There seems to have been considerable interest in Nicholas of Cusa in England in the middle of the seventeenth century. Two of his works were translated into English at this time: *The Idiot in Four Books...By the famous and learned C. Cusanus. London, Printed for William Leake...*1650, and Ὀφθαλμὸς Ἁπλοῦς *or the Single Eye...Penned by the Learned Dr Cusanus, and published for the good of the Saints by Giles Randal... London,* 1646.

and that only one Being truly exists. He calls the Being God and also "the universall *Being*" or "*Eternity*". His God is the Absolute or Reality of philosophy rather than the God of simple-minded religion. "God", he writes, "is *Being it self* in its *simplicity* and *absoluteness*, the first, the supreme, the universal *Being*.... Being *it self* in its absoluteness, undivided, unrestrained, unconfined, unalloyed by any differences of mixtures;...Being *it self* in its Truth, in its substance; the only *true Being*, the *universal Being*." The existence of this True Being is proved by the imperfection of all things that we know, since "Nothing that is imperfect can subsist, exist *of it self*, or by it self; so far as it is imperfect, it *is not*". Just as the Platonic Socrates (the image is Sterry's own) would lead his hearers from the imperfect beauties of this world to the One True Beauty, so Sterry would lead his readers from the imperfect existences around them to the supreme and abso-lute existence which is "in All, thro' All, on every Side, beneath, above, beyond All, ever, every where the same, equally entire, equally undivided...that Sacred Circle of All Being,...whose Center is every where,...whose Circumfer-ence is no where Bounded". "God", he declares in one of his sermons, "is the only Substance." It is important to notice, however, that Sterry's God is not, like the God of much spurious Platonism, a mere abstract unity which on the last analysis turns out to be equal to Not-Being or Zero. He insists again and again in his writings that the Unity of God includes Multiplicity and Variety in the highest degree. "Unity", he writes with true philosophic acumen, "without distinction or variety, is a *barrenness*, a melancholy, a solitude, a blackness of Darkness." But God "is not a Broken, Barren, but a perfect and pregnant Unity". "*God is not a Solitary Unity, without Society or Solace; but a Unity richly Replenished, and Eternally entertain'd, with a Variety, as true and boundless as the Unity itself.*" He includes in himself not only every degree and variety of being but even of not-being also, "privations of Being...as darkness, night, absence and death". Unity in

Diversity may in fact be said to be the great principle that pervades the whole of Sterry's theology. In the terminology of modern philosophy his Absolute is not abstract Being, but Being in its most concrete form. It should be noticed also that it is conceived dynamically rather than statically. He calls God "a Vital Act", "life it self, life pure, absolute unmixt, unconfined..., a Fountain equally unexhaust, a Sea unbounded".

Unlike Milton, Sterry is a Trinitarian. The Trinity for him is the supreme example of Unity in Diversity. He makes an imaginary Objector argue quaintly: "If God, by being Infinite, and so all Forms of Things in one be a Trinity, he is upon this account equally a Duality, a Quaternity and Centenary, any Form of Numbers and Things, as a Trinity." Sterry's reply is the contention that three is "the most perfect Number, being compleat in it self". It is "the essential Form of each Number, having its Beginning, its Middle, its End in itself". In fact for Sterry the rhythm of the triad pervades the whole universe. But his conception of the Trinity goes far beyond this mathematical mysticism. It is for him a union of "Life, Light and Love". The First Person, God the Father, symbolized as Light, is the One of the Neoplatonists, the ineffable perfect Being, perfect Unity. The Second Person or Christ is Life, the image of the First. If the Father is the perfect example of Unity, the Son is the supreme example of Diversity, "Distinction or Variety", to use Sterry's words. He is described as "the effulgency of the Godhead, shining out into an essential Image, a clear distinct Image of it self in the fulness of its Divine Essence". He is eternally generated by the Father's "contemplation of Himself, which is the *Beatifical Vision* of the most beautiful, the most blessed *Essence of Essences*. This *Act* of *Contemplation* is an Intellectual and *Divine Generation*, in which the Divine Essence, with an eternity of most heightened Pleasures, eternally bringeth forth it self, within it self, into an *Image* of it self". This Eternal Son, the perfect Image of the Father, is the Universe, not the imperfect Universe that we know through the senses, but the ideal Universe (which is the real one), where all things exist in their true and perfect forms, the World Yonder (ἐκεῖ) of Plotinus. "This", writes Sterry, "is the Heaven in which Christ is, or rather which Hee is" and "Jesus Christ is always in Heaven, Himself is Heaven." The Eternal Son or Ideal Universe is, in fact, the actualization of the Absolute. In Sterry's words the Father is the "Manifester", the Son, "the Manifested". The question might be asked why, if the Absolute is the most real of things, does it need to be actualized. Sterry's answer would probably have been that the Son, or Ideal Universe is not to be conceived as separate from the Absolute, but as an essential part of it. If the Father is the "Manifester", the Son, the "Manifested", the Holy Ghost or third person of the Trinity is the "Manifestation",, which is conceived by Sterry as Love, the principle of harmony which unites the Father and Son, the Divine Love of God for the Universe, "The Love Knot, or the Love Union between the two."[1] It is noticeable that like many ancient thinkers Sterry tends to speak of the relationship between the Father and the Son, between God and the World, in terms that suggest the relationship of the sexes. These erotic images may seem offensive to the modern reader, but there was plenty of authority for them in the mysticism both of the East and of the West. The traditional interpretation of the Canticles made them acceptable to many minds of the Middle Ages and the Renascence, and the most orthodox Catholic mystics had no hesitation in speaking of the Divine Lover in terms which sound very strange to modern ears. Sterry is fond of speaking of the Trinity as "the first Marriage and glorious *Prototype* of all Marriages". "Here the *Father* is the Lover and the Bridegroome, the *eternal Word* or Wisdome is the Daughter and Bride, his essential Image, in which his own

---

[1] This interpretation of the doctrine of the Trinity is very similar to those given by John Scotus Erigena, Eckhardt and Nicholas of Cusa, to which it is probably indebted.

glories and sweetnesses offer themselves to his Divine View and Embraces." "All his works are *love-sports* with this his Son and Bride, various parts of Divine Love which he acteth." Sterry, as we have seen, lays particular stress on the beauty and sanctity of marriage. For him, as for Milton, marriage has a very special significance. For Sterry indeed it is nothing less than an image of God Himself, and the love of the sexes is one of the keys to the mystery of the universe. He would doubtless have agreed entirely with R. L. Nettleship's words on this subject: "I can't help believing that somehow or other there *is* a real point of contact between 'the love of mankind', as represented by Jesus and as concentrated in the idea of 'God is Love', and 'das Ewig-Weibliche zieht uns hinan' of Goethe: and that the world won't be happy till it finds it".[1] Another notion concerning the relationship of God to the Creation which runs all through Sterry's writings has already been noticed in another connection. It is the conception of God as an artist, who satisfies himself by the creation of the world as a human artist satisfies himself by the creation of a work of art. The mystery of artistic creation is one that seems to have fascinated Sterry and he saw in it a repetition on a small scale of the mystery of the universe. This doctrine is, of course, closely allied to the conception of God as a great "artificer" or craftsman, and to the "argument from design" so dear to theologians of the seventeenth and eighteenth centuries. But Sterry invests it with a lofty poetic charm, which is absent from the theory in the dry, abstract form in which it was commonly presented. His God is an artist rather than an "artificer". He compares him to a painter, a musician, a poet, and even, as we have seen, to a jeweller. The world is "ποίημα τοῦ θεοῦ, God's poem". It is a great drama, a great picture, a great piece of music, not a piece of mechanism. As we shall see it is in the light of aesthetic experience that

---

[1] R. L. Nettleship, *Philosophical Lectures and Remains* (London, 1897), I, 90.

Sterry tends to seek solutions of the major problems of metaphysics. A third notion concerning the Creation which occurs in Sterry's works is the curious one, found often in occult lore, that God is asleep and that the world is a dream of God that will pass away when he awakes: "When God", he writes, "shall awaken himself upon the World, then shall it be known, that he alone is the Eye, the Light, the Life of the World...a long sleep hath lain upon Men, upon the whole World for many generations". He interprets *Psalm* lxxiii, 20, in this sense: *As a dream when one awaketh, so, O Lord, when thou awakest, thou shalt despise their Image*. His explanation is that "God the supream and eternal Spirit is here presented, bringing forth this World, as a man doth a *dream* in his sleep....When this Eternal Spirit, in whose sleep, like painted forms in a dream, they [the things of this world] vainly flutter about, awakeneth himself, he at once dissolveth them into their *own nothingness* and *despiseth them*, as having never been anything". "As Dreams are imaginations in the Fancy which act their parts while the Man sleepeth: such was this Image after which Man with the whole world was made." He quotes with approval a saying of Ficino, the Italian Platonist, that he "esteems him a great Person, who saith to himself of all things here, it may be that all this is a dream". It is, perhaps, significant that, while God appeared to many of Sterry's contemporaries to be a Mathematician, to him he seemed rather a Lover, an Artist and a Dreamer.

If the Triune God is the only Reality, all other existences, from the Angels downward, are comparatively unreal or, to use Sterry's expression, "shadowy". Like Plato he has a strong sense of the unreality and fleetingness of the phenomenal world. Phenomena are for him, as for Plato in the *Republic*, mere shadows seen by the dwellers in the Cave of Life, the Army of Ghosts that Carlyle saw in broad daylight. In this respect he differs very widely from Milton, for whom there was nothing ghostly, or unsubstantial in heaven, earth, hell or chaos. "*Fiunt non sunt*" Sterry writes of the appearances of this world: "They are sent forth, but subsist not. They *are* only in the *making*; in the same moment in which they are brought forth, they *are no more*. This is universally true of all creatures, Men and Angels". They are compared to the reflections cast by "the Heavenly Bodies moving over the Sea" or by "Buildings standing, Men or Horses going on the Earth, besides a River". They "fly away, and are no more; like Lightning, or the shadow upon any part of the Dial". He quotes with strong approval the Greek phrase "τὸ μὴ ὄν" as applied to the world of appearances distinguished from "τὸ ὄν", that which truly exists or reality. Yet, if phenomena are unreal, they contain an element of reality too, for God, the Absolute, is present in them all. Nature, even Nature as seen by our imperfect eyes, is an image of reality. In one place Sterry calls it "the painted lid before the cabinet", and elsewhere, using a more pregnant and beautiful image, he writes that "The *Creation* of the World was a *Vail* cast upon the Face of God, with a figure of the Godhead wrought upon this Vail, and God Himself *seen* through it by a *dim transparency*; as the Sun in a morning, or Mist, is seen by a refracted Light through the thick *medium* of earthly *Vapours*". This description calls to mind the power described by Shelley in *Adonais* as

> that sustaining Love
> Which through the web of being blindly wove
> By man and beast and earth and air and sea,
> Burns bright or dim.[1]

The doctrine of divine immanence plays a very prominent part in Sterry's teaching:

"God", he writes, "is present...in every Creature....He is *entirely present* with all the Joys and Glories of eternity, ever undivided, His own Heaven to himself, in the *Depths* of *Hell* beneath as in the heighth of Heaven above, in the *dust* of the *Grave*, in a wave of the Sea, as in the most shining Cherubim, or flaming Seraphim."

[1] *Adonais*, LIV.

There is not the lowest thing which hath not God in it; for God fills all. Yet as the Sun-beams fall on a Dunghill, and are not polluted, but shine on the Dung-hill; so God is still himself, to himself, high and glorious in the lowest Things.

The Creature is nothing of itself, or by it self, but a *momentary emanation* from God, sent forth by him, . . . and filled with him.

We seem to be listening to a seventeenth-century version of the words of F. H. Bradley:

. . . the Absolute is immanent alike through every region of appearances. There are degrees and ranks, but, one and all, they are alike indispensable. We can find no province of the world so low but the Absolute inhabits it. Nowhere is there even a single fact so fragmentary and so poor that to the Universe it does not matter. There is truth in every idea however false, there is reality in every existence however slight; and where we can point to reality or truth, there is the one undivided life of the Absolute.[1]

The last words of this passage recall three of the best lines of verse that Sterry wrote:

> Thou first, & last of things in all yᵉ Same;
> Nothing before, beyond doth thee confine;
> Nothing within divides thine unmixt flame.

It should be noticed that Sterry guards himself very carefully against any confusion of his doctrine with the cruder kind of pantheism. "Do we make the Creature nothing? Do we make God all? Do we confound God and the Creature?" These are questions which he places in the mouth of the Objector.

"Far be it", answers Sterry, "we speak the Language of the general stream of *Divines, Philosophers, Poets*,[2] Heathen and Sacred, through all Ages. . . . Our design and desire is to establish most firmly and clearly the immutable and everlasting bounds between God and the Creature. The Creature truly *really is* in the proper *rank* and order of its own Being, but all that is, in the presence of the Divine Being, in comparison with it, is like a *dream*, when one

---

[1] *Appearance and Reality* (ed. 1925), p. 487.
[2] Notice that "*Divines, Philosophers, Poets*" are cited as authorities of equal importance.

awakes, less than nothing...The Creature is nothing of it self, or by it self but a *momentary emanation* from God, sent forth from him, and filled with him. God is *not the Creature*, yet he is in the Creature, not...confined to the Creature, or defined by the Creature, but...filling all in all, every Creature."

Sterry's doctrine of immanence really springs from his profound sense of wonder and mystery in all things, a sense that he shares with his contemporary, Traherne. It finds expression in some fine aphorisms: "All things in Heaven above, and Earth beneath, meet in the Constitution of each Individual". "Nothing is *mean and vile* seen in a right and universal Light." "...look on each Being, ...you will see it as a *spacious Palace*, a sacred Temple, or a new and distinct Heaven." Sentences like these may be compared with Spinoza's great saying, "the more we understand individual things, the more we understand God".[1] They anticipate Blake's great proverb: "Everything that lives is Holy".[2]

The link between the Absolute and the World of Appearances is found by Sterry in the Ideas. The Ideas are the perfect and ideal forms of all things, "Eternal Truths of Things" in his own words, existing in the mind of God which generates them in endless variety and multiplicity. In this respect Sterry is a true Platonist. For him the Ideas are the realities, while the appearances of this world are mere shadows of them. The Divine Mind in which the Ideas exist is itself the Idea of Ideas and this is Christ, the Son, who is also the Idea of Man. "Angels", he writes, "and all other Creatures have their destined Ideas in the *Divine Mind*. But God himself in his own essential Image, in the Person of the Son, the *Idea of Ideas*, is the *Idea of Man*." Elsewhere he calls God "the proper Idea of the Humane Soul, that is its most inward and inseparable Principle, which hath in itself the Pattern, the exemplar form of the Soul". In such passages he

---

[1] Spinoza, *Ethics*, v, xxiv: "Quo magis res singulares intelligimus, eo magis Deum intelligimus".

[2] Blake, *The Marriage of Heaven and Hell* (Nonesuch Ed. p. 204).

comes very close to the opinion expressed by Blake in his
blunt couplet:

> Thou art a Man, God is no more;
> Thy own humanity learn to adore.

All things, it would appear, have their Ideas in the mind of
God, but the only Idea which is actualized in the concrete is
the highest Idea of all, the Idea of Man or the Eternal Son
which was incarnated as Jesus of Nazareth.[1] This incarnation
is the central point of a world history that is governed by the
rhythm of the Triad. The first creation is called by Sterry "a
kind of Incarnation; for in that the Image of God was made
Flesh". This was the first stage of cosmic evolution, which
Sterry calls "The Kingdom of Nature". It is a "shadowy
state", beautiful and innocent but unreal. "All the beauty,
Joy and Life of it", he writes in a striking phrase, are "the
Divine Seede Asleep". Man, "the first Adam",[2] was then
living in perfect harmony with all the other creatures, and
was "the Blessed Fountain of Divinity to them". This happy
unity of the Kingdom of Nature was ended by the Fall. The
Fall is the work of the Devil, who, like Blake's Urizen, is the
principle of disunion, division and selfishness, breaking up
the unity of the world. We are reminded of the German
mystics and especially the *Theologia Germanica*[3] by the statement that "The Devil is Self-love; a particular Being cutting
off itself from the rest of things", "a divided Kingdom, a
Duality, a ruinous Thing". "By the Fall the frame of Nature,
within and without us is now a Glass broken into so many
pieces". The image of the first Adam is shattered: "the
Image at the Fall vanisheth into a counterfeit Image, breaking it self into innumerable false Images full of disorders,
confusion and contradictions". Yet we must notice that
Sterry regards the Fall as necessary. Its purpose was in his

---

[1] Cf. the very similar Christology of Nicholas of Cusa, *De
Doct. Ign.* III. 2.
[2] The "Adam Kadmon" of Jewish occult lore.
[3] See *Theologia Germanica*, Caps. II and III.

own words to change "the *shadowy happiness*" of the creature
into "a *substantial* one". It is due to the application of the
great principle of Unity in Diversity. The original unity of
things must be broken up into the greatest Diversity before
the higher unity of the spirit can be reached. The achievement of this higher unity is the work of the Eternal Son, who
becomes incarnate as Jesus of Nazareth, the perfect man or
Idea of Humanity in the concrete. At this point the second
stage of world history called the Kingdom of the Son or the
Mediator begins. The Crucifixion is the consummation of the
process by which God, the Absolute, is separated from the
world. It is the supreme example of the "diversity" or
"variety" of God, and is necessary in order that the diversity
may be absolutely complete. Now "the *Sun* of the eternal
Image and glory, having by its course, touched the *utmost
bound* of distance from it self...begins to return". The
Resurrection and Ascension are followed by the Second
Coming, which, unlike the First Coming, is spiritual, and is
now in progress. The Second Coming is the formation of a
new Unity of the Spirit among believers, the Heavenly or
Spiritual Man in place of the shadowy "Natural Man", who
was destroyed at the Fall. Christ, the Eternal Son, is now a
spirit which "goes out into the spirits of men" and forms
"a New Root of Immortality below the Natural Root of each
Creature". By participation in this spirit of Christ they
become Saints and together build up the "Heavenly Man"
or complete and final manifestation of the Son: "All the
Saints become one *heavenly Body*". This is the Greater Man of
Milton's *Paradise Lost* who shall

> Restore us and regain the blissful seat.

It is what Sir Henry Vane calls "*Christ's mystical Body*" of
which the "Saints" are "*Branches* that abide in him, and
whose Fruit is permanent unto Life Eternal".[1]

---

[1] *An Epistle General to the Mystical Body of Christ on Earth...
written by Sir Henry Vane, Knight....Printed in the Year* 1662, p. 36.

The process of the formation of this Heavenly or Universal Man is going on at present. The Eternal Son is now spreading throughout the whole world and turning it into "An Universall Paradise". Sterry describes this event in memorable language: "He [Christ] hath by this means filled every point of time with Eternity, every spot of Earth with Heaven". The final effect will be to purge away all the grossness of "flesh" or "matter", which is merely another name for unreality, and turn all things into "spirit": "Christ subdues the World to himself. He takes away the dark Grossness from it, works it to a Spirituality, a transparency, like a Crystal Glass, that the Beams of God may fill every Point of it, and the Person of God be seen thro' every Part".

It may be noticed that, like Milton, Sterry does not seem to draw a hard and fast line between "matter" and "spirit".[1] But, if the general doctrine is similar, the emphasis is different in Sterry. For Milton "spirit" seems to have been a refined form of "matter". For Sterry "matter" is a "shadowy" or unreal form of "spirit". In some places indeed he writes as though all things were material except God: "Divines say that every Creature; even the highest Angel hath something of materiality, darknesse, grosnesse, composition, carnality; and so it is flesh, compared with God who only is a spirit". But elsewhere he shows clearly that he believes "matter" only to exist in relation to mind. "There is no such thing as *Picture, Prospect, Person, Life, Love,* or *Joy, Death* or *Suffering*. All is an unimaginable heap of *inconceivable Atomes* which have no Relation to, no Commerce with each other, if there be no indivisible *Unity*, in which things meet, in which they are *compared, judged* and *proportioned*." In fact the world for Sterry really consists not of matter but of a multitude of minds or spirits: "What we call materiality or corporeity", he declares, seen in its true state is "A Divine Company of beautiful Spirits".[2]

---

[1] *Comus*, 453–63, and *Paradise Lost*, v, 469–83.
[2] Cf. J. M. McTaggart, *Some Dogmas of Religion*, London, 1930, pp. 247–50.

The third and last stage of cosmic evolution is the passing of the Kingdom of Christ into what Sterry calls the Kingdom of the Father. All things are now absorbed into the timeless and spaceless life of the Absolute. But this is not conceived as a Nirvana where all individuality is annihilated. On the contrary Sterry insists that then and then only will each individual find its true being. Commenting on the petition in the Lord's Prayer, "Thy will be done on Earth, as in Heaven", he writes, "When God shall answer this *Petition*, the *Godhead* shall not swallow up the *Creature*; nor *Heaven*, *Earth*. But the *Creature* and the *Earth* shall have together with a full *Community* in Glory; as Distinct a Property and Unity in themselves, as *God* and *Heaven*. *Heaven* and *Earth* shall be in those Days, as *Husband* and *Wife*, tho' *one Principle*, *Nature* and *Shape*; yet two *Sexes*, *one* the Image of the *other*". In fact Sterry calls his God or Absolute a Person, and even the only real Person, but he speaks often as if he were rather a Unity comprehending a multitude of separate spirits, a community rather than a single Person. "God", he writes, "is the Heavenly *Hierusalem* where all Things are *Fellow-Citizens*." Sterry, like his contemporary Traherne[1] and like Wordsworth and the great poets of the nineteenth century, has a strong conviction of the greatness of the human soul: "The Soul is a Unity comprehending it self, and all created forms of things in one substantial individual Act". "Thus is the Soule or Spirit of every Man all the World to Him, the World with all varieties of things, his owne body with all its parts, & changes are himselfe, his owne Soule or Spirit...." We can notice from this passage that for Sterry as for Spinoza body and soul are simply different aspects of the same thing. He insists like Wordsworth that the Soul is "not *Passive* but Active". He calls it "Pure Act", "a substantiall Act, or Spring of life".[2] He loves to compare it to a mirror or to a

---

[1] See Traherne, *Cent. of Meditations*, I, 15; II, 23, etc.
[2] Cf. Wordsworth, *Excursion*, IV, ll. 1058-77.

palace made of looking glass in which all things are reflected.[1]
He frequently speaks of a "depth" in it. One of his great
sayings is that "the Soul of man hath a seminal infiniteness".
He gives several divisions of the soul following well-known
authorities. One is the threefold division into "sense",
"reason", and "spirit". "Sense" is shared by the brutes,
"reason" is the quality of a man. "Spirit" is a faculty above
reason which turns a man into a "Saint". The "coming
forth" of the Son forms a fourth element within or beneath
"spirit" called "the spirit of Jesus" by which a saint becomes
part of the composite personality of the "Greater Man".

Another division is into four "Orbs". The lowest "Orb"
is again the "*Sensitive*", where "the Soul...is all set and
adorned with the sensitive and shadowy shapes of things".
The second is "the rational Orb", "a more ample and more
Lucid". The third is "the Intellectual", where the Soul
beholds "The Intellectual Forms of things, the immortal
Essences and Substances". The fourth is the "*Divine Orb*".
It is called "The Unity of the Soul", "in this it hath the most
immediate resemblance to and conjunction with the supream
Unity, the *Divine Nature*". Elsewhere Sterry teaches the
doctrine that the soul has a "highest point", and "apex", or
a "spire top", a "supream part" as he calls it with which it
has direct communion with the divine. This notion is part of
the mystical tradition which goes back to Plotinus.[2] It is
interesting to find that Sterry has a good word for the imagination, which was generally regarded rather scornfully by
seventeenth-century thinkers as mere "decaying sense". For
Sterry indeed it is connected with "sense", but it has high
functions. It is the "*first* and *highest* faculty of the *sensitive
Soul* where it is in its *perfection*, is *as* ample as the *universal
object* of *sense*, the whole *Corporeal world*". "It not only takes

---

[1] "Thus is the Essence of the soul, as a Christalline Heaven, or
as a Palace composed all of purest and firmest *Looking-Glass*",
Discourse, p. 83.

[2] Plotinus, *Enn.* III, viii, 5.

in and *enjoys* the *sensitive forms* of all the *objects* of *sense, uniting*
and *varying* them according to its own pleasure, but also...it
espouseth in it self the *spiritual* and *corporeal world* to each other,
receiving the *impressions,* the *similitudes,* the *illapses* of the
invisible Glories as the *Originals* into their *sensitive Image,* and
heightning the *sensitive Image* to a greatness and glory *above* it self
by this communion with its invisible patterns". Sterry's
Imagination includes both the "Fancy" and the "Imagination" of Wordsworth and Coleridge. On the one hand it is
the faculty that varies and rearranges memories of sense
impressions; on the other it is a power which is in communion with the spiritual world, the world of reality, and it
irradiates our perception of the world of appearances with
"the light that never was on sea or land".

Sterry regarded man as an image of the Trinity, and the
relationship of soul to body as an image of the relationship of
the Father to the Son, another "divine marriage" in which
the soul is the bridegroom, and the body the bride. He
considers the body to be as important as the soul, and as
equally divine in nature and origin, a Temple of the Holy
Ghost in which "all things...are divine Figures of a Divine
Glory". "Thy Body", he writes, "O Believer, so far as thou
standest in a Spiritual Principle, is a Fellow-member with thy
Soul in the Body of Christ." In this connection we can notice
his curious views on eschatology. Unlike Milton, who
believed both soul and body to be mortal, Sterry declares
that both soul and body are immortal. He explains, however,
that he does not refer to the corruptible body that we know
through the senses, but to the idea of the body, which alone
truly exists. Like Origen he refuses to believe in the doctrine
of eternal damnation. The body and soul of a saint at death
pass immediately into the presence of God. The body and
soul of a sinner go to a hell which consists of the "sense of
their losse, restlesse desyres, and pursuites, perpetuall frustra-
tions, & disappointments with the feares, cares, anguishes
& torments that accompany these". These things according

to Sterry are the "knawings of that worme that never dys". The fire of hell is the "Light of Heaven" as it appears to sinners. To them it is a burning and purging fire. When they are sufficiently purged, "the seed of God immediately puts forth itselfe into them", and ultimately they are redeemed, passing "thorough sufferings into Rest, & Glory". Sterry's hell is in fact a place not of damnation but of education and regeneration.[1] To the objection that it is identical with the Popish Purgatory he replies that it differs from Purgatory because the Papists make Hell and Purgatory two separate places and distinguish between mortal and venial sins, and because in the Popish Purgatory sufferings are "expiatory, & satisfactory to the Divine Justice" and souls can be freed by "good works of their saints and churche". In Sterry's hell Pardon, Redemption, Justification" come from Christ only, and the wicked are simply made to endure the sufferings that Christ endured, so that ultimately they may be redeemed.

Sterry's most important and interesting book, *A Discourse of the Freedom of the Will*, deals with the great problems of Free Will and Determinism which were so much debated throughout Christendom in his age. He may well have been in Milton's mind when he wrote of those spirits among the Fallen Angels whose fate so closely resembles that of the fallen Independents after the Restoration:

> Others apart sat on a Hill retir'd,
> In thoughts more elevate, and reason'd high
> Of Providence, Foreknowledge, Will, and Fate,
> Fixt Fate, free will, foreknowledge absolute,...

Sterry, like Spinoza and unlike Milton, is a thorough-going determinist, and he is much more logical than Milton in this respect. For Milton, like Sterry, believed in divine immanence

---

[1] Sterry's views on eschatology are set out in his printed essay "The State of a Saints Soul and Body in Death" (*The Rise, Race and Royalty*, etc., 1683, pp. 434–515) and his manuscript discourse headed "That the State of wicked men after this life is mixt of evill, & good things".

and in the unity of the universe, but his strong sense of individuality and human dignity would not allow him to make the obvious deduction that the actions of all finite beings must be determined by the divine will. Sterry's determinism, however, is of a very different character from the juridical and mechanical determinism of his Calvinist contemporaries. Moreover, he could understand the attitude of his opponents, and nothing is more admirable in his writings than his tribute to their motives: " *Persons engaged in both sides in this question...* *are highly honoured by me, and truly dear to me...* ", he writes, and he attributes to the defenders of "Free Will" " *the design...to heighten the Grace of God by its* freedom *and* peculiarity *...a holy jealousy...lest God should be imagined* like the natural day *... made up of* two Contraries *...a ground of* Holiness *and a ground* of Sin ".

His own arguments are extremely interesting both for their own sake, and because of their strong resemblance to those of Spinoza. True liberty for Sterry is perfectly consistent with complete determinism. He contends that liberty is simply "a *relation* or *harmony* between the *essence* or *nature* of each thing and its *operations*". It means something different for the "Elements and Celestial Bodies", for plants, for "bruit Creatures" and for "*intellectual* beings". Liberty in fact is simply freedom to follow that "endeavour wherewith a thing endeavours to persist in its being", which for Spinoza was the actual essence of the thing. As God is in all things, all action is necessarily determined by Him.[1] An arbitrary or

---

[1] Cf. "Every thing, every where, lieth within the bounds of this Divine Harmony, is measured and governed by it, springeth forth from it, beareth a part in it, *is Harmony* in this Harmony... This is God...Harmony it self...diffusing it self through all things, endlessly and boundlessly unfolding it self into all forms of things...Can there be now any one thing in the nature of things, any one thing in the *will* of any Spirit, any one essence, form, power, act...which lies not in, which flows not from this first and universal spring, the Divine Unity?" *A Discourse,* etc. p. 13; and "If God be the first Cause, if the Will be a second Cause,

indetermined freedom is not true liberty, and is quite inconsistent with God's attributes of omniscience and omnipotence.[1] It is also inconsistent with Sterry's conception of a harmonious and divinely ordered universe, into which it would introduce elements of chance and contingency. The Objector is made to seek "How otherwise doth Man excel bruit Creatures and natural Agents? and how otherwise is man free and not necessitated in his actions?" Sterry in his answer distinguishes between two kinds of necessity: "Coaction...from an *outward power*" and an internal necessity, "A reason from *within*". The Will of man is determined from within, not without. It is "*divinely free*", for it acts "according to its own proper Nature", "after the manner of the inward Principles of its own Essence". In its healthy state it is "a *rational inclination* to the...*supream* good". God Himself is a being "perfectly free" and "*absolutely necessary*". His acts are determined by no cause from without but by "a reason from *within*", "the Glorious Secret of his own Essence".[2] The great difficulty of such a doctrine, as Sterry clearly perceived, is the problem of the existence of sin and evil. If the will of man is determined by God, why does he sin? If he sins, how can he justly be held to be guilty? Sterry deals very candidly with these questions. He boldly admits God's ultimate responsibility for all evil and sin. But he contends that evil and sin have no real existence. Sin is "nothing positive...a meer privation". Evil is caused by a "withdrawal" of God from his own creation, a well-known

---

if the Acts of the Will, and the determination of the Will in these Acts, be the effects of the Will, then is God the universal cause of all these, then is he more truly and effectually the cause of each act and determination of the Will, than the Will it self." *Ibid.* p. 43.

[1] Cf. *Theologia Germanica*, Cap. LI.

[2] Cf. John Smith, *Select Discourses* (1660), p. 394: "Such an inward living principle of virtue and activity further heightened and united with Light and Truth we may call Liberty".

doctrine found in Milton and derived from the Jewish Cabala.[1]
It is part of the divine plan, and due to the divine wisdom,
which has designed a universe with a place for all degrees of
being and not-being.[2] Similarly for man, who is the microcosm and the image of God, to attain to divine perfection, he
must experience evil and sin. The Fall is necessary that man
may rise from the "shadowy" state of innocence to true
wisdom and virtue. The weakness of this contention seems
to be that it involves the contradiction that, on the one hand,
it is said that evil has no real existence, while on the other it is
declared to be a necessary part of the universe and even of
God. So we are faced by the illogical position that something
which does not exist is a necessary part of Reality. But some
such contradiction is probably inherent in all the monistic
systems which descend from Neoplatonism. Sterry seems to
be on much firmer ground, when he declares that the problem of evil could only be solved if we could judge God's
works as a whole "sub specie aeternitatis". It is interesting
to notice that he almost reproduces Spinoza's famous phrase
in this connection. "In this light of eternity alone is the
Work of God seen aright, in the entire piece, in the whole
design from the beginning to the end", "God worketh all
things from eternity in eternity, and for eternity; Thus he
maketh every thing beautiful, as it is seen in the light of
eternity, which alone is the light of Truth: Time being the
shadow of Eternity, and a Vail upon it".

The Objector is made to ask, "How then doth shame or
guilt lie on the Creature? Why is God yet angry? How is he
just in punishing?" Sterry acutely points out that, if the
existence of an omnipotent and omniscient deity is accepted,

---

[1] Cf. D. Saurat, *Milton, Man and Thinker*, London, 1924,
p. 286–9. Notice, however, that Milton uses the doctrine of
"withdrawal" to explain the existence of Free Will, while Sterry
uses it to explain the existence of evil.

[2] Cf. Spinoza's letter to Blyenbergh q. L. Roth's *Spinoza*,
London, 1929, p. 163.

these difficulties arise just as much out of the doctrine of Free Will as out of that of necessity. In one case he compares God to a father who gives a child freedom to run "into a pleasant Field, or a Devouring Flood", foreseeing that he will run into the devouring flood, and yet not attempting to prevent him. In the other case he is a father who holds the child over "the cruel flood", "taketh away his arms", and "leaves him to fall into the Flood and perish there". Both fathers are equally responsible for the drowning of the children. Sterry has the courage to face the fact that belief in an omnipotent being necessarily involves belief in the ultimate responsibility of that being for all the evil in the Universe. He considers that both sin and punishment are part of the divine order. Man is guilty and feels shame because guilt and shame are the inevitable accompaniments of evil doing and indeed part of it. Anger is attributed to God "*per Anthropopathiam*"; it is a "*metonymical* way of speaking, which expresseth the effect by the cause". Sterry's God is as free from human passions as the God of Spinoza.[1] Like Spinoza's God he can only strictly be said to love Himself, and all his actions are due to this love: "When wicked men suffer from their sins, when innocent persons are refined by their sufferings; the Eye of God is fixed upon his own Divine loveliness and Glory in both. The purest and most perfect Love acteth him towards this most pure and perfect Loveliness and Glory alike in both;..."

Sterry clearly perceives the dangers of this doctrine, and the facility with which it might be misinterpreted. These are the "prickels" on the Divine Rose-Tree of Truth. He is very careful to dissociate himself completely from the "Ranters", the sect mentioned by Bunyan in *Grace Abounding*, which justified every kind of moral licence on the ground that all human actions are the work of the divine wisdom. "But you

---

[1] Cf. Spinoza's *Ethics*, v, Prop. xvii: "Deus expers est passionum, nec ullo Laetitiae aut Tristitiae affectu afficitur".

will perhaps say, All these things seem hitherto to confirm the *Ranters* in their *licentious Principles* and Practices. For, why should not *Sinners* with the freedom of all sinful pleasures, *rest* and *rejoyce* in the *absoluteness* of the Divine Conduct, the Perfection of the Divine Order and Beauty...?" Sterry is sensible of the difficulty of answering this question, and of "*initiating*" the reader into "these holy mysteries", which can only darken and dazzle the "profane Eye and Heart". His reply is in effect that the question is an improper one. Sin is to be avoided because it is a negation of true order and harmony, and cuts men off from the sight and the fellowship of God. If a Spirit "form to itself an heavenly Image" of the "Divine Order", it will "thus far...be *sanctified* by this sacred Light", "but if a spirit do take from hence *arguments to sin*, encouragements to sin; now it no more seeth a right Image of this heavenly Glory". In other words, if we form a right conception of God and the universe, we shall not want to sin, and it is only if our conception of these things is inadequate that we are likely to use them as an excuse for moral license. A man who can contemplate the divine harmony of the universe will himself partake of that harmony, and be free from the discord of sin. While Sterry obviously realized that the existence of evil is the supreme intellectual difficulty in any theological system, and devotes much space to it in his *Discourse of the Freedom of the Will*, it cannot be said that he shows any deep feeling in his treatment of the question. His theory of the unreality of evil is part of the neoplatonic tradition, and he would find it amply expounded in such writers as John Scotus Erigena, Nicholas of Cusa, and Campanella. He accepts it wholeheartedly and it must be admitted that it suits his clear joyous outlook, which forms an extraordinary contrast to the intense and often morbid consciousness of sin that characterizes many of his contemporaries, as, for example, Bunyan. To use Matthew Arnold's terms, he is a Hellenist by temperament, a rare spectacle in the ranks of the Hebraic Puritans of the seventeenth century. In this connection it is interesting to notice his tendency, already mentioned, to regard metaphysical problems from the aesthetic standpoint. His universe is a work of art, a great picture, in which the shadows of evil play their part as well as the high lights of good,[1] a great piece of music, where the discords of sin help to build up the perfect harmony, and finally in one of the most impressive passages in his writings he compares it to an epic poem in which the plot "conveyeth things down by a gradual descent to the lowest Depths and deepest Darknesses; then bringeth them up again to the highest point of all most flourishing Felicities". Elsewhere he compares God to a spectator at a tragedy who takes pleasure in the most terrible deeds enacted on the stage. It might almost be said that according to Sterry mankind is to be saved according to the rules of Aristotle's *Poetics*.[2] Indeed this doctrine was more than a mere analogy or illustration. He had an opinion of the nature of poetry that was as exalted as that of Milton or that of Wordsworth. He considered "that *Divine Poets*...delight the best Minds by awakening in them the richest, the liveliest Images of the Divine Work, the Divine Mind". He even goes so far as to say "That the Works of Poets, in the excellencies of their imaginations and contrivances, were imitations drawn from those Original Poems, the Divine works and contrivances of the Eternal Spirit...that Excellent Poets in the heighths of their fancies and spirits were touched and warmed by a Divine Ray, through which the supream Wisdom formed upon them, and so upon their work, some weak

---

[1] Cf. Nicholas of Cusa, *Ecce Ascendimus*: "Dico Deum gloriosum cognoscere bona et mala (quia alias perfecte non cognosceret) sicut oculus cognoscit lumen et tenebras."

[2] Cf. Donne, Sermon xxxvii in *Eighty Sermons*, London 1640, p. 370: "They would beleeve it in their fables, and would not beleeve it in the Scriptures; They would beleeve it in the nine Muses, and would not beleeve it in the Twelve Apostles...They would be saved poetically, and fantastically..."

impression and obscure Image of itself. Thus it seemeth to be altogether *Divine*". These words are close to Shelley's definition of a poem as "an image of life expressed in its eternal truth", and Coleridge's description of the act of poetic creation as "the repetition in the finite intellect of the infinite I AM".

Sterry's ethics have many points of contact with those of Spinoza and also with those of his great contemporary at Cambridge, John Smith. On the theoretic side they may be said to spring directly out of his metaphysics. Man is a microcosm containing within himself the whole universe, and the whole divine drama of the Creation, the Fall and the Redemption is re-enacted in the mind of each individual. Each man and each woman is at first the "shadowy" image of innocent nature. That image is shattered by the principle of selfishness and disintegration, which is the Devil. The good man or "saint" reintegrates in his own mind a new "image", the "divine image" just as the Son is building up the divine image throughout the universe. The divine image in the human mind is indeed boldly declared by Sterry, as by John Smith, to be Christ himself.[1] Religion for Sterry as for John Smith is essentially the discovery of a divine life, a life of spiritual beauty and happiness, "a royal beauty of holiness" as he calls it. The man who lives "as a *Son* under the Gospel" instead of "as a *Servant* under the Law" lives in "a *Divine Principle*". He is "naturally good". "It is his Nature to be so." He is in St Peter's words a "*partaker of the Divine Nature*". His life has the beauty and spontaneity of the work of a great artist. For such thinkers as John Smith and Peter Sterry there is no distinction between "Faith" and "Works". The living of the divine life is the concrete act of Faith. "Faith", Sterry declares emphatically, is for him "no Empty Image or thin Persuasion. It is a *substantial incorporation* of

---

[1] Cf. no. 96 in this selection and John Smith's *Select Discourses*, 1660, p. 21.

the *things* themselves with in the soul." The divine life is
distinguished by calm, serenity and joy, "Care" is said to be
a sin because it "defaces Spiritual beauty". We are bidden
to "live unconcerned in this world" and regard all its images
and happenings in their true light as essentially unreal. The
objector is made to ask, "may ye enjoy the delights of the
Creature, which is an Inferiour Image?" Sterry's reply is full
of high wisdom and poetry: "Yes,...Please thyself to the
full with every Content. Only let it be no Cloud to cut off;
but a *Christal* to take in the Divine Glory, that this may be
thine and flame in them." The fruits of the divine life for
Sterry are love, forgiveness and toleration. Love is simply
the healthy state of human will. Forgiveness is a re-uniting
of the different parts of the divine Image just as selfishness is
a dissolution of the original unity. Toleration, it seems,
should be extended to all. Almost the only harsh or contro-
versial words in Sterry's works are to be found in the single
sermon on the Roman and Presbyterian Churches, but these
words, we may notice, are directed not against Catholics and
Presbyterians, but against what Sterry believed to be the
intolerant spirit of ecclesiasticism that dominated the Catholic
and Presbyterian hierarchies. From his other writings it is
clear that his noble universalism embraces not only Puritan,
Anglican and Romanist, but Jews and pagans as well. He
cites pagan poets and philosophers and Jewish rabbis and
mystics as authorities in every way equal to the most orthodox Christian divines. Indeed in several passages he lays
particular stress on the profound truths embodied in pagan
mythology. "Confus'd dreams of Christ" is a fine phrase
that he applies to the Greek myths. For Sterry Truth was
something "Heavenly and Divine", far beyond any human
doctrines, however good,[1] and he appears to have held the

---

[1] See no. III, pp. 201, 202. Cf. Professor W. Schirmer's
suggestive remarks on the use of classical mythology in English
literature of the sixteenth and seventeenth centuries in his *Antike,
Renaissance und Puritanismus*, München, 1933, pp. 24–71.

very modern opinion that all religions contain some element of truth. In his great appeal for toleration in the Preface to the *Discourse of the Freedom of the Will* he lays down a principle which few dared to defend publicly in the seventeenth century, that religious opinions have very little connection with the worth of the individual, and are mainly the result of education and upbringing: "Had my Education, my Acquaintance, the several Circumstances and Concurrances been the same to me, as to this person from whom I now most of all dissent, that which is now his sense and state, might have been mine. Have the same just, equal, tender respects and thoughts with the same allowances of another, which thou requirest from him to thy self."

It is not easy to determine whether we can correctly describe Sterry as a mystic. He certainly uses the language of the mystics and was steeped in the writings of the great mystics from Plotinus and the Pseudo-Dionysius to Nicholas of Cusa and Jacob Böhme. We have noticed that he held the central belief of Christian mysticism that the soul has "a supreme part" or "apex" above rationality with which it can have communion with the divine. If mysticism means the doctrine that teaches that the universe is incomprehensible, and that we must give up the attempt to understand it, and regard it with childlike awe and veneration, Sterry is no more a mystic than Spinoza or Goethe. It is true that he speaks of "the bright deep" of the divine purpose, and "the holy mysteries", but he boldly attempts to penetrate the "bright deep" and to find a rational explanation for the mysteries. That indeed is the whole purpose of his great *Discourse of the Freedom of the Will.* Delacroix describes "the states of the mystics" as "among the exalted states of what we may term the unprecise series of psychological states".[1] Sterry's "moments of vision" certainly do not seem to belong

---

[1] H. Delacroix, *Études d'Histoire et de Psychologie du Mysticisme,* Paris, 1908, p. 393.

to this order. They are the experience of a powerful and penetrating mind which, when it becomes kindled by enthusiasm, soars above the intricate structure of logic which it has itself created. If we use the word "mysticism" in a wider sense and apply it to the experiences of such men as Dante, Spinoza, Goethe, and Wordsworth who begin with rationality, and then transcend its limits, Sterry is certainly a mystic. His mysticism is not the mysticism that is based on emotion, and which is only too easily lost in vagueness and "mysticality". It is the quality so well described by McTaggart in his *Hegelian Cosmology* as "a mysticism which starts from the standpoint of the understanding, and only departs from it in so far as that standpoint shows itself not to be ultimate, but to postulate something beyond itself".[1]

Many passages in Sterry's writings recall the expressions and the experiences of the medieval and Catholic mystics and their predecessors, the Neoplatonists. There is evidence in his letters to his son that he practised the traditional exercises of mystical religion. In many places in his writings he refers to the "Prayer of Quiet" found in the whole line of European mystics from Plotinus to William Law: "Put out every spark of Creature Light or Life and you shall find yourselves immediately in the presence of God". Like St Teresa and many others, Sterry speaks of God as a hunter pursuing the soul, of the bitter-sweet of the divine "love-play", the paradox of the "musical discord", the mystical marriage of the soul with God, and similar experiences. Nevertheless, Sterry's mentality is, I believe, fundamentally different from that of the Catholic mystics, and is much closer on the one hand to that of his contemporary Thomas Traherne and on the other to that of the great nature poets of the nineteenth century, Wordsworth and Shelley. His states of exaltation do not seem to occur when the mind is abstracted from the world of sense. On the contrary, as in Wordsworth and Shelley, they seem to arise from a heightening and purification

[1] McTaggart, *Hegelian Cosmology*, London, 1918, p. 292.

of sensuous experience. Sterry is fond of speaking of "spiritual senses" and "the spiritual eye". Such phrases sum up
much of his philosophy. For him as for Wordsworth the
state of beatitude seems to come from the reaching out
through sense to a world beyond sense. In words that
anticipate in a remarkable degree the spirit of the romantic
poets he writes of "that Sympathy, wᶜʰ seemes to be in
nature between a Divine State of things, & the fieldes, or
groves;...we generally find the nativeness, the Springing
Life, the freshnes, & flourishing lustre, the Solemnity, the
Quiet, the Purity, the Sweetnes, the Liberty, the Pleasures,
the Mixtures of Light & Shade, the Openness of the Light,
the Depths of the Shade, the Murmurings of windes, the
Clearnes, & Course of Rivers, all conspire together to awaken
in the Soule a certain sense, & Image of an Immortall, &
Divine State...".

In another passage in one of his sermons he asks his
hearers to "Suppose a Man by Miracle, Borne and Growne up
in One Midnight. Day now begins to come on: This Man
to whom all things were almost alike before; now perceives
Barren Shores, Hanging Cliffes, Devouring Seas on one Hand;
on another, Pleasant Fields, Faire Buildings, a Peacefull
Country. As the Light increaseth, the Face of these Things
still Changeth, Presenting fresh Horrours, and fuller Beauties.
Would not this Man Amazedly Wonder...? Who is not
amazed to see the Changes that are made in the Garment of
This Earth?"[1] Sterry himself seems to have looked upon the
heavens, and the earth changing with the changes of night
and day, and "amazedly wondered". For him as for Traherne the visible universe was invested with a perennial
splendour. Sometimes that vision became intensified, until
all things were irradiated and aglow with a heavenly light so
that they became "A New World of Glories", to use his
own great phrase, in which "Each Dust is known in the
bright form of a beautiful Star: each Star is discovered to be

[1] *The Clouds in which Christ Comes*, pp. 37, 38.

an Heaven of Stars". This is an experience less akin surely
to the visions of the old saints than to the experiences of the
modern poets, to the "bliss ineffable" of a Wordsworth,
when he

> felt the sentiment of Being spread
> O'er all that moves and all that seemeth still;

and to the ecstasy of a Shelley when he was made "one with
nature" and saw how all things

> Interpenetrated lie
> By the Glory of the sky:
> Be it love, light, harmony,
> Odour or the soul of all
> Which from Heaven like dew doth fall.

Another experience described by Sterry is one that he also
shares with Wordsworth and with Shelley. It is the over-
powering sense of the unity of all things felt with something
of the rapture that the medieval saints experienced in their
visions of Christ or the Saints: "This Harmony comprehendeth all particular Musick and Beauties of the Creature....
Blessed is he who hath a *seeing Eye* to discern this Beauty in
every Appearance, the most rugged, black: blessed is he who
hath a hearing Ear to take in this Musick from every motion,
the most sharp, the most confused. Yea blessed is he who
lies with his whole Person, and Life wrapt up in this Harmony; who moveth, as always carried on in the Chariot,
upon the Wings of this Harmony". Finally it may be
noticed—and here again we shall be reminded of Wordsworth—that an exaltation of spirit similar to that produced
by the contemplation of nature is found in Sterry's writings
when he is pleading the cause of charity and toleration. The
ecstatic love of the believer for God is deliberately identified
by him with the love for humanity. Just as at certain times
he saw the world in what he believed to be its true light, as
"a New World of Glories", so at others he could see all men
as he believed them really to be, divinely beautiful and worthy
to be loved. The commandments to love God and to love

our neighbours as ourselves are said by him to be one commandment only, because Christ and God are in all men. Sterry cannot be labelled as philosopher, theologian, visionary or poet. Like some other great Englishmen he partakes in some degree of all these characters. His doctrine is no mere "bloodless ballet of abstractions" on the one hand, nor is his writing a mere series of purple patches of beautiful and eloquent language on the other. His thought is concrete and imaginative like that of the poets, and hence it is inseparable from its expression, from his "verba ardentia",[1] his living language, which at its best has the inextinguishable life of high poetry. Now that the mist of political and ecclesiastical prejudice which has obscured his fame for two and a half centuries has lifted, he should take his rightful place in the goodly fellowship of the English prophets.

---

[1] The phrase applied by Dr Johnson to the language of Sir Thomas Browne.

A

DISCOURSE

OF THE

FREEDOM

OF THE

WILL.

By *PETER STERRY*,
Sometimes Fellow of *Emmanuel* Colledge in *Cambridge*.

HEB. 13. 2.
*Be not forgetful to entertain STRANGERS: for thereby
some have entertained ANGELS unawares.*

LONDON:

Printed for *John Starkey*, at the *Miter* near *Temple-
Bar*, in *Fleetstreet*. 1675.

PASSAGES SELECTED FROM
THE WRITINGS OF
PETER STERRY

NOTE ON THE TEXT

In the following extracts I have endeavoured to reproduce all the peculiarities of the original printed or manuscript texts of Peter Sterry's writings with the following exceptions: (1) I have substituted the modern s for the old long ſ wherever that letter occurs. (2) In the few places where the archaic v for u and u for v have been used by the old scribes or printers I have made my text conform to the modern usage in this matter. (3) In reprinting prefatory matter (such as the Preface to *A Discourse of the Freedom of the Will*) which was printed in italic type in the old editions with quotations, etc. in roman type, I have restored the normal relationship between the two founts, using roman where the original has italics and *vice versa*. (4) I have corrected printer's errors in the old texts, but have drawn attention to such corrections in the notes except where they consist of the elimination or insertion of a single letter. Alterations of the original texts are indicated by pointed brackets.

LIST OF ABBREVIATIONS

USED IN REFERRING TO PRINTED BOOKS

S.C.S.   *The Spirits Conviction of Sinne*, 1645.

C.C.C.   *The Clouds in which Christ Comes*, 1648.

T.C.S.   *The Teachings of Christ In the Soul*, 1648.

C.F.C.   *The Commings Forth of Christ In the Power of his Death*, 1650.

E.D.N.   *England's Deliverance from the Northern Presbytery*, 1652.

T.W.U.   *The True Way of Uniting the People of God in these Nations*, 1660.

D.F.W.   *A Discourse of the Freedom of the Will*, 1675.

R.R.R.   *The Rise, Race, and Royalty of the Kingdom of God in the Soul of Man*, 1683.

A.G.M.   *The Appearance of God to Man in the Gospel*, 1710.

Roman numerals indicate MSS., see Bibliography, pp. 223–26.

1. *Preface to* A *Discourse of the* Freedom *of the* Will

Christian and Candid Reader,

I Intreat some few things of thee, for thine own sake and for
mine.
  1. *Study the Love of God,* the *Nature* of God, as he is *Love,* the
Work of God, as it is a *Work* of *Love.* *Moses* in his dying Song 5
beginneth with God, and the perfection of his Work; *He is the
Rock, his Work is perfect.* St. *Paul* descended from the Paradise in
the Third Heavens, bringeth this with him down into the World,
as the Sacred Mystery, and rich ground of all Truth, from which
all the Beauties and Sweetnesses of Paradise, of all the Heavens 10
spring; That *Love is the band of Perfection.* It is *Love* then, which
runneth through the whole Work of God, which frameth, in-
formeth, uniteth it all into one *Master-piece* of Divine Love.
  If God be Love, the Attributes of God are the Attributes of
this Love; the Purity, Simplicity, the Soveraignty, the Wisdom, 15
the Almightiness, the Unchangeableness, the Infiniteness, the
eternity of *Divine Love.* If God be Love, his Work is the Work of
Love, of a Love unmixt, unconfined, supream, infinite in Wisdom
and Power, not limited in its workings by any pre-existent matter,
but bringing forth freely and entirely from it self its whole work 20
both matter and form, according to its own inclination and complacency in it self.
  Leo Hebraeus, enflamed with the Beauty, and languishing in
the Love of the heavenly *Sophia,* the heavenly Wisdom, which is
the first and freshest life of all Beauties in one Face, immortal, and 25
ever-flourishing, is instructed by this Divine Mistress in those
excellent Dialogues between her and himself to Court and Woo
her into his Embraces, by enquiring into the Nature of Love.
Pursuing this enquiry, by the bright Conduct of her shining
Beauties, he is led through the whole nature of things above and 30
below, with all the Varieties and Changes as manifold streams of
Divine Love; in diverse breadths and depths, with innumerable,
sportful windings and turnings, flowing forth from its own full
Sea of eternal Sweetness, and, through all its Chanels, hasting
hither again. 35

Campanella teacheth us, That all *second Causes*, are *Causa prima modificata*, so many *Modifications* of the *first Cause*, so many forms and shapes in which the first Cause appears and acts. All the Works of God, are the *Divine Love*, in so many *Modes* and
5 *Dresses*. There is *diversity* of *Manifestations*, there are *diversities* of *Operations*, which compose the whole frame and business of this Creation, which are as diverse *persons* acting diverse parts upon this stage. But there is *one Spirit, one Lord, one God, one Love, which worketh all in all.*

10   It is the Divine Love, with its unsearchable Riches, which is the fulness that filleth all persons, and all parts upon the stage of Time or Eternity. If any man know not the way to the Sea, let him follow a River in the course of its stream, saith the *Comœdian*.

Dear Reader, if thou wouldst be lead to that Sea, which is as
15 the gathering together, and confluence of all the waters of Life, of all Truths, Goodness, Joys, Beauties and Blessedness; follow the *stream* of the *Divine Love*, as it holdeth on its course, from its head in eternity through every work of God, through every Creature. So shalt thou be not only happy in thine end, but in thy
20 way; while this *stream* of Love shall not only be thy guide by thy side, but shall carry thee along in its soft and delicious bosom, bearing thee up in the bright Arms of its own Divine Power, sporting with thee all along, washing thee white as snow in its own pure floods, and bathing thy whole Spirit and Person in
25 heavenly unexpressible sweetness.

This is my first Request to you.

2. *Study and practise that great Command of Love, as the Lesson of thy whole Life, with which alone thou art to entertain thy self, and all the Heavenly Company, both here and in eternity.* This is the *first* and
30 *great* Command; That *thou love God with thy whole selfe*; and then, That *thou love thy Neighbour as thy self*, which is a *second Law*, a *second Love*, like unto the first. Indeed it is so like, that it is *one* with it. Be thou thy self in thy whole Person, the Sacrifice of a whole Burnt-Offering, ascending in a Sacred flame of heavenly
35 love to God, the only and eternal Beauty. As the *zeal* of the House of God, which is *Love flaming*, did *eat up David* and *Christ*; so let this *heavenly Love* of the *Divine Beauty*, which is the Beauty it self, descending in a pure and sweet flame upon thee, by consuming thee, convert thee into one spiritual flame with it self. Now live
40 thou no where, but where thou lovest, in thy Beloved. Let thy Beloved alone now live in thee; when thou hast thus lost *thy self* by an heavenly Love in thy Beloved, in *thy God*; when thou hast

thus by the Sacred and sweet mystery of this Love found thy
Beloved, *thy God*, in the place of *thy self*; Then love thy Neighbour
as thy *self*. Love thy *Neighbour* in thy *Jesus*, thy God. Love thy
Jesus, thy God, in thy *Neighbour*. Let this *Neighbourhood* of Divine
Love be as large as the God of Love himself is. Let every other 5
Person and Spirit, which lives and moves, and hath its being in
God, within the *encompassing*, upon the *Ground* and *Root* of the
Divine Being, be thy *Neighbour*, thy *Brother*, *another self*, as *thy self* to
thy self; the Object to thee of an heavenly and incorruptible Love.

Upon this Commandment, saith Jesus Christ, *hang* all the *Law* 10
and the Prophets. This *Love* is the Centre and the *Circle* of all the
Works of God, of all Motions and Rests, of all mysteries in
Nature and Grace, in Time and Eternity. *Plato* saith, That three
sorts of Persons are led to God, The *Musician* by *Harmony*, the
Philosopher by the *beam* of *Truth*, the *Lover* by the *light of Beauty*. 15
All these *Conductors* to the *supream Being* meet in this *Love*, of
which we speak; the *first* and *only true Beauty*, being the *first Birth*,
the first *Effulgency*, the *essential Image* of the *supream Goodness*, is
also the *first*, the *supream*, the *only Truth*; the *Original*, the *measure*,
the *end* of *all Truth*; which by its amiable attractive Light, con- 20
ducteth all Understandings in the search of Truth, and giveth
them rest only in its transparent and blissful Bosom. This also
is the *first*, the *only*, the *universal Harmony*, the *Musick* of all things
in Heaven and on Earth; the Musick, in which all things of Earth
and of Heaven, meet to make *one melodious Consort*. 25

While the *holy Lover* then pursues the *tracts* of this *Beauty*,
through all the works and ways of God, he is encompassed with the
Light of *Divine Truth* shining through him, and round about him.
He is carried on in the *Spirit* by the force of the *Divine Harmony*;
He carrieth along this *Harmony* of things, *charming all things round* 30
about him, as he passeth on. So he seeth the *God of Gods* at last on
Mount Sion, the *perfection* of *Beauty*, *Harmony*, *Truth* and *Goodness*,
which all *Center* in the *Divine Love*, the *Divine Unity*, the *band* of
perfection.

3. *Let no differences of Principles or Practices divide thee in thine* 35
affections from any person. He who seems to me as a *Samaritan* to a
Jew, most worthy of contempt and hatred, most apt to wound or
kill me, may hide under the shape of a *Samaritan*, a *generous*,
affectionate Neighbour, *Brother* and *Friend*. When I lie wounded and
dying, neglected by those who are nearest to me, most esteemed 40
by me; This person may pour Wine and Oyl into my Wounds,
with tender and constant care, at his own expence, bring me back

to life and joy. How evident hath it been in the History of all times, that in Parties most remote one from the other, most opposed one to the other; Persons have been found of equal excellencies, in all kinds, of equal integrity to *Truth and Goodness*. 5 Our most Orthodox Divines, who have been heated and heightned with the greatest zeal of Opposition to the *Pope*, as the *Antichrist*, yet have believed a *Pope* to have ascended from the *Papal Chair*, to a Throne in Heaven. Had my Education, my Acquaintance, the several Circumstances and Concurrances been the same to me, 10 as to this person from whom I now most of all dissent, that which is now his sense and state, might have been mine. Have the same just, equal, tender respects and thoughts with the same allowances of another, which thou requirest from him to thy self. It is a *Rule* in *Philosophy*, That *there is the same reason of Contrarieties*. 15 Two opposed Parties or Persons, by reason of the opposition, for the most part looking through the same disturbed and coloured *Medium*, behold one another under the same uncomely form, in the same displeasing Colours. Hath there not been frequent experience of those, who by being of differing Parties, alienated, 20 exasperated, having their fansies filled with strange Images of each other, when they have been brought together by some intervening Providence, have discovered such agreeable Beauties of Morality and Humanity, such an harmonious agreement in *essential*, in *radical Principles* of Divine *Truth*, of the true and everlasting good, 25 that they have conversed with highest delight, they have departed with an higher esteem of each other, their Souls have been inseparably united with Angelical kisses and embraces? *Some entertaining Strangers, have entertained Angels.* Do thou so believe, that in every encounter thou mayest meet under the disguise of 30 an *Enemy*, a *Friend*, a *Brother*, who, when his Helmet shall be taken off, may disclose a beautiful, and a well known face, which shall charm all thy Opposition into love and delight at the sight of it.

But now, *Reader*, I fall at thy feet, I take hold of thy knees, by all things moving and obliging I beseech thee, *If there be any* 35 *Bowels*, or *comforts* of *Love*, any *Peace, Pleasantness, Strength, Prosperity* in *Union*, any *good* in *Unity*, that thou wouldst take deeply into thine Heart, and treasure up safely there, and frequently with fixed, studious eyes, contemplate this (as I humbly conceive it) *most sure* and *reconciling Truth*, which I shall now, as I am able, 40 represent to thee.

Often, yea for the most part, two *opposed Parties* have something on *each side*, excellently *good*, something exorbitantly *evil*;

although perhaps in unequal degrees. *Both* mutually set after an unmoveable manner before their eyes, *their own good,* the *evil* on the *other part. Thus* they blind their minds to all sense of belief of any good *there.* Thus they lift up themselves above all sense of their *own evil.* So they heighten themselves by self-justifications, by 5 mutual Condemnations, unto an extinguishing of every beam of good, to an encrease of their evils, unto a blackness or darkness, until by these mutual mistakes they have drawn on upon themselves mutual and absolute ruine. How much better were it to obey that Precept of the *Holy Ghost,* which offereth it self to us, 10 like an *Olive-branch* in the mouth of this Sacred *Dove, To look every man not to his own things, but to the things of another.*

O that now I had an hundred Mouths, an hundred Tongues, a voice like Thunder, like the Voice of God, that rends the Rock to cry to all sorts of Persons and Spirits in this Land, in all the 15 Christian World through the whole Creation; *Let all that differ in Principles, Professions,* or *Opinions,* and *Forms, see that good which is in each other, and the evil in themselves. Joyn in this, to extirpate the evil, the common evil, your common enemy, and so quench that fire which burns upon your Estates, your Houses, your Relations, your Bodies, your* 20 *Souls, even to the nethermost Hell. Unite the good which is in you, so shall the good on one side make up that which is imperfect and defective in the good on the other side, unto a perfection of good in both. So shall the good on one side be as a proper Anti⟨dote⟩ to extinguish the evil on the other side. Thus while the evil is the privation, the loss of your selves, and the good your* 25 *true-selves,* (*as* Horace *calls* Virgil, Dimidium animae meae,) *you will meet like two halves of each other, filling up the circle of each others Being, Beauties, Joys, and be now compleated in one. How unexpressible would the fruits of this Union be? How would it heighten you in all the Beauties and Blessednesses of Truth and Goodness, in which your im-* 30 *mortality and conformity to God are placed? yea, how would this Union strengthen those outward Interests, and sweeten those natural Enjoyments, for whose sake, now like Adders, you stop your Ears to the Wisest Charmer, and the most potent Charms, that would draw you home into the bosom of each other, for whose sake now you cast down to the ground* 35 *all ingenuity and integrity. You make your way over their sweetest Beauties and tenderest Bowels, to the heart-blood of one another, until you have drowned in blood those very darling Interests and Enjoyments, together with your own Lives and Persons, your native Country, the Christian World, the face of the whole Earth?* But ah, when will poor 40 Mankind on Earth be *wise,* to understand its own *good* or be *good,* that it may be *wise? Blessed is he that cometh in the Name of the Lord.*

We wait for thy Salvation, thy Jesus, O God! To him shall the gathering of the people be, the true Shiloe, *for whom this Glory is reserved.*

It seemeth indeed, according to my humble sense, necessary to divide those *Principles* and *Practices*, which divide Mankind
5 into *three Heads*:

   1. *Some* seem to be of a nature perfectly *indifferent*, neither good nor evil, but according to the intention and spirit which acteth them.

   2. *Some* differ in the *degrees, mixtures*, or *varieties* of *good* and
10 *evil.*

   3. *Others* differ in the *whole kind* of *good* and *evil.*

In this last state of things, it is the part of every Child of Light, to maintain the Divine Love in his Spirit, like the Sun in the Firmament, encompassing the whole Earth, from one end to
15 the other, shining upon all, both good and bad, upon dry and sandy Desarts, the Habitations of wild Beasts, and venemous Serpents, as well as cultivated Gardens, flourishing with wholesome Herbs, pleasant Flowers, and all sorts of fruits. Thus God himself is propounded to us for a Pattern by the Son of Good.
20   *Distinguish* between the *good* and *evil.* Love takes pleasure in the *good.* Hate the *evil.* Advance the *good.* Oppose the *evil* upon all occasions, with all your forces. But every where *distinguish* carefully, with all tenderness of Spirit, between the *person*, and the *evil* of the person. *Be wise as Serpents, but innocent as Doves*, according
25 to the Counsel and Command of *Jesus Christ*, who is the supream *Wisdom* and *Love* both in one. Discern the *evil* with a quick and curious eye, guard your selves with all your might from it, maintain an aversion, an enmity to it, eternally irreconcilable. Thus be a *Serpent* to the *evil*, but at the same time be a *Dove* to the *person*,
30 without gaul, without any thing to offend, moaning over it, groaning for it, as your *Mate*, till it be recovered from the evil, which captivates it into a fellowship with you, in the purity and love of the Divine Nature.

Have always most tender bowels for, and a most sensible
35 sympathy with all Mankind in their greatest Deformities and Defilements, as thy Brethren tyed unto thee by a *double Consanguinity.*

   1. *All men are made of the same blood in* Adam.

   2. *All men are redeemed by the same blood of the Lord Jesus, who*
40 *hath given himself a Ransom for all, to be testified,* ἐν ⟨καὶ⟩ροῖς ἰδίοις, in the proper times. Each person which hath his part in this Ransom, hath its proper time for its discovery in him. Thine may

be now sooner. This person also now most of all lost in the depth of all evils, may have his proper time yet to come, for the taking off the disguise of these filthy Rags from him, for the discovery of the Glory, as of a Son of God in him. As his time comes later, so it may come with a *fuller Glory*. As *Zipporah* said to *Moses*, whether 5 bitterly, or in the sweet sense of a Sacred mystery, pointing to the *Messias*, *Thou art an Husband to me in bloods*. So look thou on every man, as a *Brother* to thee, in *both these bloods*, of which *one* was once pure and precious, as that of the *Sacred Image of God in Paradise*. The other is eternally pure and precious, as the blood of *God* 10 *himself*.

Forgiving one another freely for Christ's sake, is the language of *St. Paul*. Look upon every person through this *two-fold Glass*, *the Blood*, and the *Beauties* of *Christ*. *Christ hath died for all*. The *natural Being* of *every person* hath his *Root* in the *Grave of Christ*, and 15 is *watered* with his blood. *Christ lives in all*. His *Resurrection* is the *life* of the *whole Creation*. He is the *Wisdom*, the *Power*, the *Righteousness* of God in every work of *Nature*, as well as of *Grace*. He is the *Root*, out of which every *natural*, as well as every *spiritual*, Plant springs, which brings forth himself through every 20 natural existence, and brings forth himself out of it, as the *flower*, the *brightness of the Glory of God*. He is the *Root* and *Truth* of all things. *All things are by him, and for him, to the praise and glory of God in him*. *His name is excellent through all the Earth*. Read then this *Name* of *Excellency*, of *Glory*, the *Name of Christ* in every *part* 25 and *point* of the Earth, the *darkest*, the *lowest*, the *least*; forgive the *spots* upon this *Name* in every person, for the *Names-sake* engraven upon it.

Receive one another into the Glory of God, is the Rule of *St. Paul*. *Divines* distinguish between the person, together with the *nature* 30 of the *Devil*, and the *evil*. The *person*, the *nature*, springs forth from God, and so is good, hath a *Divinity* and *Glory* in it; a *Divine Root*, a *Divine Image*. It stands in the Glory of God, as a Flower in the Garden, a Beam in the Sun, it is maintained by a continual emanation from the bosom of the supream Glory. Thus thou art 35 to receive every person, clouded with the greatest evils, as he is the *work* of *Nature*, and of *God* into the Glory of God. Thus every other person is to be thy *Neighbour*, thy *Brother* in the Glory of God; and the Object of a Divine Love.

No evil, as evil is the *nature* or *choice* of any person, but the 40 *mishap*, and the *disease*. *Truth* is the only Object of every *Understanding*, the only *white* at which it aims. Like the *Mary-gold*, it

opens it self only to this *Sun*, or that which shines upon it in the glorious *form* of this Sun, and so descends in seeming beams of this Divine Beauty into its bosom. Good is the only Object of the *Will*. As the Needle toucht by the Load-stone, is governed in
5 its motion and rest by the North-pole; so is the *Will* moved and attracted by that alone, which toucheth it with a sense of *good*. It resteth in no bosom, but that which courteth and wooeth it under the Divine Form of good, with the seeming Charms of this its only *Beloved* and *Bridegroom*.
10   St. *Paul* saith, *Sin deceived me, and slew me*. No person is willingly deceived in his belief of *Truth*, or disappointed in his expectation of *good*. Every *evil* is a degree of *death*; a *disease*, in the end *death*. When it appeareth like it self, all things fly from it, as from death. But as *Cupid*, in the form of the young and flourishing
15 Prince *Ascanius*, by treacherous embraces and kisses, breath'd a fatal poyson into the veins of the *Carthaginean Queen*. So doth sin and evil by the hellish enchantments of the Prince of Darkness, form it self into the most alluring resemblance of the heavenly Image, composed of Truth and Goodness, meeting in one im-
20 mortal form. It adorneth it self all over with the most curious and sparkling Counterfeits of all its most amiable, most Divine Sweetnesses and Beauties. Thus it insinuates it self into the eyes and hearts of the Sons of God, and fills them with its false sweetnesses, enflames them with a false Love, as the poyson and fire from Hell.
25 Yet still in the midst of these enchantments and deaths, as the Athenians in the midst of their Atheism and Idolatry, had an Altar inscribed, *To the unknown God*; The Understanding and the Will, according to their own proper natures, stand in every natural Spirit, as Altars in a Temple, shining and burning, with
30 continual fires by night and by day, aspiring to the highest and clearest Heavens, through all opposed Clouds of Darkness, while this inscription in clear Characters appeareth engraven round these Altars, *To the Unknown Good*, the *Unknown God*, to the *unknown Truth*, the *unknown Jesus*.
35   If any person then be faln into any evil, *Let those that are spiritual restore him with a spiritual skill, with a spirit of Meekness and Divine Love*. Apply Reproofs, Chastisements to evil persons in their seasons, as a *Brother* gives an Antidote to a beloved *Brother*, that by a mistake hath been surprized and drunk in poyson; or as
40 one hand applies a Medicine to the other hand, or to the eye, when it suffers by any wound or distemper.
    If thou art an *Angel*, and hath to do with a *Devil*, use no

reviling Language, for so the Angel himself is by the Spirit of God markt with a Character of Honour for this, that he *used no reviling Speeches to the Devil.*

Preserve thy self from that *bitter zeal*, which St. *James* mentioneth, upon which he setteth so evil a mark, branding it 5 deeply with the fire of Hell; as a *Devil* transfiguring himself into the form of an *Angel. If there be* (saith he) *amongst you bitter envying; this wisdom is not from above, but earthly, sensual and devilish;* We read it, bitter envying. In Greek it is, πικρὸς 3ῆλος, bitter zeal. Take heed of suffering thy *zeal* against the *evil*, to be mingled 10 and tempered with a bitterness against the *person*. As *Lightning* from Heaven melts the *Sword*, but doth no harm to the *Scabbard⟨,⟩* discover thou in all thy Reproofs and Chastisements an equal love to the person, and hatred to the *evil*, an equal desire to destroy the *evil*, and save the *person*. Or rather, let thy *zeal* against the *evil* be 15 *love* to the *person*, flaming forth, and burning with a great, but with a sweet, and Divine force, that it may consume the Dross for the Golds-sake, to which the dross cleaves, that of the Gold, thus refined, it may make a Jewel for the Bosom, or a Crown for the Head of Jesus Christ. Suffer not thy zeal against evil, to be 20 like the *Locusts* from the bottomless-pit, which have faces like *men, hair* soft and delicate like *women, Crowns* of Glory upon their heads like *Angels*, but venemous and killing *stings* in their *tails*. Let it not be like *Culinary fire*, or the fire of Hell, black, sooty, and devouring; but like the fire from the *golden Altar*, mingled with 25 sweet Incense, filling all round about, and carrying up that upon which it feeds, as a Sacrifice to Heaven, with the rich Odours and Perfumes of a Divine Love.

If I be lifted up to Heaven by manifold excellencies, together with *Corazin* and *Bethsaida*, from whence I look down upon another 30 far beneath me, lying like *Sodom* and *Gomorrah*, in a loathed and hated deep of darknesses, defilements, disgraces; Let me then think, That this *Sodom* may have a better Spirit, a better ground of good at the bottom of its Spirit than my self. That if the seed of Love and Light which hath been sown in me, had been sown with 35 the like advantage there, it would have far excelled me in its fruits. Yea, let me think that it may not only have a better ground, but a *Divine seed*, hid deep in that ground beneath all this soil and dung, beneath all this darkness, deformity, and deadness of its Winter-season, which may rise up in its proper Spring into pleasant 40 Flowers and Fruits, as the *Garden of God*. Thus let me think, and let these thoughts instruct me to love every *other* person, removed to the greatest *distance* from me, cast down to the greatest *depth* beneath me, as my *Neighbour*, my *Brother*, my *self*.

This is my double Request to thee, *gentle Reader*.

1. That thou love every other person, as thy Neighbour, 5 thy Friend, thy self, with that Divine Love, in whose flame thou sacrificest thy self, and all things to receive thy self again, and all things together with thyself in a more excellent and durable form.

2. That thou suffer nothing to stain the Candour of this Love, 10 whose Reasons being altogether Divine, subject all other reason to themselves. Give me leave to strengthen this *twofold Request*, by presenting to thee thine own *Interest*, after the highest manner contained in it, after a *two-fold form*.

This *Divine Love*, at this heighth, in this Latitude, is all that 15 is *true* in *Religion*, all that is *good* in *Man*, all that is *acceptable* with *God*, all the *hope* of *future Glory*, and of *blessed immortality*. *If I give all my Goods to the Poor, and my Body to be burnt, and have not Charity, I am nothing.* Is there any *Charity* or *Love* to *Man* greater than this, to give all my Goods to the Poor? Is there any Charity or Love to 20 God more Divine than this, to give my Body to be burnt for him? Yes, there is a *Charity*, a *Love*, which transcends all this, which, if I want, I may yet have all this, and be nothing. This is that *Divine Love*, of which I speak, *which lifteth not it self up above any of the works of God*, but keepeth the *Unity* of the eternal *Work-* 25 *man*, of his *Divine Design* and *Work*, in the golden band of an universal Peace, and Divine Amity. This is that *Divine Love* which *behaveth not it self uncomely, seeketh not its own things*, breaketh not the Harmony of the whole, dividing it self from the whole, by a particular *self-love*. In the universal Beauty and Melody of the 30 Divine Wisdom and Work, it respecteth it self as a *part*, and all *parts*, as it *self*, having one Beauty and Joy together, in the Beauty, Joy, and harmonious Perfection of the Divine Figure in the whole piece.

This Love *beareth all things, believeth all things, hopeth all* 35 *things, suffereth all things*. This we read of the Divine Love, 1 *Cor.* 13. 7. The first expression in that verse is, πάντα στέγει, which we render, beareth all things. I have three Reasons against this translation of it.

1. It makes the last Clause of this verse a *tautology*, a vain 40 repetition; *It suffereth all things*, which is the same with the *first*.

2. It is the remotest sense of the *Greek word*, two senses being nearer:

1 To *cover*.

2. To *contain* or *comprehend*.

3. These two nearer senses are more agreeable, more full and Divine.

  1. The *Divine Love* covereth all things with the *Divine loveliness* 5 and beauty of the universal *Harmony*, which is the *Righteousness of God in Christ*, the *first*, the *fairest Image* of the *invisible God*, in which every other Image of God standeth, as in the Original, the all-comprehending Glory. This is that which *Solomon* saith, *Love covereth all sin*. And *St. Paul*, of the *Divine Workman*, of the 10 *Divine Love*; *He putteth the highest comeliness*, that is, the *universal Comeliness* of the *Divine Image* in its entirety and perfection upon every part, even *upon the most uncomely parts*; *That there may be no schism or division in the Body*, that there may be one glory of all.

  2. The *Divine Love* in every *Person* or *Spirit* lives not in *it* 15 *self* as a *part*, but in the life of the *whole*, in the *Divine*, the *Universal Spirit*, the *Spirit* of *Love*, the *Spirit* of the *whole*. *I live not*, saith *St. Paul, but Christ liveth in me*. Again, *If you live in the Spirit, walk in the Spirit*. Thus the Divine Love having its life in each person, in the life of the *whole*, the *Universal Spirit*, being one Spirit with 20 that Spirit, which is the *Unity* of the *whole*, comprehendeth all things with strictest tenderest imbraces in it self, as *one self* with *it self*. So saith the *holy Apostle*, *All things are yours, you are Christs and Christ is Gods*. *All things are yours*, as *you* are *Christs*, as *Christ* is *Gods*; that is, in the *Unity* of the *eternal Spirit*, which *is Love* it 25 self.

  Now from this *covering Beauty*, and *comprehensive Virtue*, in *Divine Love* these effects naturally flow; *To believe all things, to hope all things*; We easily believe and hope that which we desire. The *Divine Love* hath a *complacency* in all things, as it comprehendeth them 30 in their Divine *Root*. It hath a *good will* to all things, as they stand in the same *Divine Root* with it self. From this *Complacency*, this *Desire*, this *Divine* Root it *believeth*, it *hopeth* all things. It believeth all things to be *Divine Tabernacles*, like that in the Wilderness, which though moving through *Desarts*, through a *Land of Graves*, 35 through a Land of fiery Serpents, yet answer to their *Pattern* on the top of the Mount; though covered with a course Tent, exposed to the fury of the Sun, and tempests in the midst of Clouds, of dust; yet are all-glorious within, composed of rich materials, bearing a Divine Figure, filled with the Divine Presence 40 and Glory. It hopeth all things, light in the midst of darkness, a flourishing Garden of Lillies and Roses, in a ground covered,

and bound up with all the darknesses and rigours of the hardest
Winter; a treasure of *Honey-Combs* in the body of a *Lion*.

The *Master of the Sentences* hath such a high esteem of this
Charity, or *Divine Love*, which is the subject of *St. Pauls* Discourse
5 in this Chapter, That he affirmeth it to be the *holy Spirit himself*,
the *third Person* in the *Trinity*, which is the *Love* in the Divine
Nature, and so the *Virtue*, the *Power*; As the *second Person*, the *Lord
Jesus* is the *Beauty*, the *Wisdom*.

St. James reasoneth after this manner, *Can the same Fountain*
10 *bring forth sweet and bitter waters? with the same mouth you bless God,
and curse man, made after the Image of God.* If from the same heart
thou bringest forth that Love to some men, by which thou givest
all thy Goods to them to supply their wants, and ragest with
wrath or hatred against others, who as they have any *making*, are
15 *made* after the same Divine Image with the rest of Mankind; Who
as they have any *Being*, have the same *Divine Root*, are sealed with
the same *Divine Impression*, thou hast not *Charity*, thou hast not
Divine Love, thou hast not the *Spirit*; the *universal*, the *eternal
Spirit*, thou art *nothing*. If thou hast the gift of *Prophesie*, if thou
20 understandest all *divine Mysteries*, if thou hast a *divine Faith*, if with
the same heart thou lovest God to so high a degree, that thou
givest thy Body to be burnt for him, and yet burnest in rage
against any man, made after the Image of God; All these Divine
Gifts or Graces in which thou gloriest, are nothing; thou art
25 nothing, thou hast not *Charity*. Thou hast not the *Divine Love*,
thou hast not the *Spirit* of *Christ* and of *God*, which is the *universal
Spirit*, the *Spring*, the *Seal*, the *Band* of the Divine *Unity*.

Dear Reader, follow after this *Divine Love*, without which all
that, which thou hast, is *nothing*, which if thou hast, it is the hand
30 of perfection, *never faileth, never falleth short* of the Glory of God;
but by the incorruptibleness of a meek spirit, preserveth in it self
a Divine Beauty and Sweetness, which is ever perfect, which
never passeth away, in the midst of all changes of Life, in Death, to
Eternity.

35 This is thy *first Interest*, in preserving the *Divine Love* entire
in thy heart.

⟨3⟩ *The measure which thou measurest to others, shall be measured to
thee again. If you do well, who will harm you? St. Paul* distinguisheth
between a *righteous man* and a *good man*. *This doing well* is that good-
40 ness of *Divine Love*, pouring forth round about it, heavenly beams
upon all things, which maketh men to be so far from any inclination to harm the person, in whom this *goodness* discovereth it self,

that they are willing to *die* for him. St. *John* giveth us a lively figure of the Divine Love, in a light of Glory, by these words, He *that loveth his Brother, walketh in the light, and there is none offence in him.* The last words are capable of two senses, which very agreeably meet here. 5

1. There is nothing in this person, at which any man taketh any offence.

2. There is nothing, of which this person receiveth any Image, into his Spirit, which offends him.

He, who is this *Divine Lover*, walketh always in those blessed 10 *Regions* of *Divine Light*, where everything presenteth it self in his heart, as it lieth in the heart of God, springing forth from the womb of an *eternal Love*, acted by that *eternal Spirit*, which is *Love* it self, cloathed with an ever-flourishing loveliness, lying in the *universal Harmony* of the Divine Wisdom, being one piece with it, 15 having the Glory of God resulting from it, and resting upon it. He, that is, this *Divine Lover*, shines forth in all his Discourses, Conversation and Actions, upon all eyes and hearts, with such a sweet light and heavenly lustre of the Divine Nature, of the supream Love it self, the *Unity*, the *Mother*, the *Sister*, the *Desire* of 20 all things, the *Joy of the whole Earth*, that nothing takes offence at this Person, nothing can harm him.

O what a Conquest had we attained, if we once did so live, that we convinced all persons, that we loved them in truth and in deed, that we had a *Divine Love* for them, that we esteemed all 25 things in our selves of no value, of no effect to our present Beauty and Peace, to our eternal Life and Glory, to be altogether *nothing*, except this *Divine Love* alone? How would this demonstration of an *heavenly Wisdom*, in an *heavenly meekness of Divine Love*, disarm all hands of the weapons lifted up against us, and all hearts 30 of their wrath conceived against us, like the *Musick* of *David's Harp*, the sweet force of this *Love* would chase away every evil Spirit from every Breast?

There is no power in Nature like to that of *Similitude*. Everything draws and attracts its like to it. Where this Divine Love 35 flourisheth in any person, all the blessed immortal Spirits of heavenly Love above, in eternity, with all the joys and glories of Love resort to this Person, to this Heart, planting themselves round about, as *heavenly Guards*, and *heavenly Ministers* to it, inhabiting in it, as their proper *Paradise*, and *Heaven* here below. In 40 all things below, through all their differences, distances and divisions, the *Spirit* of *Love*, which hath in it the *Root* and *Idea* of each

Creature, which is in each Creature, as the *proper Root* of that *Creature*, as its *Ideal*, and primitive Form, *discloseth* it self to, shineth forth upon, and in all forms of things circleth in this person, this heart, being attracted by it, drawn to it, as its proper 5 Centre.

Some *Divine Philosophers* teach us, That according to the property or power which predominateth in us here, such will that *Divine Idea* be, which shall be our eternal Habitation and Palace above, in which we shall enjoy all things, being sealed to us by this 10 *Idea.* If the Divine universal Love reign in thee here, Love, which seems to be the highest and sweetest of all *Ideas*, in the *Divine Nature*, the *Divine Nature* it self in its most proper and perfect *Idea*, uniting the Ideas of all Perfections, of all Beauties, of all Sweetnesses, of all Lives, Loves, Joys, and Glories in it 15 self, at their greatest heights, with the most ravishing agreeableness and harmony; this shall be thy proper *Habitation* and *Palace*, set up for thee in thine own person, in every Creature, in every Created or Uncreated form of things, to dwell unchangeably in both, *here* and *above*. Here shall all things present themselves to 20 thee, cloathed and sealed with this *Idea*, with this pure and perfect *Love*. *With the measure with which thou hast measured unto others, shall it be measured unto thee*. Thou hast loved all things with a *Divine Love*, looking upon them stedfastly, through all seasons and changes in a *Divine Light*, in the incorruptible form of a *Divine* 25 *loveliness*. As thou hast looked upon them, so shall they all, in all seasons and states, *appear* to thee in a *Divine Light*, full and overflowing with a *Divine Love*, cloathed all over with a *Divine loveliness*. Love all things, O *Reader*, after a *divine* manner, that thou mayest be the beloved Object of all *divine things*, and *divinely* 30 *beloved* by all things, that thou mayest shine with a *divine loveliness* in all *eyes*, and be received with a *divine loveliness* into *all hearts*.

These are the *Requests* which I make to thee for thine *own sake.*

I have *one Request* only to present to thee, for *my self*, which 35 is, That thou wouldst come with this *Divine Love* to the reading of this Discourse.

Come with that love *which thinketh no evil*. We read in the *Revelations* of an *Angel descending from Heaven, who enlightned the whole Earth*. While thou readest, let this *heavenly love* be as a 40 *Seraphim* flying down upon its flaming wings, from the Throne of Love into thy Bosom, to enlighten thy whole Soul with its beams, unto a Divine Candour, that there may be no dark corner left for any suspitious Jealousies, Prejudices, Animosities, or ill will, like poysonous Toads in the hollows of some old wall.

Come with this love which *believeth all things*, all the good that every subject, either person or thing, is capable of. As Bees extract the virtue out of the commonest Herbs, and convert it to 5 Honey in themselves: So do thou believe every thing here to be intended in the best sense, of which it is capable: Draw forth this sense from it, and improve it in thy self with the utmost advantage, to the sweetest satisfaction, and the richest treasure in thy own mind. 10

Believe this Piece to be the fruit of Love, springing from a *Root* of *Divine Love*. We read in the Revelations of an *Angel standing in the Sun*. *Plato* somewhere saith, something like this, that if we stood in the Sun, all things, even this dark mass of Elements, and elementary composition to us, beholding them 15 from that center of Light, would appear in a *Sun-like Glory*. Be thou this *Angel*, or in this an *Angel-like* Spirit, stand in this *Sun*, the glorious circle of *divine Love*. From thence see the Fountain of Love opening it self to thee in this Discourse, all the parts, all the lines as so many streams flowing forth from it to water thy 20 Spirit, and make it a Garden of Divine Sweetnesses and Beauties. If the *rich man* in Hell, next to the quenching of those flames, which burnt upon himself, made this his Request to Heaven, That *his brethren might be preserved from coming to that place of torment*; How much more do the *blessed Inhabitants* of Heaven sweetly burn 25 in pure and precious flames of most ardent desires, that other persons, dear unto them, may be brought into the same blessed place, to partake of the same incorruptible Joys and Glories? Let Love instruct and prompt thee, *gentle Reader*, to think that the worthless Authour, according to the inexplicable sweetness, the 30 unconfined freedom, and fulness of this *eternal Law*, the *Divine Love*, which guildeth without difference the *Cottage* and the *Palace*, the *Dunghill* and the *Throne*, may have been led by a Sacred beam of this Love, touching his heart from on high, so near unto the borders of the happy Regions and Kingdoms of Divine Truth, as 35 to discover all to be *Heaven* there. Let the same sweet Instructor teach thee, to think that he, as he may have been by the same gracious beam led farther into the blissful Continent of this Love, may have met with *Heavens*, which open themselves into Sweetnesses and Glories, ever increasing, ever extending themselves to 40 a more vast amplitude and compass which heighten themselves in Joys and Glories, in Sweetness and Beauty, past all description,

or belief, except to him alone who hath been by the same shining guide led into the same places. Then let the sweet waters of this Divine Love, from its own Fountain sprinkled upon thine heart, raise this candid belief in thee, that as a pair of silver-feathered
5 Doves flying before *Æneas*, guided him to the Tree laden with golden-boughs, in the midst of a thick and obscure Wood; So this Discourse, aiming at a resemblance of those beautiful and lovely Birds, sacred to love, in a whiteness of unspotted Candor, may be a birth of Love, though weak, and flying low, sent forth
10 to allure and guide thee into those everlasting Heavens of Divine Truth and Goodness, which as thou entrest into the discoveries of the Divine Love, and passest on farther in them, thou wilt find in the obscurities and tumults of these earthly shades, of this life of dreams, opening themselves to thee, with inexplicable delights and
15 satisfactions, with transcending glories, endlessly raising themselves to greater heights, and spreading themselves to a wider compass.

But you will say, what connexion hath the *Divine Love* with *Free-will*, the subject of this ensuing Discourse?
20   Very fit and harmonious in two respects:
   1. The *Will it self is Love*. *Thomas Aquinas* defines the *Will* to be the *inclination of the Soul*. The Object of the Will is good. The inclination of the Soul to *good* is *love*. St. *Augustine* calls *Love*, *Pondus Animae*, the *weight* of the Soul, by which it moves to its
25 attracting *Object*, as to its Center. The Object of *Love* is *loveliness* or *beauty*. *Beauty* in its *Essence* is *good*, in its effulgency, in its *proper* and *essential Image*. Thus the *Will* and *Love* are both *one* in their *Object*, and in their *proper formality*; both are the Souls *vital spring* or *principle* of *motion* to good. The *Understanding* receives its *Object*
30 into it self, to be a *living Light* shining within it, and illustrating it. The *Soul* in the *Will* flyeth forth upon the wings of Love, into the bosom of the beloved Object, to live there where it *loves*.

He, who with a clear eye distinguisheth the curious and close workings of the *will*, may find all its motions or affections to be the
35 *same love* in various postures, as it rests with sweetest complacency, in the embraces of the beloved Beauty, or faints under a dispair of fruition, or an irresistable opposition in its prosecutions; as it sails on smooth Seas, with soft and prosperous gales to its haven in its eye; or wrestles with tempests of Waves and Winds,
40 with chearful courage raising it self to surmount them. As the colours of the *Rainbow* are the same light variously reflected from the Sun, and variously falling upon the watry Cloud; so are all

the motions of the Will the same *Love*, raised from the same good, beautifully shining forth, and reflecting it self variously upon the Soul in different postures of *presence* or *absence*, *of doubt*, *difficulty*, *impossibility* in the attainment, or *facility* and *assurance* of fruition.

The *freedom* then of *Love* is the *freedom* of the *Will*. We 5 frequently say, *What so free as Love?* yet what so *inevitable*, as the *golden-headed darts* of *Love*, like beams shot forth as from a golden Quiver, from the face or bosom of the amiable and shining *good?* What so inevitable, as the sweet wounds made by these darts? *God is love*, the *Soul* is the *Image* of God. According to our dis- 10 tinctions, *God* is *Love* most peculiarly and properly in his *Divine Will*. The will of man then is also a *Divine Love*, being the *Image* of the *Divine Will*. If that be true, as it appeareth so to many of the greatest *Philosophers* or *Divines*, that the *Soul* in its essence and faculties, are really one. The *Soul* it self is *essentially* a *Divine Love*, 15 being in its essence an *Image* of that *God* which is *Love*.

Behold then the *freedom* of the humane *will* in the *freedom* of the *Divine* Love; where as, in the *Godhead* it self, the most *perfect freedom* and the most *absolute necessity* are joined together in a *Marriage*, to which the whole Heavens and Earth, with un- 20 utterable joy, sing eternall *Marriage-Songs*. Where *liberty* and *necessity* meet in *one*; while the Will is carried most *freely* and most *necessarily* to its *Object*, which is *goodness*: Goodness at once becometh the essence and election of the Will, for the highest *necessity* is that of our *natures* and *essences*. According to which 25 ground *Logicians* make those *Propositions* most *necessary*, where there is the most *essential connexion* between the *terms*. In like manner *Love* being the *principal* act of the Soul, and carried most freely, most necessarily to goodness in its proper and essential Image, which is the first, the most true, the highest beauty; 30 Beauty, the beauty of *Goodness*, the beauty of *Holiness*, become at once the *essence* and *election* of *Love*. Thus the *Divine Will* and the *Divine Good*, the *Divine Love* and *Divine Beauty*, are made *one*, by the golden knot of the same heavenly and eternal *Marriage*, diffusing themselves from this marriage-bed in Divine embraces, and 35 inconfined enjoyments, through all things of Time and Eternity, through finiteness and infiniteness it self.

Let me add to these a *third Marriage*, making up the joys and triumphs of the other two; between the *Divine Loves*, the *Father*, the *Brother*, the *Bridegroom*; And the *Daughter*, the *Sister*, the *Bride*; 40 the *Divine* and the *Humane will*; the *Soul* and her *God*; the *Image* and her *Original*. Is any freedom to be compared with this, which takes

up the *Image* into the ample glories of its *Original*; which determining and espousing the *Humane* will, the *Divine Love* below, to the *Universal*, the *Divine Good*, as its dear *Object*, and delightful *Bridegroom*; taketh it up also into one uncontrouled, unlimited
5 Sweetness and Liberty, with the *Divine Love*, the *Divine will above*.

Yea, now the *will* and *love* enjoy a *two-fold*, full and glorious *Liberty*, while *Goodness* and *Beauty* are their *Essence*, as well as their *Election*.

1. They freely and unconfinedly rove through all the fields of
10 *Goodness* and *Beauty* in their greatest amplitude, in their richest and most unbounded *Varieties*, as freely, as through their own proper *Essence* and *Being*.

2. Their *Liberty*, in this unconfined amplitude of all Goodness and Beauty, becomes most ample and triumphant, while it is free
15 from all fear, danger, suspicion, possibility of change to any degree of confinement or constraint, by this essential Connexion between it self and the highest *necessity*. O good, O beautiful, O *blessed* Will, which sits upon the Throne of Eternity, which governeth us and all things! While in being good, beautiful,
20 blessed, with a perfect *Liberty*, thou art such also with the highest necessity. Thou art now as delightfully and complacentially; so unchangeably, absolutely universally, supreamely, soveraignly, essentially Good, beautiful and blessed in thine whole Nature, Person and Duration, in all thy works and ways. O Good,
25 Beautiful, Blessed, is that will also, in whom *Liberty* and *Necessity* are after the same manner united by its *Union* with the *Divine Will*.

Nothing seems to present the Divine Face of Truth, and the whole nature of things with such *harmonious* and *charming Beauties*
30 to the eye of the mind, as the *determination* of the will by its *essential* and *universal Causes*, seen in *one view* with the *Divine Love*. A *single light* seen by Mariners resting upon their Ship, which, as I remember, was of old called by the name of *Helena*⟨,⟩ threatneth a dreadful storm. But two Twin-Lights, known by the name of
35 the two Brothers, *Castor* and *Pollux*, infuse a new life into the hearts of the Sea-men, by the sweet hope of a sudden and gentle Calm. After the same manner, these *two*, the *divine Love*, and the *determination* of the *will*, shining together, as *twin-lights*, entertain us with a most beautiful composure, a golden Calm, and Sun-
40 shine, a Divine Amity spread through the work of God in all the parts of it. But either of these alone exposeth all to stormy gusts, flawes, and wracks.

We read of the Spouse in the *Canticles*, That the *Joynts of her thighs are Jewels, the work of a curious workman*. The indeterminate motions of the Will, render the work of *God*, a dis-joynted piece, exposing it in its most principal parts and motions to an un-governed *contingency*, without joynts or bands, which may knit 5 them together one to another, and to the whole, as *one piece*. If the will with its motions, by a necessary connexion in the *Order* of *Causes*, be joynted into the *whole*, and compose with the rests of the parts *one entire work*, answering to *one entire design*, framed in the *heart*, and brought forth by the hand of that supream and eternal 10 Spirit, which is *love* it self; the pure, unmixt, entire *Spirit of love*; How sweet? how beautiful? how full of all Divine Charms and Perfections through all the parts of it? What a Princely Daughter and Spouse, worthy of the great and eternal King must we think this *work* to be; which is the compleat and full contrivance of so 15 rich and so high a Love formed in its own *Bosom*. In the midst of all its most amiable and delightful treasures; which is the *outward work* of a most pure and Almighty Love, wrought entirely from end to end by its own hand, with fingers dropping its own pure incorruptible Myrrh upon every part of it, as it wrought it, 20 forming it for a *compleat* Image of *it self*, and a *continual delight* to *it self*? What *Jewels* now must we think all the *Joynts* of the *Thighs* of this Divine Image and Birth? How harmonious the *motions* by these *Joynts*, when the joynts and motions are all the work of so skilful, so curious, so faithful a Workman, as *Love* it self, the 25 supream and eternal Love?

I humbly acknowledge, that to my weak Understanding, a created *Will*, absolute and *arbitrary*, *determined* in its course by no *light* of *Truth*, no *light* or *life* of *good*, seemeth to lead my Spirit into a Wilderness, where there is no way or guide; or to thrust me 30 forth without Ballast or Rudder, without a Pole-star, or Needle toucht with the loadstone upon the face of an unknown and stormy Sea. What a golden-thread of Harmony guides us through the nature of things? and leads us into all Truth? (*Harmony* being the very *Essence* of all *Natures* and all *Truths*) when we understand 35 the whole nature of things, from the greatest to the least parts and motions of it to be determined, and that determination to be the work of the *Divine Love*, the firmest band of sweetest Union, the sweetest Life of all beautiful proportion, being only Wise, only Powerful, inasmuch as it is the highest *Unity*, containing all 40 *Variety* Originally in it self, sending it forth from it self, and diffusing it self through all!

We are taught in *Metaphysicks*, That *Being*, *Truth* and *Goodness*, are really *one*. How sweet a rest now doth the Spirit, with its Understanding, and its Will, find to it self in every *Being*, in every *Truth*, in every *State* or *Motion* of *Being*, in every form of *Truth*.
5 When it hath a sense of the *highest Love*, which is the same with the *highest Goodness*, designing, disposing, working all in all, even all *Conceptions* in all *Understandings*, all *Motions*, in every *Will*, *Humane*, *Angelical*, *Divine?* With what a joy and complacency unexpressible doth the Will, the Understanding, the whole Spirit now
10 lie down to rest everywhere, as upon a bed of Love, as in the bosom of goodness it self?

Let not any question the close and Divine Contexture of the whole Work in all the parts and conduct of it; by a firm connexion of *Causes* and *Effects*, like links in a Chain, from its
15 *first beginning* of its *last end*; because he meeteth with an *Hell*, as well as an *Heaven* in this work of God. *Divine Love* (which transcendently excels in all Wisdom and Prudence, beyond all the highest wits of men, the richest Contrivances of Poets,) knoweth how to joynt an *Hell* into its work, with such Divine Artifice,
20 incomprehensible to Men or Angels, that this also shall be beautiful, with delights in its place and shall give a sweetness a lustre to the whole piece. *St. Paul* saith to the Saints, *All things, this World, Life, Death, things present, things to come are yours, you are Christs, and Christ is Gods*, and *God* is *Love*. See a golden
25 *Chain*, see the *Order* of the precious *Links*, see how in a beautiful *circle* the beginning is fastned to the *end*.

All *Philosophy* agreeth in this, that the *last end* is the *first mover*. In *God* then, who is *Love*, the first and the last links of this Chain *meet*. *All things*, this *wicked World*, *Death* it self, even the
30 *second Death* and *Hell*, *deaths to come*, as well as *deaths present*, are *shining links* in this *golden Chain*, fastened to that superior *Link*, the *Saint*, the *spiritual man*; *He* is linkt by heavenly embraces to *Jesus Christ*, *Jesus Christ* to *God*, the Father of *Lights*, and the spring of *Loves*.

35 *Homer* tells us of a *Chain* fastned to the Throne of *Jupiter*, which reacheth down to the *Earth*. He speaketh to *Neptune*, *Minerva*, and the rest of the *Powers* about him, which reign in the Skies, in the Seas, in the Earth, in Hell below. *If ye should all hang with your whole weight upon the end of this Chain, I would at my pleasure*
40 *draw you all up to my self.* The *Throne* of the most *High* God, is a Throne of *Grace*, of *Love*. Like a *Chain* doth the whole Nature of things descend from this Throne, having its top fastned to it.

What-ever the weights may be of the lowermost links of this Chain, yet *that Love* which sits upon the Throne, with a Divine delight as it lets down the Chain from it self, so draws it up again by the Order of the successive Links unto a Divine Ornament, an eternal Joy and Glory to it self. All things of *Nature* in its 5 *Beauties*, all things of *Nature* in its *Ruine*, *Life* and *Death* in all forms, are a *Saints*, a *Saint* is *Christs*, *Christ* is *Gods*.

But, *gentle Reader*, this is enough to set forth the suitableness between the *two Subjects* of my *Epistle* and my *Book*; the *Divine Love*, and the *Will of* Man, the *Daughter*, and the *Bride* of this *Love*, 10 by its immortal *Birth* and *Espousals*, *essentially*, *inevitably* determined to its *heavenly Father* and *Bridegroom*. To this *Love* the *only Good*, in all appearance of it, the Will turns it self, as the Needle toucht with the *Loadstone* to the *North-pole*. *Beautiful* and *blessed* is this Will, when its own Bridegroom shines upon it, and 15 attracts it by beams, by sweet glimpses of it self, spread through all things, more *clear*, or more *obscure*, but *true*. Then do her *beauty* and *blessedness* both change into *deformity* and *misery*, when by hellish enchantments she is deluded, and drawn into the embraces of a wrinkled *Witch*, or a *Spirit*, from the *darkness* below, *trans-* 20 *formed into the likeness of her heavenly Love.*

There are now a few things only remaining, of which I would briefly give thee some accompt.

Persons engaged on both sides in this question, which is the ground of my *Treatise*, are highly honoured by me, and truly dear 25 to me in an high degree. *A natural Understanding, Ingenuity, Integrity, Learning, Wisdom, Knowledge,* an *heavenly mind,* set a great price and lustre upon them. The *ends* at which these persons on both parts profess to aim, are truly *Spiritual* and *Divine*. It is the design of one part to heighten the Grace of God by its *freedom* and 30 *peculiarity*. Of the other, to enlarge the Glory of this Grace by its *extent* and *amplitude*. *One* admires and adores the *absoluteness*, the *soveraignty* of *God*, the *other* his *goodness*. On *one* side is an holy jealousy, for the *Unity* and the *Beauty* of the Divine Nature, lest God should be imagined like the *natural day* in the Creation, made 35 up of *two Contraries*, co-ordinate and equally predominate, as *Day* and *Night*, *Love* and *Wrath*, a ground of *Holiness*, and a ground of *Sin*. The *others* are equally jealous of the same *Unity* and *Beauty* of the *Divine Nature*, lest the *eternal Power*, and so the *Godhead* should be divided between the *Creator* and the *Creature*; least in effect 40 *two Gods* should be set up, like those of the *Manichees*, a Fountain of *Good*, and a Fountain of *Evil*; lest the *Divine Glory* should be darkned in its work, and the *Harmony* broken, in which the *Divine Unity* and *Beauty* most sweetly shine, by taking away in any part of the work the *fix'd subordination* of *Causes* and *Effects*.

O what Joy and Glory would crown the Earth, and the
5 Church of God on Earth, if those Divine Persons who have fix'd to themselves ends so Divine, instead of opposing each other in their way, perhaps sometimes mistaken to those ends, would unite their Divine Will and Forces mutually to advance the ends of each other! *St. Paul* saith, *If the falling away of the* Jews *be the*
10 *bringing in of the* Gentiles; *what shall the return be, but life from the dead?* If the dividings, the disputes of these Parties have brought much light to the Church, what will the reconciling and uniting of their *glorious ends*, and their *Spirits* in the glory of those *ends* be, but as a *Marriage*-day shining from on high, which shall fill the
15 Angels themselves with a new joy? The day will come, when men shall say, *Blessed is he who comes in the Name of the* Lord⟨,⟩ who reconcileth the *freedom* and *peculiarity* of the *Grace of God*, unto a full *amplitude* and *extent*, so raising its *sweetness* to a perfect heighth; who shall bring into mutual embraces the *soveraignty* or *absoluteness*
20 of *God*, and his *goodness*, that the *soveraignty*, the *absoluteness*, may be *soveraignly* and *absolutely good*; that the *goodness* alone may be *absolute* and *soveraign*; who through the whole compass of the *Divine Nature* and the *works* of *God*, shall discover to the eyes of men in the evidence of a Divine Light, the *Unity*, the *Beauty* of the
25 *Godhead* in their clearest *Purity*, their highest *Perfection*; springing and shining through *all*, making *all*, in the whole, *one entire piece, pure and pleasant, perfect* in the *Beauties of Holiness*.

The Rules which I have desired to govern my self by in this Discourse, are these, *Right Reason*, the universally acknowledged
30 *Principles* of all sober *Philosophy* and sound *Divinity*, the *Analogy* of *Faith*, the *Letter* of the *Scriptures*, the *Spirit* of *Christ*, in the *Head* of the Church *Christ* himself, in the *Scriptures*, in the *Church*, in the *Spirits*, and *experiences* of each *Saint*. As all these answer each other in a mutual *Harmony*, like the several strings upon a well-tuned
35 Lute: So shall I ever (as I humbly believe) take it for granted, That what-ever jars upon any of these strings, is also out of tune to all the rest. That what-ever is not conformable to any one of these Rules, crosseth them all. If any thing of this kind shall have faln from me, I do here humbly repent of it, and recant it.
40 I humbly desire all those, who shall stoop to read what I have written, to believe that no Gift can be so acceptable to me, as the displacing of any *Errour* or *Falshood* in my Mind, with the gentle

hand of Love, by bringing in the *Truth* which it hath *counterfeited* and *vailed*. If any Errour have seemed sweet, beautiful, or desirable to me, in any kind. I humbly undertake to have a confident assurance of this, That the Truth it self shining forth, will bring along with it far more transcendent Sweetnesses, Beauties, Agree- 5 ablenesses and Satisfactions to all my Desires, excelling it in all the impressions of a Divine Pleasantness, Power and Profit, as the true *Sun* doth a *Parelius*, or a counterfeit Image of the Sun in a Cloud.

If any shall undertake to answer this Discourse with reviling and reproachful Language, I shall endeavour to imitate the example 10 of the *Marquess de Rente*, fixed with much dearness and esteem upon my heart. He came to a City, filled with Reproaches cast upon him. I (saith he) *spake not one word to clear my self, I received gladly the Humiliation.*

Now, *gentle Reader*, I will seal up my *Epistle* to thee with that 15 golden Sentence of St. *Paul, Let all your things be done to all in Charity, or in Divine Love.*

Let me add this one short Direction, as a gloss upon it, bear always clearly, and deeply engraven upon thy Soul, these and the like Precepts, *Love all Men, Honour all* men. *Love your Enemies,* 20 *Love another as thy self.*

Study to know God, as he is the *Pattern,* and the *Perfection* of the *Divine Perfection* included in these *Precepts; Be you perfect* saith Jesus Christ, *as your heavenly Father is perfect.* So he setteth before his Disciples the rich ground, out of which these Precepts Spring, 25 as Plants of *Paradise.*

Study the *Reason* and the *Equity* of these *Precepts.* The *Precepts* of God are *true,* saith David, and *righteous altogether.* Every *Divine Precept* is founded in a *Divine Truth.* The only *reason* of *Love,* is *loveliness.* Thus shalt thou be every where led into a 30 *Paradise,* and into *Heaven,* while thou shalt now understand that God is *Love,* a *Godhead* of *Love; That while thou livest and movest,* and *hath* thy *Being* in *God; thou livest,* and *movest,* and *hast thy Being in Love* it self; That while *God works all in* all, *fills all in all, all within thee, all without thee,* is a *work* of Love, is *full* of Love. 35

Thus these *Precepts,* in the *reason* of them, which will shine out upon thee more and more, as thou growest in the *practice* of them, shall be an anointing upon thine eyes, by virtue of which thou shalt see in all things, *every where, which way soever thou turnest thy self, a Divine Loveliness* presenting it self to thee, continually 40 entertaining, enflaming thine heart with a Divine Love, crowning thy thoughts with a *Divine* Peace and *Joy.*

Gentle Reader, There were in the *Temple* Vessels made of *Wood,* but these were over-laid with pure and massy *Gold.* This Treatise is no *Temple,* thou wilt certainly meet with many things of wood, and perhaps of the lowest sort of wood, worthless, the
5 subject of Frailty and Corruption. Let it be thy part and glory to over-lay it with the *Gold* of the *Temple* above, *Divine Love, which covereth all Sin.* So my humble Prayer is, That thou mayest be together with my self, yea, so shall we both be, if we abide in the *Divine Love, Priests,* consecrated by an *heavenly Blood,* and an
10 *heavenly Unction,* to mini*ster* to the God of all *Loving-kindnesses,* by day and by night, in the *Temple of Love.* Here now *death* is no more, here from our *Death-beds,* as from the *golden Altar,* like the *sweet* and *costly Incense,* we shall ascend in a *pure* and *glorious flame* of *heavenly Love,* kindled from the *Face* and *Heart* of *God above,*
15 unto the *Throne* of *God,* the *Throne* of *Grace* and *Love,* to be ever in the *circuit* of that *Throne,* where the *eternal Spirit,* like a *Rain-bow,* shall encompass us round, as the *seal* and *band* of *eternal Love* shining with *all, innumerable beauties* and pleasantnesses, ever full, ever fresh and flourishing.
20   Perhaps some one will say, Who is this that thus preacheth Love to the World? Is he himself a *Dove washt in Milk?* Far is he from pretending to the praise and perfections of that Spirit, the Bride of the heavenly Bridegroom, which sitteth in the Garden of Divine Purities, Sweetnesses and Light, making her Beloved,
25 and his Companions to hear *her Voice,* while they return their esteem, affections, and admiration in Songs, saying to her, *Thy Voice is pleasant, thy Face, thy Person is lovely.* No, the only Character here is that of a *Voice in the Wilderness,* a Wilderness of many Deformities and Distractions within, as well as *without,*
30 Crying, *Prepare ye the way of Divine Love, make streight paths* for it, by *bringing down every Mountain of Vanity and Pride,* by *filling up* the *Vallies* of *low, dejected, lost, dispairing Spirits.* He who thus cries to you too frequently, too deeply, hath pierc'd the side of this Love; yet still from the wounded heart, through the wounds, *water* and
35 *blood* flow to wash off the stains of this blood *upon him,* and by this *blood,* as a *Balsom,* as a *Cordial,* as a *Spring of Life,* all at once to *heal* his Wounds, to *infuse* new vigour and joy into his Spirits, to *renew* life in his heart, even out of *Death, it self* unto *Immortality.* This is the *Innocency* and *Wisdome* which maketh them *blessed,* who
40 aspire to it; who, as often as they fail in their duty of loving *every other person* as themselves, are sensible of the *guilt* of breaking the *whole* Law, which is summed up in these *two great Commandments,*

and maketh them inseparable as the *substance*, and the *shadow* in the *Sunshine*, or as the *Fountain* and the *stream*, the *Sun* and the *similitude* of the Sun, in the light surrounding it.

> *To love God, with all our selves,* and
> *To love our Neighbour, as our selves.* 5
>
> D.F.W. Sigs. a–d₃ᵛ.

2. *An Universal Being*

Everything that *IS* beareth written upon it this *Name* of God, *I AM*. All things that *be* declare a *Being*: While all things agree in this, *That they be*, they demonstrate an *universal* Being. *Being,* as it is 10 divided and *restrained* by particular Differences (in all things particular and different one from another) by being lessened, *contracted*, and obscured, is *imperfect*. Nothing that is imperfect can subsist, exist *of it self*, or by it self; for so far as it is imperfect it *is not*. Imperfection is so far a *privation* or negation of Being. 15 *Before* then that which is *imperfect*, is that which is *perfect*, from which and by which that which is imperfect existeth. Thus *Socrates* in *Plato*, from the beauties of sense *scattered* and divided among divers beautiful Subjects or Persons, leads us to all the beauties of sense *united* in one Person compleatly beautiful. From this 20 perfection of beauty, where it is an *accident* seated in a *subject* of dark matter, ever changing, he raiseth us to the innumerable forms of beauty, the unchangeable essences and immortal substances of beauty, where beauty is the whole *substance*, pure, and immaterial. These manifold forms of immaterial and essential 25 beauties, awakened in the intellectual Spirit, he maketh as golden wings, by which we fly upward into the bosome of that *first* Beauty, where all beauties meet in an entire and transcendent *Unity*.

Thus all particular and imperfect *Beings* carry us up to the 30 perfect and universal *Being*, abstracted from them all, set on his *Throne high and lifted up above them all*, from which, as their proper *Head*, they flow, by and in which, as in their proper *Root*, they subsist, being the beams of this glorious Sun, and Rivers from this full Sea. This is God in his *high and holy place of Eternity*. This 35 universal Being, where all Beings meet in one, *is Eternity*. This is the *holy place of Eternity*. *Being it self* in its most exalted Purity abstracted and separated from all differences, mixtures, allayes,

from every thing foreign. This is the *high place of Eternity. Being it self* in its first and supreme Unity, comprehending all *Beings,* all perfections of Being, heighthned to a perfection so far above themselves, that no Being, the most perfect, is able to look up
5 to it.   *D.F.W.* pp. 9, 10.

3. *The Unity of God*

God is so one, as that he is the most simple, the most pure, the most perfect Unity; the first, the Supream Unity: Otherwise he should be one, by an Unity distinct from him, before him, and
10 above him; Then should this Unity be the only true God. Thus is God the most Pure, the most Perfect Unity, far before, far above all Divisions, Compositions or Mixtures, by which all the Creatures, all Things beneath him, and besides him, descend and come forth from him. He then hath nothing within him, nothing
15 without him, to limit, or confine him. The Unity of God is his Infinitness. By the Purity and Perfection of this Unity, he is in All, thro' All, on every Side, beneath above, beyond All, ever every where the same, equally undivided, equally unconfin'd, full of himself, encompassed with himself, that Sacred Circle of All-
20 Being, of Infinitness, of Eternity, whose Center is every where, in the smallest Point of Things; whose Circumference, is no where Bounded, spreads beyond all Bound or Measure; which yet with its whole Circumference, in its full Amplitude, lies every where compleat in its Center, altogether undivided in the
25 lowest, the least, the last Division of Things.   *A.G.M.* p. 388.

4. *The Trinity*

The Unity of the Divine Nature in its Proper Form and Essence is a Trinity, God is not a Dark, Dead, Melancholy, Barren or Solitary Unity. He is in the Language of the Scripture, Light,
30 Life, Love, all Fulness. Every one of these unveil'd opens itself into the beautiful Face of this blessed Trinity.   *A.G.M.* p. 426.

5. *Not a Solitary Unity*

God is not a solitary Unity, without Society or Solace; but a Unity richly Replenish'd, and Eternally entertain'd, with a Variety, as true and
35 *boundless as the Unity itself.* We read in the Scripture, of *all Fulness,*

*the Fulness of the Godhead dwelling in Christ, of the unsearchable Riches
of Christ, of the manifold various Wisdom of God, of Treasures of
Wisdom and Knowledge.* Power and Wisdom agree in that definition
which *Proclus* makes of Wisdom, that it is a *Fulness of Things*: As
both these are at their height, so is this Fulness and Variety of   5
Things at its utmost extent in God.   *A. G. M.* p. 433.

6. *God is Love*

The *Divinity* and *Poetry* of the *Heathen* from their most ancient,
most sacred mysteries, teach us, that *Love* is the *Eldest* and
Youngest of all the *gods*. Our God, the God and Father of our 10
Lord Jesus, is the God of *Love* in the truest, the sweetest and the
best sense. He alone is Love it self, in an abstracted eternal
Divine *Essence* and *Substance*, pure Love altogether unmixt, having
nothing in it self different, or divers from it self; thus is an *infinite
Love*, a sweet and clear *Sea*, which swalloweth up all bounds, all 15
shore and bottoms, into it self. This *Love*, as it is every way the
same, is the *ancient of Dayes*, the *eldest of all the Gods*. Thus is this
most high and holy *Love*, the *God of Gods*, the *First* and the *Last*,
containing all things within its own blissful bosome, as the bound
of all, but being it self every way beyond all bounds, without 20
all bounds, *infinite*.   *D. F. W.* p. 41.

7. *A Vital Act*

God is eminently, transcendently a vital Act. The *Psalmist*
saith to him, *With thee is the Fountain of Life.* *St. John* in the close
of his first *Epistle* saith of him, *This is the true God, and eternal life,* 25
He is life it self, life pure, absolute, unmixt, unconfined, eternal,
infinite, a Fountain ever equally unexhaust, a Sea unbounded.
          D. F. W. p. 198.

8. *God and the Ideas*

The prime operation of every *Intellectual Spirit* is *contemplation*. 30
The first and immediate *Object* of its *contemplation* is its *own
Essence*. In this *Glass* of living and immortal Light, all other
things, according to their proper *essences* in their several and
essential forms, appear to it most clearly and delightfully, as its own

Births and *Beauties*. *God, the first*, and most *perfect*, the *Father* and *King* of all *Intellectual Spirits*, is the *truest Person*. He alone in truth subsisteth in himself, existeth without, and above all things. He truly containeth the whole *compass of things* in their *unchangeable* 5 *Truths* and *Substances* within himself, although he Himself be the most *absolute*, and most *abstracted Vnity*. *Angels* and *Men*, in the perfection of their Natures, are no more than *shadowy persons*. They have only *shadowy Essences, a shadowy comprehension* of *shadows*.

10 God then alone most perfectly and substantially enjoyeth Himself in the contemplation of Himself, which is the *Beatifical Vision* of the most beautiful, the most blessed *Essence* of *Essences*. This *Act* of *Contemplation* is an Intellectual and *Divine Generation*, in which the Divine Essence, with an eternity of most heightned 15 Pleasures, eternally bringeth forth it self, within it self, into an *Image* of it self.

According to the Perfection in which God knoweth Himself, and enjoyeth Himself, so is the Perfection of this Image. As those are, so is this clear, distinct and full. The more distinct the beam 20 is from the first Light in its emanation, the more strong and full is the reflection. This *Divine Image* then is at once most perfectly *distinct* from its *Divine Original*, most exactly *equal* to it, and most perfectly *one with it*. As then God is, so is this essential, eternal Image of God, a compleat and distinct Person in it self, in every 25 point with the highest and most ravishing agreeableness, answering the Divine Essence in its spring out of which it ariseth.

If this Image were not a *Compleat Person*, Gods *knowledge* and *fruition of Himself* would be *incompleat*, without the pleasing and proportionate *returns* of an equal *Loveliness, Life* and *Love*. If this 30 Image were not perfectly *distinct* from the bosome out of which it flourisheth, the knowledge and enjoyment of God would be *confused*, more like to the blindness, the barrenness, the cold of darkness and death, than the life and fruitfulness, the warmth of beauty, life and love, which all have their Perfection and their 35 Joyes in the propagation of themselves into most distinct forms, and the reflection upon themselves from these forms.

This is the *first*, and so the most *universal Image*, the *first seat* of all *Images* of things. In this all the fulness, the unchangeable riches of the Godhead display themselves in their first, their 40 fairest, their fullest *glories*. All forms of things are here most proper, most perfect, most distinct, substantial and true. Philosophers and Divines call the first Images of things, as they rise up

from the Fountain of eternity in the bosome of this universal and
Eternal Image, *Ideas*. The *Idea*, in this sense, is the first and distinct
Image of each form of things in the Divine Mind; The *universal
Image* of which we speak is that *Divine Mind* or *Understanding*. This
is the *proper Idea* of the Godhead, the *universal Idea*, the *Idea* of *Ideas*, 5
and so that *Mother of us all, which is above*. Every Idea of each
Creature is this *Idea*, bringing forth it self, according to the
inestimable Treasures of the Godhead in it, into innumerable
distinct figures of it self in the unconfined Varieties of its own
Excellencies and Beauties, that so it may enjoy it self, sport with 10
it self, in these, with endless and ever new Pleasures of all Divine
Loves.   *D.F.W.* pp. 48, 49.

9. *The One and the Many*

As the Heavenly Bodies moving over the Sea, as Buildings
standing, Men or Horses going on the Earth, besides a River, 15
cast their Images into the *Waters* of the Sea, or a River, and beget
upon them *new Appearances* in their own Likeness; so is the State
of Things in *Nature*.

The *Spirit* is the *Truth* of Things in their Eternal Principle.
This *Spirit* stands *above* this Creation, which is as a Water receiving, 20
not the *Substance* of Things, but only the *empty Image*.
                                                    A.G.M. p. 87.

10. *Omnipresence*

God is present to himself in every Creature, after the manner
of a God.   25

Where-ever he is present, He is *entirely present* with all the Joys
and Glories of eternity, ever undivided, His own Heaven to
himself, in the *Depths* of *Hell* beneath as in the Heights of Heaven
above, in the *dust* of the *Grave*, in a wave of the Sea, as in the most
shining Cherubim or flaming Seraphim.   *D.F.W.* p. 75. 30

11. *Immanence*

God, in the presence of his Glory, *resides* in every Creature,
beneath the form of that Creature, as a Vail wrought with a Figure
of himself. Thus he constantly resides in each Creature, as the
Root, and Being of its Being; In the pure nature of man, he shines 35

through the Vail of the Angelical or Intellectual Image, as a *transparent* Vail of finest Lawn, or sweetest Light, sprung from his own Face.   *D.F.W.* p. 117.

12. *In the Lowest Things*

5   *There is not the lowest Thing, which hath not God in it*; for God fills all: Yet as the Sun-Beams fall on a Dunghill, and are not polluted; so God is still himself to himself, high and glorious in the lowest Things.   *A.G.M.* p. 276.

13. *The Gate of the Creation*

10   Is there any thing so dark, so low, as that the *Wisdom* of God reacheth not to it, and shines not in it? If the Wisdom of God is there, then is there the *Center*, the *Concurrency*, the *Union* of all Things, of all Glory.

     If the Wisdom of God shine there, then is there a *Spiritual*
15   *Light* opening all Divine Beauties, making that Thing, the *Gate* of the Creation, of Paradise, Heaven, and the Divine Nature. This is that Traffique of *Wisdom*, which makes the Merchandize of it, better than that of *Silver*, *Gold*, or *Pearl*.   R.R.R. p. 163.

14. *The Olive Tree*

20   In the mystical Fables of the Heathens, the Goddess of Wis-dome contending with the God of the Seas, for the *tutelage* of *Athens*, made suddainly at once to spring up out of the Earth an Olive-tree in its perfection, with its branches and leaves all green, laden with ripe Olives. When an Olive-tree or an Apple-tree
25   riseth up by degrees from its Kernel to a perfect Plant, when it successively putteth forth it self thorow the Spring and Summer, in buds, in leaves, in blosomes, in fruit, unto a full ripeness in Autumn; then in that state of maturity, with its leaves, and fruit in full growth and beauty upon it, it standeth up immediately and
30   entirely out of its Ideal, or first Cause, out of the Divine Omni-potency or Almightiness, as it had never before existed, as if no Summer, no Spring had ever gone before. Yea, the whole Creation round about that Olive-tree, in its present posture with all Plants on Earth, with the present face of Heaven, with the present con-
35   figuration of all Bodies, of all Humane or Angelical Spirits comes

forth from God, as immediately, entirely, absolutely, as when on
the *third day*, all Herbs, Flowers, and Trees first appeared, and rose
up in a moment, at once perfect out of the Earth; or as if the
present Autumn had been the *first*, and the *beginning* of the World,
as some suppose that season to have been.   *D. F. W.* p. 64.   5

15. *To the Pure*

No Object, however low, however base, *embaseth* the Divine
Understanding. The figures of *Mice* and *Emraulds* formeth in Gold,
lessen'd not the lustre, or preciousness of the Gold, neither did they
detract any thing from the sacred Worth, Majesty, or Divinity of 10
the *Ark*, by being put into it. This *Ark* was the Figure of our
Jesus, the essential Image, the Divine Mind, Understanding, and
Wisdome of the Father. *Lazarus* with his Rags, his running
Sores, and the Dogs licking them, represented to the life in an
excellent Picture done by the hand of *Vandike*, of *Titian*, or some 15
great Master, is a worthy and most agreeable entertainment for
the eye and fancy of any Princess, a rich Ornament and rare Jewel
for the Chamber or Cabinet of a Prince. The *Plague* with all its
loathsome and horrid attendance, conceived in the mind, formed
to a most exact Image in *Virgil's* fancy, from thence transferred 20
into his inimitable Poems, becomes worthy of the Ear, the Fancy,
the Mind of that great and most polite Prince, *Augustus Caesar*;
yea, cloathed thus with this Image, the mind and fancy of the *Poet*
transfuse, and present themselves to the spirit of that Prince, as of
all learned and judicious Readers, with a heightned Beauty, and 25
kind of Divinity.

That is a certain Rule, *That every thing received, is received according
to the nature and manner of the Recipient.* The Divine Understanding
cloathing it self with the Images and Forms of all Objects,
deformeth not it self, but maketh them Divine: *To the Pure all things* 30
are pure, but to the Unclean nothing is pure, but even their minds (the
Angelical part,) *their Consciences* (the Divine part of their Souls,)
is defiled.   *D. F. W.* p. 28.

16. *Nothing is Mean and Vile*

Nothing is *mean and vile*, seen in a right and universal Light. 35
Every degree of Being to the least, the narrowest, and obscurest
Point, hath Being it self in its amplitude and *majesty* in it, without

which it could not be. Every thing that is in any kind or degree,
hath the *Throne* of Being set up in it, with God the supream King,
and Fountain of Beings, sitting upon it, and filling it with the
train of his Glories. Thus look upon each Being, and you will see
5 it as a *spacious Palace*, a sacred Temple, or a new and distinct
Heaven.

Being it self, in its universal Nature, from its purest heighth, by
beautiful, harmonious, just degrees and steps, *descendeth* into every
Being, even to the lowest shades. All ranks and degrees of Being,
10 so become like the mystical steps in that scale of Divine Harmony
and Proportions, *Jacobs Ladder*. Every form of Being to the
lowest step, seen and understood according to its order and
proportions in its descent upon this *Ladder*, seemeth as an *Angel*,
or as a Troop of Angels in one, full of all Angelick Musick and
15 Beauty.

Every thing as it lieth in the whole piece, beareth its part in the
Universal Consort. The Divine Musick of the whole would be
changed into Confusion and Discords, All the sweet proportions
of all the parts would be disordered, and become disagreeable, if
20 any one, the least, and least considered part, were taken out of the
whole. Every part is tyed to the whole, and to all the other parts,
by mutual and essential *Relations*. By virtue of these Relations,
All the distinct proportions, of all the parts, and of the whole,
meet in one, on each part, filling it with, and wrapping it up in the
25 rich Garment of the Universal Harmony, curiously wrought, with
all the distinct and particular Harmonies.   *D.F.W*. p. 30.

17. *The Anima Mundi*

Plotinus teacheth, That the first Soul, which is the immediate
Workman of this World, in the order of its procession, from the
30 separate Intelligences or Angels, and from God, the only supream
Father of all, hath its face *ever turned* to the face of God, and un-
moveably fixed upon it⟨;⟩ from his Face, it continually takes in,
as the Nectar of the Gods, the Divine Light, the Divine Life and
Love, it continually takes in, as at an heavenly Feast, as the
35 heavenly Ambrosia, the Ideal Beauty, the first, the Archetypal
Forms in their most immediate, sweetest, freshest, fullest Effulgency or Images. This *God-like Soul* thus bred, thus divinely
formed, thus nourished, thus impregnated, sends forth from it self
this whole visible World, in the figures of those first Glories, in the

similitude of their Unity, Variety, and Order, *without thought*, care,
or trouble, without ever turning a look to this World; as a Person
with his Face to the Sun, casts his shadow upon the ground behind him. There is only this difference, as this great Soul casts the
shadow of this Corporeal World from it self, there is no *ground* 5
for it to fall upon, besides the Soul it self.   *D. F. W.* p. 97.

18. *Millions of Angels*

A bright or light Body, like the Sun, sends forth Millions of
Beams round about from every Point of itself. Such a Brightness,
such a Fruitfulness is there in the Person of Christ; Millions of 10
Angels every Moment spring and sparkle forth from him.

A. G. M. p. 249.

19. *The Mediatory Kingdom*

God in the Creature is seen by a *shadowy Image* alone, which lies
as a Vail upon the pure Glories of his Divine Face and Person. 15
He now shines forth like the Sun in a cloudy day, by that obscure
Image of his Coelestial Form, a reflected, refracted Light.

God in the *Kingdom* of the *Father*, (the Father of Lights in the
simplicity of the Divine Nature) is the *eternal Sun* at its heighth, at
its Noon-sted, in its Meridional Glories.   20

God in the *Mediatory Kingdom*, (which is properly the Kingdom
of Christ in his *personal Reign*) resembles the lovely Morning, the
golden Hour of the Day, when there is no more shades or pure
Light, but both are mixt, and sweetly married into the pleasant
Flowers of Saffron or Roses, breathing their sweetnesses thorow 25
the whole Air and Universe. God in Jesus Christ is now the Sun
ascending, shining forth in its strength, but not at its full heighth.
God and the Creature are like two Lillies or Roses joyned upon one
stalk in a fair Morning, or a bright Forenoon; or like *two Friends*
in this sweet season, in a Garden of Roses embracing. These 30
mutually possess, enjoy the full Beauties, the *full* sweetness each
of other, but not *fully*; *clearly*, but not *compleatly*, until the Sun
come to its full heighth.   *D. F. W.* p. 205.

20. *The Sun's Sun*

Thus the Lord Jesus in his spiritual Glories, as he is the Divine Understanding, is the *Original* form of the Sun, the *Suns Sun*. To him agrees that, which *Plutarch* delivereth to us from the ancient 5 Philosophers, that the God of the Sun, which inhabits the Sun, excels the Sun in the sweetness, beauty, and glory of his Light, ten thousand times more, than the Sun doth this Earth, or the darkest Cloud. The Sun it self shining in these visible Heavens is the essence or essential form, framed by this pattern, sprung forth 10 from it. The Light, the Sun-shines, and Suns which we severally take in our eyes, are so many figures, and pictures, or shadows rather of this Sun flowing from him.   *D.F.W.* p. 39.

21. *The Chariot*

The Body, & Seate of this Chariot is the Unity of the Godhead. 15 This is the Unity of Glory, Love, Power, Wisdome, Life. The Glory makes it rich, fine, and shining more than ten thousand Suns in One. The Love makes it all soft & delicate beyond the perfumed beds of Roses, or the doune of Swans. The Power renders it firme, impregnable, incorruptible, eternall. By the 20 Wisdome it becomes a curious Worke with all beautifull, & various contrivances, figures, proportions, & harmonies. By ye Life it is heightned to a supreame, & immortall Spirit; a composure of all immortall Spirits of Musicke, Beauty, Joy, & Delight.

The Wings, or winged horses, or living wheeles of this Chariot 25 are the Varieties in this Unity. Every Change wch wee call the change of person, state, place, or appearance, is a variety springing up in this Unity.

Each Varietie hath the proper forme & so the perfect fulnes of all Varieties in it. Thus is it at once Wings to this Chariot, & also 30 all desyrable, delightfull Companions, Prospects, & Entertainments in the Chariot.

The Chariot hath five Coverings. 1st The Divine, & Eternall Glories. 2. A Contexture of Angells, & their Glories. 3. Cælestiall Suns, & Skies. 4. A Composure of elementary formes, & 35 Beauties. 5. The Shades of all these.

The Superiors, & Inferiors of these comprehend one another, shine through each other, are full of each other, as Originalls, &

figures joined together most harmoniously in one pure, immortall
Spirit.

The Angells with their Glories are pure, transparent figures of
sweetest Light, through wch ye Godhead with all it's Glories
clearly shines. The Cælestiall Suns, & Skies are pure figures of 5
finest Gold transparent, as glasse, in which the Angells with all
their splendours sit, & sing, & shine. The elementary formes are
clear, chrystalline figures of these Suns, & Skies filled with the
reflexions, & divine formes of the Suns, the Skies, the Glories
above residing in them, & looking forth with smiling Beauties, 10
as so many immortall Beauties thorough them. The Shades of all
these meet in One, partaking of the Purity, Life, Transparency, &
Immortalitie of that Spirit, & his Unity, in wch all these stand.
This Divine Shade is enriched, heightned, & filled with all the
superior Glories, wch descend into it, & compose it. 15

These are the five Coverings of this Divine Chariot, among
which the Inmost, is also the Outmost, in wch ye superior is y^e
inmost Center, & outmost Circle to the inferior.

This is the Chariot, in wch ye heavenly Bride together with
her Bridegroome rideth along through all changes of Light, & 20
Darknesse, Life, & Death. This is at once a Chariot of divine
State; a bed of divine Loves, a Pallace of divine Glories, a
Paradise of divine Delights, & Pleasures, carrying them along with
itselfe, as it passeth thorough them, & transforming them all into
unchangeable Beauties, & Delights. 25

The Spirit of a Saint, as it is in ye Spirit of Christ, moves
thorough all things in this Chariot. The Spirit of a Saint, as it is
one Spirit with Christ, is itselfe this Chariot, where all things in
the formes of beautifull, & immortall Spirits ride along together
through all formes of things, in every forme making a Divine 30
spectacle, and entertainment for a Saint. When he awakes in his
owne proper Spirit he ever finds himselfe with his beloved in this
Chariot. This is the Voice of ye Spouse in ye Canticles. ere I was
aware my Soule made me as ye chariot of my princely people.
Thus if any man be in Christ, He is a new Creation: behold s^th 35
Christ, I make all things new in the newnesse of the Spirit. The
New Heavens, & ye new earth; Life, & Death made new meete
together in this Chariot described by Ezekiel in his first Chapter,
when he saw the Glory of God. MS. III, ff. 180–184.

22. *Fiunt Non Sunt*

It is affirmed of all things material and visible, *Fiunt, non sunt*;
they are sent forth, but subsist not. They *are* only in the *making*;
in the same moment in which they are brought forth, they are *no*
5 *more*.

This is universally true of all Creatures, Men and Angels. They
have only a transient, no permanent Being. No eye ever takes in
twice the same beam of Light. No man standing upon the bank
of a River sees twice the same water present with him. Before he
10 can cast his eye upon it the second time, it is past by and gone: So
is no Creature no appearance the same two moments. We can
never say of created Beings or Beauties, of our sweetest Solaces,
or bitterest Sufferings, *they are*. For while we are saying it, they
fly away, and are no more; like Lightning, or the shadow upon any
15 point of the Dial.   *D. F. W.* p. 63.

23. *The Book of God*

In a *Book* the most *Beautiful* Things are represented by *Black*
Lines, the *straightest* Things by *crooked Scratches*, the *Greatest* and
most *Glorious* Things by little *Spots*. It were impossible for a Man
20 by all that he saw, or read in a Book, to understand those Things,
if he had not some Image of *Beauty*, *Greatness* and *Glory* before in
his Mind.

This *World* is such a *Book* of *God*, in which you have a *Representation* of him, but so *confus'd*; that it is impossible to know any
25 thing of God aright by the *Natural Image*, except you have first the
Spiritual Image, which is God himself form'd in your Souls.

A. G. M. p. 89.

24. *Body, Soul and Spirit*

The *Body* is an Outward Image made of Dust, *Gen.* 2. 7. *God*
30 *formed Man of the Dust of the Ground.*

The *Soule* is a Breath of Life Inclosed in This Image, Clothed
with It, and Giving Life to It: *He breathed into his Nosthrils the
Breath of Life, and Man became a Living Soul.*

The *Spirit* is the Fountain of Life, which flowes forth from God,
35 to Feed, and Maintain the Breath of Life in the Body. When the
time of Death Comes, This Spirit draws back to their Head again

Those streams of Life, by which It went forth into the Body. Then the Outward Image falls to the Ground, and moulders away. Thus doth *the Dust return to the Earth, as it was; and the Spirit returns to God that gave it. Eccles.* 12. 7.

Now of These Three the Higher lives In the Lower, and Above 5 It. The Lower lives By the Higher. And the Highest of all Three, the Spirit of Man hath a higher than That, by which It Self lives, even the Spirit of the Lord Jesus, who is the King and Father of Spirits. *T. C. S.* Epistle Dedicatory, A 3ᵛ.

25. *The True Orpheus* 10

The rectitude of Reason, was the Image of God, the Crowne, and Glory of Man. By this he grew up streight in the midst of the Creatures; uniting heightning them all by a Harmony into the same Image. So he subdued them to himselfe, himselfe with them ascended into, and rested in the Divine Image. 15

Thus Man was the true *Orpheus* with his Divine Hymnes in the midst of Beasts, Trees, and Stones dancing to his Musick.

T. C. S. p. 24.

26. *The Three Kings*

Plato saith, That there are *three Kings*, round whose Thrones all 20 things dance; *God*, the *Mind*, the *Soul*; this continual procession of the Soul from the Divine Mind, through the Angelical Mind, in the entire Image of it, with all its Divine Forms, and their Order, their Harmony, their Unity in the whole compass of their Variety, is the *mystical Dance* of the Soul round the Throne of her King, 25 her Bridegroom, by which at once she contemplates, enjoys, springs up into his Divine Form in all its Beauties, and is filled with him. *He* in like Manner hath her ever before him, as the *Looking-Glass* of his own Beauty, lying and playing in himself, as the Image of a Flower or Tree in the Water, every way circled in 30 by him, as she is *centered* in him.

As the Divine Mind, through the Angelical is in the Soul, so are the Divine, the Angelical Mind through the Soul in this visible World *centring* it in themselves, riding forth upon the Circuit of the Heaven and the Earth, as the *lowest figure* of themselves, at once 35 standing up out of them and standing in them.

The Soul, as the Exemplar Form, as the Unity, the *inmost*

Center, the outmost Circle, sendeth forth this Corporeal Image, as a *figure* of it self, formeth, moveth, acteth it throughout, *sustaineth* it in it self, filleth it with it self, every way boundeth and containeth it within it self.

5 The vast all-containing Unity of the Soul figureth it self, the circular, globous, round form of the Heavens and the Earth, in the Union and Harmony of all the parts, suffering no where any *discontinuity*, or *vacuity*, nor any deformity or discord in the whole.

From the variety of invisible Forms within it self, the Soul
10 springeth up into all the innumerable Army of heavenly Bodies in the Cœlestial Orbs, into all the diversity of *Elementary shapes* and figures in the Regions below. The Harmony and Order of the Soul in all its forms and motions through them floweth forth, figureth it self, as a Light of Beauty shineth, as a Divine Musick
15 soundeth through all the parts and changes of the Cœlestial, the Elementary Sphears, *charming* those Souls that have *awakened and purified senses* to take them in.

As the Soul within it self springeth up into each form, in its proper Order, bringing forth it self at once with the entire Unity
20 of its whole undivided Essence anew, in that distinct form; so doth the Soul from that Original, in the likeness of the same Image, each new moment, spring forth *anew* according to the *innate Law* of the universal Order and Harmony into the whole Heavens and Earth, in a new posture and figure. Thus after the similitude
25 of its own circlings through all forms within it self, the Soul *incessantly* turneth round the Heavens, and the Elementary Orbs, which by their perpetual circling through each other, turn about by day and by night the restless wheel of *Generation* and *Corruption*, as of all change. Thus as the Soul danceth round the Throne of
30 the Divine and the Angelick King, these Heavens and the Elements dance round the Throne of their King the Soul.

D. F. W. pp. 93, 94.

27. *The Waggon and the Horses*

At our Birth, which is the morning of this life, and our entrance
35 upon our Journy through this weary world, our Souls and Bodies are joyned to this fleshly Image by the natural Spirit, the spirit of this world, as Horses put into a Waggon, to which they are fastned by their Harnes, and Traces. The Body is as the fore-horse, but the Soul as the filler, which draws most, and bears the chief

weight, All the day long of this life we draw this Waggon heavy laden with all sorts of temptations, and troubles thorow deep ways of mire, and sand. This only is our comfort, that the divine will, which is love itself in its perfection, as a hand put forth from Heaven thorow a Cloud, at our Birth put us into this Waggon, and governs us all the Day. In the evening of our life, at the end of our Journey Death is the same divine will, as a naked hand of pure love shining forth from an open heaven of clear light, and glory, taking ⟨both⟩ our Souls, and Bodies out of the Waggon, and Traces of this fleshly Image, and Spirit, and leading them immediately into their Inn, into a place of freedom, rest, and refreshing into the unity of the eternal spirit into the Bosom of our Lord Jesus.   R.R.R. p. 435.

28. *A Priest in the Temple*

In the Tabernacle, and Temple every part, every pin answered to the Pattern on the Mount, which were the Heavenly Things themselves in the Spirit, in Eternity. All objects, all actions in the Temple, the Beasts, the cutting their throats, the taking off their skins, the taking out their Entrails, the cutting them in pieces, the boyling, the burning them were sacred Figures of Divine and Immortal Glories, to which the Musick of the Levites round about upon the walls with their Instruments, and voices kept time.

Thou, O Man, art set in this World, as a Priest in this Temple. Behold! Both the Intellectual, and the Bestial part in it; Love, and hatred; War, and Peace; Joy, and Grief; Light, and Darkness; Weepings, with Howlings, Laughter with Shouts; Life, and Death with all that is delightful, or dismal belonging to them; all these Heavenly, and Divine Mysteries. Every one answereth to a purpose in the Heart of God; to a Pattern in the Eternal, and Essential Form of God. Every one answereth to the Musick of the Holy Angels, which stand in Quires in the uppermost parts of this Creation, as the Levites upon the walls of the Temple. The basest, the bloodiest Persons, and Offices; those that kill, and those that are killed, bear the Figure of *Jesus Christ*, like the Beasts for Sacrifice, or the Sacrificing Priests in their linnen Garments stained with Blood.   R.R.R. p. 285.

29. *The Temple of the Holy Ghost*

All the parts of your Bodies themselves, the lowest, and least,
even to a hair of your Heads, every thing that befals you in every
part of your Body in the meanest, and slightest circumstance, is
5 formed exactly by the Divine Wisdom, and Power, according to
the Divine Will, to answer the Pattern in the Mount, to be the
holy figure of an eternal Glory in Christ. We read *Psal.* 29. 9.
Every thing in his Temple speaks Glory. Every thing in thy Body, O
Believer, so far as thou art a Believer, speaks Glory. For this is
10 his Temple. O live alwaies in the Spirit, that thou maist alwaies
be in thy Body, as in the Temple, that there thou maist see,
understand, and enjoy the Glory in every thing!

The Temple of God is filled with the Glory of God. There is
a Prophesy in *Malachy*, concerning the times of the Gospel, that
15 he shall come into his Temple. You, O Saints are the Temple,
which is here Prophesied of Jesus Christ, as God in the Glory of
the Father, in the Third Person, the Holy Ghost, comes into you,
into your Bodies also, and fills them with his Glory. The same
word in Hebrew signifieth a Temple, and a Pallace. The name of
20 a Temple in Greek, signifieth an Habitation, or dwelling place. It
is a note of a learned Divine, that the Temple had Tables, and a
Throne, and a State in it, which was the Golden Mercy Seat called
in the Gospel, the Throne of Grace, to signifie that the Temple of
God was his Pallace, as he is the great King. The Eternal Spirit is
25 present in the Body of a Believer, as in his Pallace. He keeps his
Court there. There is his Throne, with all the blessed Angels, and
all the Heavenly Company, waiting round about it.

R. R. R. p. 461.

30. *The Earthly Paradise*

30 Q. *What was the Image of God in Man?*

A. The Image of God in Man consisted of Righteousness and
Blessedness.

Q. *What was Righteousness in Man?*

A. Righteousness in Man was a conformity to the Divine
35 Nature. All the Creatures stood together in Man, as in the Head,
in a Divine Harmony of their Essences and Operations, of each
with itself, of each with other, of all with God. From Man as the
Head, this Harmony was propagated and maintain'd thro' the

Creatures, subsisting apart by themselves. One Divine Life, mov'd, shin'd, sounded in and thro' all, as an unexpressible Love, Beauty, Musick, made up out of all, compleat in all, beginning and terminating in Man, as the Head of all.

Q. *What was the Blessedness of Man?* 5

A. The Blessedness of Man was Communion with God himself, and in all the Creatures.

The Divine Life and Love in Man, in all Divine Forms, every where met with itself, touch'd, embrac'd, enjoy'd itself, open'd its own secret Springs upon itself, awaken'd its own Powers 10 within itself; the motions of which are all Sweetnesses and Pleasures. This is the Joy, which is the result of the Harmony.

Q. *Where did God set Man so made?*

A. God plac'd Man in Paradise.

Q. *What was Paradise?* 15

A. Paradise was the Similitude and Presence of God in the whole Creation. The Creation was a Garden: All the Creatures were Divine Flowers in this Garden, animated with a Divine Life, cloth'd with a Divine Beauty, breathing a Divine Sweetness. Every one did bear the Figure of, and answer to a Glory in the 20 Face of God: The Face of God was a Sun, shining with all its Glories upon these Flowers, distilling its own Influence upon them, attracting their Sweetnesses to itself; descending into them, drawing them up into itself. Thus was the Divine Similitude, and the Divine Presence in the Creation, the Earthly Paradise; In the 25 midst of Man stood this Paradise; In the midst of this Paradise Man walk'd. *A. G. M.* pp. 463, 464.

31. *Seminal Infiniteness*

The Soul of man hath a *Seminal Infiniteness*, by which her desires grow endlessly. She therefore is delighted most with 30 those things, which least *bound* her, which still draw forth fresh desires by opening fresh delights. R. R. R. p. 157.

32. *Narcissus*

Thus is the Soule, or Spirit of every man all the World to Him. The world with all Varietie of things in it, his owne body with 35 all it's parts, & changes are himselfe, his owne Soule, or Spirit springing up from it's owne ffountaine within itselfe into all those

fformes, & Images of things, which it seeth, heareth, smelleth, tasts, feeles, imagineth, or understandeth. In the supreame, & inward part of itselfe it conteineth all fformes of things in their Originall, Eternall, Glorious Truths, & substances. In it's lower,
5 & more outward part, which is still itselfe, & within itselfe it bringeth forth itselfe sportingly into a shadowie ffigure of itselfe & in this shadowie ffigure into innumerable shadowes, & ffigures of those glorious fformes in it's superior part. This shadowie ffigure is that, which wee call this world, & the body. The Soule
10 often looking upon this, like Narcissus upon his owne fface in the ffountaine, forgets it to be itselfe, forgets that itselfe is the fface, the shadow, & the ffountaine, so it falls into a fond Love of itselfe in it's owne shadowie ffigure of itselfe. So it languisheth, & dys becoming only a Shadow of itselfe, in which itselfe with all it's
15 superior, and true Glories ly buried.
Of the Nature of a Spirit. MS. III, pp. 70, 71.

33. *Truth*

The Philosopher describes Truth to be that which *sistit intellectum, stayes* the *Understanding.*
20 If you lay your Souls to rest upon any Opinion, or Principle; besides the sweet Breathings of this Master: your Souls will sink thorow them. So let them sink thorow every Creature, till they fall below all, into the Spirit of Jesus Christ.

This Spirit is the *golden Girdle* of Truth, which will bind you
25 fast, and hold you in on every side.

This Spirit, is the *bed,* which God makes, on which you may safely repose your selves.

Here an eternall Certainty shall be under you, to sustain you: an Infinite Cleernesse round about you, as *Curtains* of Light,
30 shining upon you, and shewing you all things in their lustre.
T.C.S. p. 38.

34. *A Rose-tree*

Divine Truth is as a *Rose-tree,* which as it hath its beautiful and perfumed Roses, so it hath *prickels* to guard those Roses from
35 rash and rude hands.   *D.F.W.* p. 157.

35. *Semele*

The *Heathens* have a Fable of *Semele*, a Lady, who had the chief God for her Lover. She desired that she might see him in the Form, and Majesty of a God. She had her desire, and Dyed, *opprest* by the weight of Glory. In like manner, if you should 5 shew the mysteries of God, and the Gospel to low, and legal Spirits by *their own Light*, without the *Shadowings* of *Fleshly* Similitudes, and Parables; you would undo their Religion, confound their understandings, drive them to *despair, deadness*, or *profaneness*.   R. R. R. p. 71. 10

36. *The Wounds of Messias*

The *Jews* say that their *Messias* lies sick in Paradise of the wounds, which the Children of *Israel* have given him by their sins. Alas! how true is it that our *Messias*, our blessed Savior, who is our only Paradise, while he is indeed in Himself, and to 15 Himself an Eternal Paradise, yet in the midst of us and by the vertue of his Relation to us, lies bleeding, sick, and dying of the wounds, which he receives by our Contentions, and Enmity. Thus we blast our own Paradise, and turn it into a Wilderness.
                                                       T. W.U. p. 9. 20

37. *The Night of the Cross*

Philosophers ador'd the Night, accounting it to have some great Mystery and Deity in it. The Night of Christ's Cross hath very much Mysterious and Divine in it. *They that go down into the Deep, see the Wonders of the Lord*, Psal. 107. 23. 'Tis true of a deep 25 of Woes, as well as Waters. He that is content to enter into the Cloud, and the saddest Retreat of it, meets with Wonders and Secrets of Glory.

They that Travel to the Southern Parts of the World, see Stars, and a Face of Heaven, with which we are unacqu⟨a⟩inted. When 30 God leads us into the sadder Parts of Things, he discovers to us Beauties, Constellations of Excellencies unknown in a State of Pleasure.   *A. G. M.* p. 279.

38. *The Fall*

While we were Innocent, our Nakedness was our Purity, as a
beautiful Face unveil'd, as a Jewel drawn forth from the Case. By
the Fall we are naked, as a Sheep, when his white Fleece is torn
5 from him by the Briars; we are shamefully naked.

A.G.M. p. 233.

39. *God's Strange Work*

God bringeth forth his works in *Subordinations. Heaven* is a work,
on which he layes out much cost and *skill*, to make a *Throne* for
10 Himself. The *Earth* is a *cheaper* and *courser* peece of *Work* for a
foot-stool. Hell is his *strange Work*: A *work* in which he *estrangeth*
himself from himself; in which he goeth to the vastest Distance,
to bring forth a *Work* most unlike himself, in which he hides the
Workman in the Horror of the Work, and *shews* him, by *hiding* him
15 so deep.   *C.F.C.* Sig. a 3 v.

40. *God's Poem*

A Poetical History, or work framed by an excellent Spirit, for
a pattern of Wisdom, and Worth, and Happiness, hath this, as a
chief rule, for the contrivance of it, upon which all its Graces and
20 Beauties depend. That persons and things be carried to the
utmost extremity, into a state where they seem altogether uncapable
of any return to Beauty or Bliss: That then by just degrees and
harmonious proportions, they be raised again to a state of highest
Joy and Glory. You have examples of this in the Divine pieces of
25 those Divine Spirits, (as they are esteemed and stiled) *Homer,
Virgil, Tasso,* our English *Spencer,* with some few others like to
these; The *Works* of these persons are called *Poems.* So is the
Work of God in Creation, and contrivance from the beginning
to the end, named ποίημα τοῦ θεοῦ, God's Poem. It is an elegant
30 and judicious Observation of a learned and holy Divine, That the
Works of Poets, in the excellencies of their imaginations and
contrivances, were imitations drawn from those Original Poems,
the Divine works and contrivances of the eternal Spirit. We may
by the fairest Lights of Reason and Religion thus judge; That
35 excellent Poets in the heighths of their fancies and spirits, were
touched and warmed with a Divine Ray, through which the

supream Wisdom formed upon them, and so upon their work, some weak impression and obscure Image of it self. Thus it seemeth to be altogether *Divine*, That that work shineth in our eyes with the greatest Beauties, infuseth into our Spirits the sweetest delights, transporteth us most out of our selves unto the 5 kindest and most ravishing touches and senses of the Divinity, which diffusing it self through the amplest Variety, and so to the remotest Distances, and most opposed Contrarieties, bindeth up all with an harmonious Order into an *exact Unity*; which conveyeth things down by a gradual descent to the lowest Depths, 10 and deepest Darknesses; then bringeth them up again to the highest point of all most flourishing Felicities, opening the *beginning in the end*, espousing the end to the beginning. This is that which *Aristotle* in his Discourse of Poetry, commendeth to us as the most artful and surprising *untying of the knot*, Διὰ ἀνάγνω- 15 σιν, or by a *discovery*. This is that which *Jesus Christ* pointeth at in himself, who is the Wisdom of God; The manifold Wisdom of God, in whom all the Treasures of Wisdom and Knowledge lie hid, in whom all the Divine contrivances are formed and per-fected. *What will you say, when you shall see the Son of Man return* 20 *there, where he was at first.*

In this God himself seemeth to place the highest Beauties, the sweetest Graces, the richest Glories of his whole contrivance and work, in bringing things down by the Ministry of the Law, to the last point, to the lowest state, to the most lost condition, to the 25 nethermost part of the Earth, to the nethermost Hell; And in ways *unexpected* by, *uncomprehensible* to Men & Angels, to raise things again by the Gospel to that first *supream Glory*, which was their *Original Patern* in eternity. The Law was brought in, *that sin might abound*; That *where sin had abounded, grace might superabound.* So the 30 Wisdom of the *Heathen*, and of the *Scripture*, both instructeth us, That God entertaineth himself universally, and divinely, with this great and pleasant Work of making *high* things *low*, *great* things *little*; of making *little* things *great*, and *low* things *high*. *He sendeth the rich empty away, and filleth the hungry with good things.* He 35 *grindeth man through pain to dust, and then he saith return again ye Sons of Men.*   *D.F.W.* pp. 179, 180.

41. *The Works of Wrath*

The Works of *Wrath* are the *Strange* Works of Christ, and God,
Es. 28. 21. This Expression, *His Strange Work*, signifies; a work
with which he is not acquainted *in His own Person*, and *Nature*; a
5 Work, which is *uncouth* to Him, in which the *Height* of his Skill,
and Power delight not to put forth themselves; a work in which
he is *descended* out of his own Form into some inferiour Form of the
Creature, and so become a *Stranger* to Himself.   R.R.R. p. 153.

42. *Divine Love-play*

10   O sweet and Divine Mystery! O musical Discord, and harmonious Contrariety! *O peaceful and pleasant War*! where the
supream Love stands on both sides, where, as in a mysterious
Love-sport, or a Divine *Love-play*, *it fights with it self*, suffering for
it self, dying by it self, and to it self, linking by death into its own
15 sweetest bosom and dearest embraces, the fountain of Life, the
center and circle of all Delights: *O bitter Peace!* disordering Melody!
broken and unpleasant Harmony! where *Love suffers* all evil, and
is slain on both sides, to make perfect the Harmony. But oh full
Compensation! O full and sweet Harmony, arising out of the
20 Discords, swallowing up the Discords themselves into the most
pure, the most perfect, most pleasant melody; whereas Love first
suffered, and was slain by the disorder and enmity of Sin; so now
Love again suffereth, and is slain for the enmity, for sin, by the
wrath of God against sin, that is, by the Love in its contrary to
25 the enmity. Thus Love it self, in the place of us all, most lovingly,
and beauty it self, most beautifully is become a Sacrifice for it self
to it self.   D.F.W. p. 163.

43. *The Ordeal of the Souls*

Souls, as they are the *Birth*, so do they bear the Image of this
30 *Trinity* and Marriage. The Soul bringeth forth within her self
this sensitive Image, which is her Daughter and her Bride. The
love which unites these two in a *Conjugal state*, which springs
mutually from both, as they are living Images each of other, as
they are one self or substance in two distinct forms, which is the
35 same in both, is the Spirit of life and motion. This makes the
sweetness of life, and of all vital motions, That *Love is* their

Spring and their *Spirit*. From this Love, as from the Marriage-
bed, doth the Soul by her own proper Bride, which is its Body,
bring forth it self into all sensitive and corporeal forms, which
furnish and fill this visible World. Thus Souls come down in a
Conjugal state, while each Soul brings down its Bride and Body 5
in its bosome, out of which it springs, as *Eve* sprung forth out
of the side of *Adam*, his fair and flourishing Image, while he
flourished in his pure and *Primitive Beauties*. I confine not that
sentence of the *Jewish Rabbies* to this sense, which yet seemeth to
me (although perhaps not the only sense) as proper in it self, as it 10
is pertinent to our Discourse. If these grounds be good and firm,
how clear will it be, That there is nothing vile or mean in the
nature of things, rightly seen, when as all things are Spirits, or
Souls in their married state; that is, *heavenly Beauties*, and heavenly
Loves in various forms and postures, where all their motions are 15
the loves of these Souls in their lovely flights. Some one may
think this to be understood and confirmed by that of the *Psalmist*,
cited in the *Epistle* to the *Hebrews*, *He hath made his Ministers
Spirits, or Winds, his Angels a flame of fire*. The Fire, the Air, all the
Elements in their various composition, the Cœlestial Bodies, *are* 20
Spirits, in their proper *Vestments*, *Vehicles*, or *Chariots*, with their
proper *Brides*.

These heavenly Beauties and Loves may be cast into a deep
sleep here, yet are they still sleeping Beauties and sleeping Loves,
beautiful and lovely in their sleep. Although, like *Abraham*, they 25
may have disorderly, deformed, distracting Dreams in their sleep.
In these Dreams an *horrible darkness* may fall upon them, strange
Visions may be presented to them. They may see dreadful fires in
the midst of this darkness, themselves, their dear Bride the sensitive Image, like Doves, lying dead, and *divided* one from another, 30
like innocent Beasts of Sacrifice slain, and cut into several pieces,
with the brands of fire, or burning Lamps passing between
them. In the horrour of these Dreams, and in this sleep, they may
lie, till they be awakened, by that joyful sound of a Trumpet from
Heaven, or of an *Arch-angel*, *Arise and Shine*, *for thy light is come*, 35
the glory of the Lord is risen upon thee; Which St. *Paul* expresseth
thus, *Awake thou that sleepest, and stand up from the dead, for Christ
shall give thee light*. Then shall these Bridegroom-Souls, with their
beloved Brides, their Bodies, appear after this dark and tempestuous night of their sleep and dreams, in the fresh and pleasant 40
morning of a *new day*, as new Heavens and a new Earth, with
their Beauties, all [new] married anew to each other.

Some have imagined, that these Souls, together with their Bodies lying yet in their bosomes above, before their *descent* and *fall*, had a *prospect* of this terrible dream in that Image of the Divine Wisdom, which did then shine clearly in their Natures and 5 Essences. It seemed to them an horrible Pit without any bottom, a vast and howling Wilderness full of deformed and dreadful Monsters, to which their sweet Beauties and Chastities, dearer than their Lives, would be exposed to be deflowred *and defiled* by them, full of Dearths and Droughts, full of fiery Serpents, which with 10 stings fixed in them, with their infused Poyson would fill them all over with pains and horrors, would subject them to that most deformed and most dreadful Monster, *the King of Terrors, Death* it self. Thus were they for their own sakes most averse to this descent and exile from their native home, from themselves, from 15 their own true, sweetest Purities, Beauties and Beings.

But in that Divine Glass, in which they saw this *Prospect*, they saw also that this terrible Dream had a Divine mystery of wisdome and love in it, that out of it was to arise from every part and circumstance in it, a far more *transcendent* Glory to the supream 20 *Love*, their Father and Bridegroom. They saw, that this *Love* it self would go along with them through all, though hidden and vailed, reserving his own Purities and Sweetnesses in the *midst* of all. They saw, that he in the midst of those hidden Purities and Sweetnesses, would preserve that Love which he had to them in 25 eternity, when he beheld them in that *first-born Image* of all loves and loveliness, and that in these loves and loveliness he would conduct them, and direct their way through this Wilderness. They understood, that he would be a *seed* of *hope* to them, by the virtue of which they should certainly in the *set time*, in their proper 30 season *ascend out* of this Pit, return home from this *Exile*: then should they be received with an universal shout of Joys and Glories, resounding from all things without them, and within them, when they should see all these sufferings break up into the most heightned Glories of the supream God, the supream eternal 35 Love, and themselves with Raptures of highest pleasures, transcending all Humane or Angel-like thoughts taken up into the fellowship of these Glories.   *D. F. W.* pp. 32–4.

44. *How art Thou Fallen*

O Man! Thy God is thy *First Principle*. Thou didst stand in him,
as in thy Root. Thou wert filled with Sap from him. Thou didst
partake of the Fatness, and Sweetness of the Divine Nature. Thou
wert a flourishing and fruitful Tree. All the Birds of Heaven; the 5
Holy Spirit, the Blessed Angels delighted to sit, and Sing in thy
Branches. All visible things rested under thy Shadow. How art
thou fallen to the ground? How dost thou lie withered, and dead
upon the face of the Earth? No good thing cometh near thee.
Sin hath done this. *Thou hast not kept thy first Principle.* 10
O Man! The Divine Image was thy *proper Habitation*. This
Image in thy Person was a *Sun* of Beauty shining in every part of it;
and a Shield of Power defending it on every side. In this Image
all Blessed things were united to make a Paradise for thee, which
thou didst carry about in thine own Person, as thy proper Form, 15
thine inseparable Habitation, like to God, who carryeth his own
Heaven into every place with him. Alas! Thou art now naked in
the Eye of God, and all the Creatures. Thou art exposed to shame,
to every storm of Rage, Malice, and Wrath from all. Sin hath done
this. By Sin thou hast forsaken thine own, thy proper Habitation. 20
Beware, O Men! Of the Evil of Sin. You cast out anew the
Divine Seed out of your Garden by every new act of Sin. You
cut off anew the Divine Form, Flower, and Fruit from every
Plant in your Garden by every new Act of Sin. As oft as you Sin;
so oft you make a fresh wound upon the Divine Unity, you make 25
it to bleed afresh, and dye in your Persons.   R. R. R. p. 359.

45. *A Little Bird*

A little Bird ty'd by the Leg with a String, often flutters and
strives to raise itself; but still it is pull'd down to the Earth again:
Thus a Soul fixt in a *Self-Principle*, may make attempts to Pray and 30
Offer at the Bosom of God; but still it is snatch'd down by that
String of *Self*, which ties it to the Ground.   *A. G. M.* p. 160.

46. *Ixion*

The Corruption of the best Thing is the Worst. All Lust is
Love degenerated, Love Corrupted. Love is the Best of all things. 35
Love in its purity, at its Height, is the Godhead in God. Lust is

the Formality, and Essence of the Devil, as he is a Devil. St. *Jude* teacheth us; that fleshly Lusts are the similitude of that First sin of the Faln Spirit, which made them of Angels Devils.

Ixion in the Poets loved a Goddess, in the place of whom he 5 embraced a Cloud formed into the Shape of a Divine Beauty. Thus he became the Father of the *Centaures,* half Men, half Beasts. Then he was cast into hell where he is fastened to a Wheel turning continually round, on which he is tormented day, and night. This Parable is meant of thee, O Lustful Spirit: Thou wert made for 10 Divine Love, for the Love of the Divine Beauty. Thus hast changed, this Love into various Lusts. Thou defilest thy self with Shadows, Clouds of Darkness formed into the Empty Shapes of Beauty. Instead of the Divine, and Humane Nature in the Blessed Harmony of an Immortal Union, all thy Births, all thy Production 15 are Horrid hateful monsters; Man, Beast, and Devil all in One Spirit, in One Person. Thy end is the Endless Circle of thy Lusts, and of the Divine wrath, as the Wheel of Eternity, a Wheel of Fire, holding thee fast tied to it, and torturing thee without any Rest, or Period.   R. R. R. p. 380.

20   47. *Gold in the Dirt*

We have the Principle of Life in us, for the most part in Sensual Pleasures; as a piece of Gold in the Dirt; as the Sun in a Cloud; as the Brain or Fancy in a Mist or Fumes. Wipe the Dirt off the Gold, scatter the Cloud from before the Sun, the Mist on 25 the Fancy; chase vain Delights out of the Soul: All these will shine in their proper Beauties.   *A. G. M.* p. 277.

48. *A Man under the Law*

A man under the *Law*, is like him, that standing on the Brink of a River, looks not up, to see the glorious *Image* it self of the 30 Skie, but looking down, sees the *Shadow* of it at the bottom of the Waters.   *C. F. C.* Sig. A4v.

49. *Catholics and Presbyterians*

Our *first enemies* pleased not *God,* but yet were agreeable to *men in* their wayes. Being false to a *divine,* and *spirituall interest,* they 35 were true to principles of *humane policy.* Being severe in the *imposall* of superstitious rites, and those *principles* which descend immediately into the *practice* of such *rites*; they take, and give a large scope to the *understanding* and *affections* in *generous contemplations*, in *mysticall divinity*. Wanting that bread of heaven, that *new wine* of the kingdom, the *beauties* and *sweetnesses* of God in the 5 *Spirit*, which should feast the *inward* man; they entertain the *fancy*, and *senses* with all objects sutable to them, with a pretence of a subservency to *devotion*, as in the *Temple* of old.

On the other side, our *last enemies* please not *God*, and are contrary to all *men*. These *contemne* the *Spirit*, and its *Impressions* 10 upon the heart when they are set up for *Pillars of fire* to go before us in this dark night of flesh, as *Enthusiasmes*. At the same they condemne *humane policy*, as *profane*. They check the delights of *sense* and *fancy*, as *vain*; rejecting also the *openings* of the glory of *Christ*, the *mutuall enterviews, walkes, embraces, kisses* betweene *God* 15 and the *Soul*, in the *Spirit*, as *Whimsicall*.

It is necessary for me here to professe, that I have no meaning to justifie the *sensualities* of the *Papacy* in its religion, while by pretending these things as *Spiritual* inlightnings, *Spirituall warmings*; they intend them for a vail upon the *Spirit*. There is no such 20 way to *draw* us up to the *glory* of *Christ*, as by his *Crosse*, to which the *pleasing*, and *heightning* of the *flesh*, for the most part, carries a very great *enmity*. Therefore do I not desire to cast any disesteem upon the *severity* towards the *outward* man. Even to the *enslaving* of it, to the *beating* of it *black* and *blue*, as *Saint Paul* used it, so this 25 bee not to *the puffing* up of the *fleshly mind*. But my *Justification*, or *condemnation* of these things, as they stand in the *comparison* between these *two parties*, and as they may stand upon the *root* of the same *Principle* or *Spirit* in each party. Upon this account, as *Samuel* was by *Witchcraft* raised up out of his grave, to appear 30 before Saul, with his *Mantle* upon him. So *both these*, the *Romish-Papacy*, the *Scotish-Presbytery*, as it hath been formerly stated by me, appear like that *Witch* of *Endor*, the *fleshly principle* dressed up in the forme of *Christianity*.

But there is this *difference*; the former is the Ghost of *Judaisme* 35 cloathed with the *Mantle* which it wore in its life time, appearing in the same *outward pompe*, with the same *delicious pleasures* of *Pictures, Musick, Perfumes*, &c. as of old. But the last is *Judaism undrest*, like an *apparition in chaines*, or *Lazarus* when he came forth from the grave with the *grave-cloathes* bound about him. 40

E. D. N. pp. 14–18.

50. *Remember Hierusalem*

Remember Hierusalem. Christ came in the flesh, and was cruci-
fied, yet *Hierusalem* stood. The *Spirit* of Christ came in the persons
of the Disciples, in the power of the Gospel, and was cast out;
5 then *Hierusalem* fell. Divided into three Factions within, be-
leaguered with a fourth enemy without; *Hierusalem* miserably fell.
O *England! London! Remember Hierusalem.* You have had the
first day of your Peace, and passed it. *Christ* hath been preach'd
among you: but as in the *Flesh*, clouded with carnall rites and
10 ceremonies. Christ hath been pierc'd among us, that is, not
beleeved on: yet we *live*, though we *bleed*. You have had the first
day of your Peace and pass'd it. Be carefull; Be carefull to know
the *last day* of your Peace; the comming of the *Spirit* among you.
  You have set me on your Watch-Tower, and made me your
15 Watchman for the few sands of these glasses; if you ask mee now;
Watchman, what of the Night? My humble answer is: *the Night is
almost past, the Day is at hand, if you will receive the Spirit when he
comes*: *If you shall refuse to heare, you will look for day; but I feare, I
feare, it will be Blacknesse of Darknesse, and Desolation.*
20 But I bend my Knees to the Father of our Lord Jesus, who
hath hitherto made you Tender in a very great measure; that he
would send the Spirit of his Son into your hearts; that you may
know him, that he may be in you; that all this people may honour
the *Spirit*, as they honour Jesus Christ.   *S.C.S.* p. 31.

51. *Thou killest the King*

25

  *How black doth every Sin appear in this Light of our Lords glorified
Body.* When a Soldier was about to kill *Cresus*, his dumb Son
cryed out; thou killest the King. So cry to every Lust in thine
heart: thou crucifiest my Jesus in his Spiritual Bodie, the Body of
30 all Divine Beauties shining like a Divine Sun upon thee, comprehending thee, as the highest Heaven. In every Creature in which
thou seest not the blessed Light of this Body, in which thou doest
not kiss it with the pure mouth of the Spirit in thee, thou doest
crucify it.   *R.R.R.* p. 255.

52. *The Sweetest and Delicatest Roses*

Having *such an Idea* of the Divine Goodness of *God*, that he is
the supream *Love*, the supream *Unity*, the supream *Good*, which
are all *divers words* expressing *one thing*: Where I meet with the
darkest, the dreadfulest appearance in his Births, his Works, I   5
find my Spirit excited to seek the sweetest and delicatest Roses
among these Thorns, a Face filled with the richest smiles beneath
these Vails, the Divinest Wealth, Skill, and Figures in the Vails
themselves, as in that before the Holy of Holies.

D.F.W. p. 214.   10

53. *The Violets and Roses of the Spring*

The Violets and Roses of the Spring are the sweeter, and more
beautiful for the Winter going before them. How sweet and
amiable is the light of life arising upon those who sit in darkness,
and under the shadow of death? As a foil beneath a Diamond, so   15
do the darknesses and deformities of Sin, the hateful stains and
insupportable guilt of Sin; the terrors, the horrors, the torments
of Death, and the Divine Wrath under the Law, make the freedom
and fulness of the Divine Grace, the Righteousness, the Life and
Glory of God in the Person of the Lord Jesus appearing to a lost   20
forelorn Soul in the midst of these black shades, unvaluably
precious, infinitely amiable, pleasant, far surpassing all the sweetness and beauties of the loveliest Morning, all the Lights and
Glories of the purest Sun arising out of the darknesses of the most
melancholy and tempestuous night.   *D.F.W.* p. 183.   25

54. *The Rose of Christ*

As all the thornes in a Rose-bush are sent forth from ye Seede
of ye Rose, & are ordained to serve the Beauty, & Sweetnes of y^e
Rose: so is this worldly Image, & Life in which wee walke here,
with all its thornes of Temptations, & troubles, ye Rosebush...   30
Let ye Rose, & not ye Bush be yor Joy & Glory. So shall your
Bush to at length, being sowne in the Grave of Christ come up as
a Rose in his Resurrection from ye Dead. It is ye Spirit, which is
ye Garden of Roses. Bee continually in this Spirit, & that shall
make you grow, as the Garden makes ye flowers spring. Bee   35
continually watering your Garden with ye Blood of Christ. Set it

in yᵉ Sunshine of yᵉ Divine Presence, Beauty, Love. Pull up every
weed of Lust, Sloath, Passion, Carnallity, which would draw away
yᵉ Life, & heart of your ground from yᵉ heavenly Plants.

Letter to his Son Peter. MS. II, pp. 30, 31 (37, 38).

5   *55. The Poet and the Thieves*

   A Poet in a clear night surprized by Thieves, as he Travelled,
when they were now about to murther him, pointing to Heaven;
so many Stars, saith he, as are yonder, so many watchful Eyes are
there witnesses of this Murther: So many Forms of things, as are
10 round about thee; so many Eyes of Heavenly Beauties look upon
thee, make the darkest night to shine bright, as day round about
thee, when thou thinkest to hide in the greatest secrecy the
practice, or thought of any Lust. When thine Eyes shall be un-
sealed, how will thy Spirit within thee be amazed, and confounded,
15 how will thine heart within thee be melted to see, that thou hast
covered thy self with the loathsom, abhorred deformities of so
many pollutions, so many profannesses in the midst of the great
Congregation of all living Lovelinesses, and Loves walking round
about thee, and seeing thee, though thou lookedst not to them?
20   R. R. R. p. 224.

                    56. The Sword of Æneas

   When Æneas in Virgil was to goe down to hell; he was taught
by yᵉ brandishing onely of his bright sword to scatter all these
troups of frightfull & monstrous shades, wᶜʰ would set upon him,
25 & encompasse him in his way; & yᵗ thus he might passe on
securely, till he came to yᵉ end of those darke regions, & arrived
at yᵉ Elysian ffields, where he should find, now unknown, glorious
lights, Beauties, & pleasures, together with yᵉ Blessed Soul of his
ffather Anchises, in yᵉ midst of an Assembly of yᵉ glorified Spirits
30 of yᵉ Ancient Heroes. This is our wisdome & worke in this world,
by yᵉ Spirit of Christ, wᶜʰ is our immortall sword & by yᵗ light
of God wᶜʰ sparkles from it, as we hold it forth, & stretch it out
in yᵉ hand of our ffaith to drive away all yᵉ alluring, or affrighting
Appearances of this Life, like so many Hellish Hags, & empty
35 shades; so to pass on, till we come to yᵉ end of them all, till yᵉ new
heavens, & yᵉ new earth appeare to us in this light, & Spirit, &
Person of Christ, who is himself this light & this Spirit, who in

himself comprehendeth & revealeth ye new heavens, & ye new earth, where all things shine with pure glories smile, with true pleasure; sound forth ye harmonious Musick of divine love, send forth perfumes of all heavenly sweetnesses, & in their Eternall Dances kisse & embrace each other in ye unity of ye holy spirit. 5

Letter to his Son Peter. MS. IV, p. 127.

57. *The Prince of God*

O; My Son open your eye, & see ye Mystery in these stormes, & blacke appearances. Jesus Christ comes to you under these Shapes, as he came to Jacob like an Enimy-Angell to wrestle with him, y^t 10 when he hath tried your ffaith, and Patience in ye Conflict, he may give you ye blessing, & set a Crowne upon your head, & stile you Israel, the Prince of God.

Letter to his Son Peter. MS. II, pp. 68, 69 (75, 76).

58. *Behold Hee is a Prince* 15

These Disguises, & shadowy Deaths have ye Resurrection, as a clouded Sun, beneath them, as an encompassing heaven round about them. Wee have our sorrowes, as well, as our Sins. But these Sorrowes are ye Reflections onely of those, which Jesus in his owne Person hath already turned into Joyes; like ye figure of the 20 Sun trembling at ye Bottom of a River tost with stormy Windes. Such are ye Dreames, wch a Prince hath of a Prison, while he sleepes in his Pallace within Curtaines of Gold, and Silke. Hee awakes, & dispiseth his Dreame, ffor behold Hee is a Prince surrounded with Power, pleasures, & Glory in ye midst of his 25 Kingdome. *Letter to his Son Peter.* MS. II, pp. 19, 20.

59. *Sub Specie Aeternitatis*

I have also attempted to open that mystery, how this Work of God, in every part of it, with its Beauty, is *for eternity*, the light of eternity, being the only light of Truth, with a golden Calm, an 30 unstained Sun-shine, of purest Perpetual Peace, Pleasantness and Glory. In this light of eternity alone is the Work of God seen aright, in the entire piece, in the whole design, from the beginning to the end. As all times appear in this light, less than a moment, a *point*, nothing, being as eternity in the undivided Unity of 35

eternity; so are all the disorders of time, no more, not so much as
a shadow in a dream that is past, but as the highest and sweetest
Harmony in the undivided Unity of the eternal Harmony.

D.F.W. p. 166.

5   ## 60. *Peace in this Heart*

Have Content in yourselves. Murthers come forth from the Heart,
saith Christ. A calm Spirit cannot put forth itself in unquiet and
disorderly Motions: Its Motions without will have the Image of
its inward Rest stampt upon 'em. Do Men gather Grapes of
10 Thistles? Fire first burns upon the Subject, in which it is seated;
before it lays hold on any other. So doth a Principle of Enmity
make the War first at home, in that Spirit, in which it is bred and
cherish'd.

Poets fable, that a vast Giant lies Buried alive under *Ætna*;
15 and that, when he moves himself, he shakes the Hill, with those
horrid Confusions, which send forth Smoke, Flames, Stones,
mingled into all the Countries about. If any Soul hurl forth the
Flames and Thunder-Bolts of War into a Kingdom, we may
assure ourselves, that this Soul is first shaken, and enflam'd herself
20 by some mighty and monstrous Evil-Spirit below, which lies hid
at the Root of Life in her.

The *Pythagoreans* were wont to rise each Morning, to go to bed
every Night, with Musick. Thus they compos'd and calm'd their
Spirits at their first entrance into Business, and their Retreat from
25 them. This is the happy way of being Peaceful abroad, to preserve
Peace at home. For this End ever have some sweet and satisfying
Delight; By this as Musick arm your Souls with a peaceful
Complacency, when you are to go into the Tumults of Actions:
By this as Musick, charm your Souls to a Peacefull Repose, when
30 they withdraw from Noise and Action.

But what Delight, what Musick can do this? Only the Knowledge of Jesus Christ made manifest in your Spirits, will be as a
Jacob's Ladder discover'd within you, which joyns Heaven and
Earth; in which every Degree and State of Things is a Step; on
35 every Step an Angel Singing; Peace on Earth; Peace in this Heart.

A.G.M. pp. 293, 294.

61. *Live Unconcerned*

Live unconcerned in this World. This Divine Lesson is taught us from Heaven by the Holy Ghost upon this Ground; 1. *Cor.* 7. 29, 30, 31. *But this I say Brethren, the time is short. It remaineth, that both they that have wives, be, as though they had none; And they, that* 5 *wept as though they wept not; and they, that rejoyce, as though they rejoyced not; and they, that buy, as though they bought not; & they that use this world, as not abusing it: For the fashion of this world passeth away.* The *Apostle* here divideth all this World into 4. *Heads*; 1. Relations; 2. Passions; 3. Possessions; 4 Employments, and 10 Entertainments. *Solomon* saith in one place; *Why shouldst thou set thine heart upon that, which is not.* There is no real Difference between having a Husband, Wife, or Children, and having none; between being in Grief, or Joy, and being without Grief, or Joy; between having an Estate, and having none; between being in the height 15 of all Employments, or Entertainments, and being out of all. This world hath nothing real. It is all a Shadow. Seeing then the various States of things on Earth have no real Difference, pass thou thorow all estates with a perfect indifference of Spirit, in a constant calm. *R. R. R.* p. 279. 20

62. *Living Beautifully*

Walk honestly, saith St. *Paul,* Rom. 13. 13. The Word is καλῶς, Beautifully. Write after the Copy of Divine Beauty, which dwells in the midst of thee, and shines forth from the Face of the Lord Jesus in thine Heart: Imitate, discover this in all thy Conversation. 25

The chief Things of Beauty, are Light and Proportion. Thy Christ in thee is both these; the Light, and the Wisdom of God. Then thou livest Beautifully, when this Light runs along thro' thy Thoughts, Affections, Actions, shining in all, and making every thing proportionable to itself. *A.G.M.* p. 49. 30

63. *Ye are the Temple*

Walk worthy of that Jesus, who is as a God in thee, 1. Cor. 3. 16. *Ye are the Temple of God*: Beware then, of Defiling, or Idolizing this Temple; for both these will God destroy it, as he did his Temple in *Jerusalem.* Holy Things only are to be brought into a Temple. 35 The Temple is to be lov'd and honour'd, for the God only that dwells in it. Pollute not then thy Soul or Body, with any thing that is unclean. Love not, value not thy Being any further, than as the Divine Being is manifested in it, and fills it.

A.G.M. p. 50.

64. *Princely Brothers and Fellow Travellers*

My dearest Brother.

Let us ever remember y^t wee are here in our pilgrimage, & Disguise; Let us have our owne country, & ye way to it ever in our hearts. Both these is our Christ alone. O My Brother, w^t a Palace is hee: what a Guest? w^t a full Glory, and Entertainment? How neare; & how true a Selfe? How deare, how sweete a Life? I Know nothing pleasanter, than that which David sung to God; Thy Statutes are my Songs in ye house of my Pilgrimage. Even in this earthly body, ye Manifestations of ye Love, & beauty, & fullnes of ye Godhead in ye Person of Christ, wch are ye Statutes of God in the truest Sense, are Songs, harmony, Musick made by ye heavenly Spheares of ye Divine Beings themselves in us, by ye Charmes of wch even our House, our Pilgrimage, & all things in it are turned into heavenly Dances, & Delights. Let us Keepe then this Mystery of our ffaith in a good concience; like shining pretious stones in a Case of pure Cristall, wch thorow it sends forth its rare vertues to carry us to our Kingdome with a glorious supply of all our wants in ye way. While wee are here let us see ye faces of each other in Christ, as Princely Brothers, & fellow travellers; when wee goe hence lett us meete above on Thrones;

Soe prays

yor aff: Brother.

Letter probably to Nathaniel Sterry.

MS. II, pp. 127–9 (134–6).

65. *The Staff of Brutus*

Our naturall Relation is ye Shadow of a Cloude, which encloses ye Divine, & Eternall Relation, as Brutus wooden staffe, which hee offered at Delphi hid in ye hollownes of it a stafe of pure, massy Gold. *Letter to his Son Peter.* MS. II, p. 30.

66. *Flowers in Water*

Seek, see, and enjoy all your pleasant Relations, all pleasant Unions in this Unity of Divine Love, the Heart of the Father, as in their proper Fountain. Here is the Truth, here is the Life of them all, in their Original. Here they are unchangeable. Here they are, as Sun-beams, before they come forth, descend, divide, grow shadowy, and fading.

As we keep Flowers fresh by setting their stalks in Water: So say of all your Relations in their shadows on Earth, of all your sweet things with their Sweetnesses; *Who is their Father?* Answer thy self; *The Fountain of Love.* Then keep them with their stalks in this Fountain. So shall they be ever fresh, ever sweet to thee.

R. R. R. p. 369.

67. *The Crystal and the Flame*

Obj. But you will say; may we not enjoy the delights of the Creature, which is an Inferiour Image?

Ans. Yes, as a Man may have a Conversation with many Women, so that he break not the *Marriage-Union.* Thy *Fountain* must be thine own. All delights abroad must be, as *Streams* of this Fountain, not divided *Springs.* All other Images must be onely reflections of this One, & *concentred* in it.

Please thy self to the full with every Content. Only let it be no Cloud to cut off: but a *Christal* to take in the Divine Glory, that this may be thine and flame in them. R. R. R. p. 17.

68. *Living in a Divine Principle*

He that lives as a *Servant* under the Law, lives in *Fleshly* Principles, which are frail, false and fading. The impressions, which he hath of goodness are made by terrour and work unkindly. They are like Images in *water*, dark; ever vanishing, if they be not maintained by outward objects, Ordinance, Duties, Sermons, Books, Men.

He, that lives, as a *Son* under the Gospel, lives in a *Divine Principle,* is naturally good. If you ask, why this man is good against the stream of all earthly things, which are evil. It is his Nature to be so. For he is *made partaker of the Divine Nature,* 2 Pet. 1. 4. If you ask, how he comes to love, imitate, grow up

into an unseen Glory, the Eternal Spirit. It is his *Life* to do so.
As every Plant hath its proper Life, by which it is formed, and
grows. So to this man his God, his Jesus is his *Life*. You may
wonder, that a Son of God should continually flow forth into
5 Spiritual Discourses; continually bath himself in high hidden
heavenly Joys; continually be mastering Lusts and Passions, in
despight of temptations without, and within him; continually
maintain a Lowly, and Lovely temper in this forward world. But
all this is no wonder for he is carried on by *the Power of an Endless*
10 (indissoluble, invincible) *Life*.   R. R. R. p. 70.

69. *Through the Darkness*

Care not to cloathe your selves with the Contents of this World, all
which you must put off, so soon as you touch the Brim of this
Darkness, into which you must return. Care not for the Cares or
15 Sorrows of this Life. Those waters of Forgetfulness, into which
we must all descend, will wash them all away. Imagine this Life,
as an *Island*, surrounded with a *Sea* of Darkness; beyond which
lies the *main Land* of Eternity. Blessed is he, that can raise himself to such a Pitch, as to look off this Island, beyond that Dark-
20 ness, to the utmost bound of things. He sees his *way before*, and
behind him. What shall trouble him, on this *Twig* of life, on which
he is like a Bird but now *alighted* from a far Region, from whence
again he shall immediately take his *Flight*?
Thou cam'st through a darkness hither, but *Yesterday* when
25 thou wer't born. Why then shouldst thou not more readily, and
cheerfully return thorough the same darkness back again to those
everlasting Hills?
Let us then ever be in Tune to sing that sadly sweet Song of
Far-seeing, and so much-suffering. *Job* 1. 21. *Naked came I out*
30 *of my Mother's womb; naked shall I return hither again. The Lord*
giveth, and the Lord taketh. Blessed be the name of the Lord. Naked
comest thou, my Soul, thorough a Darkness into this World,
strip't of all the Glories; and Griefs here. The Lord gives thee
forth thorough this Darkness into this *Life*: The Lord takes thee
35 in thorough the Darkness out of this Life to Himself. Blessed is
the Name of the Lord. Rest thou in the Blessed and Glorious
Workings of the High God, while thou art in that Darkness.
Thou shalt suddenly be pass'd beyond it; where thou shalt in an
open Light enjoy the Hidden workings there; where thou shalt

see the Highest Beatitudes and Glories, *Eye to eye Heart in Heart*;
They and Thou, being made One Life, One Spirit, and without
Partition or *Veil*.   R. R. R. pp. 7, 8.

70. *The Bread of Angels*

The Scripture saith in one place to good men: *The Joy of the*   5
Lord shall be your Strength. Such as the *Nourishment* of our Spirit is,
such will its *Constitution*, and our Conversation be. If our Food,
our Joy be Divine, and we eat the Bread of Angels, our Lives will
be Divine, and our Faces shine with Angelical Beams.
                                        R. R. R. p. 32.   10

71. *Orpheus and Christ*

Long before Christ, Writers mention'd *Orpheus*, known for the
Divine Poet: Of him they reported, that by the Power of his
Musick, he could draw the Wild Beasts, Senseless Plants, massy
Stones into Dances, round about him. Sure, as they had their 15
Mysteries wrapt up in all their Fables; so in this they darkly
pointed at Jesus Christ. The Universal and Profound Peace or
Harmony of Things in the Godhead, opening itself in the Person
of our Lord Jesus: This is the Musick by which Jesus Christ
draws all Creatures in Heaven and on Earth into one, into one 20
Figure of Harmony and Love, in himself.
                                    A. G. M. pp. 282, 283.

72. *Confus'd Dreams of Christ*

Poets fable, That their Goddess of Wisdom was Born in the
Brain of her Father, without a Mother: That, their God of War 25
and Power, was Born of a Mother by the Smell of a Flower,
without a Father. Thus they had their confus'd Dreams of Christ.
He is the Divine Wisdom, Born Eternally of his Father, according
to his Divine Nature. He is the Power of God, Born of a Woman
by the Breathings of the Spirit, without a Man, according to his 30
Human Nature.   *A. G. M.* p. 316.

73. *A Lesson from the Heathen*

The *Heathens* teach us, that the God of the Sun, is the God of
Musick; because he *tempers* with his Beams, and tunes all the
visible world. This Lord, our Lord is the God of Light, Beauty, 35

Musick, the God of all Sweetnesses, Glories, Blessednesses. For
he *tunes* both the visible, and invisible World, to a happy *Harmony*.
R. R. R. p. 49.

74. *The Wilderness Transformed*

5   While thou art a desolate Wilderness, where nothing appeareth
but Dearth, and Drouth, but Bush, and Brake, the love of Eternity
descendeth, and soweth itself, as a Heavenly Seed in thee. It
cometh down in Heavenly Showers. It breaketh forth in Heavenly
Sun-shines upon thee. The same love springeth up into all manner
10 of Spiritual loveliness in thee. Now the Grass groweth, the Roes,
and the Hinds play, where the Dragon lay. The Bramble bringeth
forth Roses. The Stony Heart is now made the Garden of God.
The Soul which wallowed in the filth of the Devil is washed by
Eternal love in its own Blood, redeemed by its own life, made to
15 bear the Fruit of its own loveliness, and ready trimmed for a
Bride to itself.   R. R. R. p. 318.

75. *The Spark and the Flame*

He will bring forth y^t divine Birth in your Soule, which is
himself in a spark of Glory, and immortality, such a spark as
20 sends forth living ravishing Beams a thousand times purer,
brighter and sweeter than those of Diamonds or of ye morning
starr; such a spark as will never die, but spread it self into a
spirituall flame, as large as heaven and Earth, comprehending y^e
lives, Beauties, Loves, and joyes of all Eternall Spirits in it self.
25   *Letter to his Son Peter.* MS. IV, pp. 54, 55.

76. *Purer than the Heavens*

The Heavens over our Heads are pure. They are free from that
gross, and dark Matter, with which all Forms of things are mixt
here on Earth. This Purity of theirs, is their Transparency, Light,
30 Lustre, Harmony, Vertue, Incorruptibility. Yet they are Corporeal,
and Bodily; their bright Beauties shall be turned into Darkness, and
Blood. The Angels are purer far, than this Heaven. They have no
Cloud, Clog, or Dross of Bodies. Yet are they mixtures of Light
and Shade. Their Glories are vails upon the true Glory. They wax
35 old, as a Garment, and are changed. Their Nature is subject to

stains, and falls. But this Principle, which is the Seed, and Heart of a Believer is Purer than the Heavens, or the Angels. It is the Spirit of God, the true Light, in which there is no Darkness; Simple, incorruptible, Unchangeable.   R. R. R. p. 198.

77. *This is to be Holy*

Let not the Name of God be as a Cloud over your Heads, shadowing all about you; or as a dark Corner to Children, in which they fear Bug-bears. This is that which we call God; *Pulcherrima rerum*, the best and greatest. The best of Beauties and Joys. The greatest in Sweetness and Love, as well as in Wisdom and Power. Such Thoughts of God will make you run often into his Arms, love to be familiar with him, and long to be like him. This is to be Holy.   *A. G. M.* pp. 277, 278.

78. *A Child of God*

There is nothing so natural, as for a Child to run to the lap of its Parents in extremities, and to have a Confidence in them. It is as natural for a Child of God in pains, or griefs to cast itself into the arms of God, and there to breath forth its sorrows after such a manner as this: *My God, thou art my Father; thou hast a greater share in me, than I have in myself. I was thine, before I was mine own. Thou gavest my Being to me, and me to myself. O how great is thy Dearness towards me thine own! How great is thy Delight in me! Thou art far nearer to me, than my Self to my Self. I have my Being not in my Self, but in Thee. I am the Branch, thou art the Sap, the Spirit that runs thorow this Branch, and quickens it. How much more quick, more deep, more full a Sense hast thou, my God, of all my Sufferings, than I can have? Thou canst do all things. Thou hast Strength, I have none. Thou knowest all things. Thou hast Wisdom, I have none. I then give over my whole Being unto thee. Bear me, as thou dost always, in thine Arms, and carry me, whither thou wilt. Comprehend me, as One with Thee. Let me be Thine; be Thou mine; and do, what thou wilt with me. I can fall no lower than thou fallest with me. When I am at lowest, I shall have thy Power, and Wisdom beneath me. As thou risest, thou shalt raise me together with thyself by These.*   R. R. R. p. 73.

79. *A Royal Beauty of Holiness*

St. *Paul* teacheth us, that if one member be honoured, all the
members rejoyce together with it. When a Crown is set upon the
head of a King, it puts a Royalty, and Majesty upon his whole
5 Person. The Head of *Man* is *Christ*, the Head of *Christ* is *God*. The
Glory of the God-Head in Christ is the *Crown* upon the Head of
the Heavenly man; this puts a Royal Beauty of Holiness, the
Majesty of that Divine Righteousness upon every mystical mem-
ber⟨,⟩ upon each Soul, how mean soever, that is united to Jesus
10 Christ in one Spirit thorow believing.   R. R. R. p. 78.

80. *As Musick*

As musick is conveyed sweetest, and furthest upon a river in
ye Night: so is ye Musick of ye heavenly voice carried most
clearly, pleasantly to ye understanding, when all ye outward
15 senses ly wrapt up in darkness, and ye depth of night.
            Letter to his Son Peter. MS. IV, p. 48.

81. *A Deep Silence*

Put out then every Spark of Creature Light or Life in your
Spirits, and you shall find yourselves immediately in the Light of
20 God. *A deep Silence of all created Objects ushers in the Appearances
of God in the Soul.*   A. G. M. p. 197.

82. *The Candle of the Lord*

Tell me, O Man! what hath kept thee thy Peace, and Plenty all thy
Dayes, and Months, and Years? *Thy God hath preserved thee.* When
25 thou hast been in a doubtful, difficult, dangerous State of things;
what then hath pointed out a clear and shining path to thee in that
darkness? When thou hast had trouble in thine Affairs, calamities
in thy Person, confusion in thy Soul; what then hath sent forth
a Beam of Comfort, and Council through thy Spirit, to light thee
30 out of all these; *The Candle of God hath been upon thy head*: God hath
look'd sweetly forth from the top of thy Spirit, through the
Principles of Nature, and this hath been thy Light. When thou
hast wash'd thy Feet as thou hast walk'd, in smooth, soft, flowing

streams of Peace, and Plenty: when thou hast seen thy Children
playing about thee, like lively Lambs in pleasant Pastures, while
thou hast been as their Sheepherd, feeding thy Spirit from invisible Spirits, and then feeding their Spirit from thine; who gave
thee all these? *The secret of the Almighty was with thee.*   5

R. R. R. p. 48.

83. *Glad Tidings*

When the Lord Jesus came a Messenger of glad Tidings from
Heaven, to fill the Air of the World with the new Song of the
Gospel, He was attended by a Choir of Angels, and with a Song,   10
to shew that the Business was now Love and Delight. The Words
of the Song declare it openly; Luke 2. 14. *Glory to God in the highest:
Peace on Earth: Good-Will towards Men. Peace on Earth* is the
Harmony of the Creatures dancing to the Measure and Musick of
Divine Love. *Glory to God in the highest*; that is, the highest Glory   15
reflects itself from Men below, on the Face of God above, *Good-
will towards Men*: The sweetest Affections flow down from the
Bosom of God above, into the Breasts of Men; or, as Glory now
fills the highest Creatures, Angels, so let Love fill the lowest,
Men. Let those bright Spirits be the Palace of his Glory; so Men   20
on Earth be the Place of his Rest: Let them have his Beams, while
we have his Heart. Let his Crown reside in the midst of their
invisible Beauties, his Head lays itself in the Lap of our poor and
afflicted Flesh.

Blessed Love! This is the Appearance of our God in the Gospel.   25
His Angels and his Glory are above, nothing but Misery on Earth,
yet he leaves them, and that, his Content, his Complacency
(εὐδοκία) is here, because we are here.

The Angels shew themselves, and sing their Song to Shepherds
feeding their Flocks; as if by this they would testifie in a Figure,   30
that God, who was formerly in the World as a Priest, or a Fire,
making the Creatures Sacrifices to his Wrath: now came as a
Shepherd, to feed them on the pleasant Pastures of his plain
Appearances, by the gentle Stream of his Love and Spirit, and at
Night to gather them up into his Fold.   *A. G. M.* pp. 8, 9.   35

84. *As at the Entrance of Kings*

You poor Members of Christ; I speak now to you, who have
been sold for Bond-Slaves to Wrath and Justice, for the Debt of
Sin, who have lain long in Chains of Darkness; look up, and be
5 comforted; behold, how it dawns to the Day of Jubilee, Hear this,
and Rejoyce; the Lord calls this an acceptable Time: It is a Time,
as acceptable to him, as it is to thee. Let this approaching Day of
Jubilee raise and revive your fainting Spirits. Christ is coming,
and as he comes he proclaims the Jubilee. Hear, what the Lord
10 Jesus saith, it is he, it is he of a Truth, who crieth to thee: Go
forth, be free; return to thy Ancient Inheritance of Love, which
thou hadst in the Heart of the Father; and to thine Inheritance of
Glory, which thou hadst in the Person of the Son, even thine own
Inheritance from Eternity. Thou art the Child of the Kingdom,
15 by Choice and Election of the Father, which is, as it were, thy
first Birth, before the World was. Be no more then a Bondman,
but go forth free from all thy Task-Masters, the Law, the Flesh,
Sin and Wrath. O Beloved! What will the Blessedness of that Day
be, when, as at the entrance of Kings, Streets, Walls, and Tops of
20 Houses are hung with rich Tapestry, and Embroidery; so Christ
at his Coming shall say to our Spiritual Man, which hath been so
long imprison'd in this Flesh; Go forth: And to the Spiritual
Glory, which hath been hid under the Darkness of the Frailties,
Follies, Filth of our Natural Man, shew thyself. *A. G. M.* p. 348.

25 ## 85. *Heavenly Armies*

The Lord *Jesus*, as Captain of the Lord's Hosts, with all his
Heavenly Armies, his ten thousands of Angels, his Chariots of
fire, and Horses of fire continually encompasseth thee, marcheth,
encampeth round about thee, as his chiefest Treasure, his Love,
30 with Banners of Love spred, and displaid over thee; on every side
of thee round about. Every step thou takest in thy way to Heaven
is in the midst of these Warriours. All Divine Powers continually
circle thee in. The Invisible, and Invincible Hosts of God under
the conduct of thy Beloved *Jesus* are thy perpetual Guard, and
35 Convoy. In the midst of these thou walkest, sittest, and lyest
down; thou wakest, and sleepest, *Psal.* 91. 11. The Angels have
a charge of thee from their Prince, and thy Bridegroom, that they
keep thee in all thy ways, that they *bear thee in their hands, least at any*

time thou strike thy foot against a stone; that thou never stumble. The
Angels of God are thy Chariots of War; thy Chariots of State, thy
Chariots of Love, thy Chariots of Travel, in which thou journiest
thorow this Wilderness to thy Kingdom, the Kingdom of Love
and Glory. All this they are in one. They make thy way thy Palace   5
in the midst of thy Kingdom for Strength, for Glory, for Delights,
for Rest in thy Love. They bear thee up above in the Light of
Life, in the Life of Divine Love. This is the way high, and lifted
up above all Powers of Darkness, and Death, in which they carry
thee along, that thou mayst never strike thy foot against any   10
stone of offence, against any hard and hurtful Form of Darkness,
Enmity, or Death.   R. R. R. p. 336.

86. *Spring O Well*

We read in *Numbers* of a *Well* in the Wilderness, which the *Princes
digged with their Staves, and sung to it*; *Spring O Well*. O wandring   15
Souls, behold your Well, which is before you in every Wilderness.
The Prince of Life, your Jesus hath dig'd, and opened it for you
from the depths of the God-Head with the Staff, the Scepter of
his Spirit. Look to no other Fountain. But sing continually to
this; Spring O Well; Spring O thou heart of the Father; Spring in   20
my heart; Spring with streams of Divine Truth; Spring with
streams of Divine Strength; Spring with streams of Divine Joy;
Send forth thy streams over all my Soul, and Body; Make all my
powers and parts to sing like the Garden of *Eden*! O thou
Fountain of Gardens, My Prince hath dig'd, and opened thee in   25
my heart, O thou heart of the Father, with the Staff of his Spirit.
Open mine Eyes, O Blessed Spirit, that by thee I may see
this Fountain, which by thee is opened in me!
                                          R. R. R. pp. 367, 368.

87. *Prayer*   30

Jesus Christ saith, *No one can ascend into Heaven, but he, who came
down out of Heaven, the Son of Man, who is in Heaven.* This is true of
the *spiritual way* of ascending into Heaven by *Prayer.* Therefore in
Prayer, the *Spirit* first comes down out of Heaven, and forth from
God into the Soul: Then *it* returns in the Company of the Soul,   35
with the Desires of the Soul into Heaven, to God: Yet all this
while *it* abides in Heaven, and God; like a Pair of *Compasses*
drawing a *Circle.*   *A. G. M.* p. 99.

88. *A Fair Summers Day*

To go forth in a fair Summers day to look upon the green Fields,
and clear Skie, is a refreshing to our Natural Spirits, and begetteth
a lightsome Joy in us. come forth ye dark, and melancholy Souls!
5 see *this Jesus* in his unvailed Person, as he rideth forth upon the
Circuit of the whole Heaven and Earth in his name *Jah*, in his
Divine Form, in which he comprehendeth and filleth all; see that
New Heaven, and New Earth, which he maketh in himself. As
Snow at the shining forth of the Sun; so will the heaps of Snow,
10 the Mist and Clouds about your Heart dissolve into an unexpress-
ible Sweetness, and light of a secret Joy and hope at this *Sight*.
By the *Light* of the Beauties of this Person cometh the *Sight* of
him: by this *Sight* cometh Faith: then cometh all *Peace* and *Joy* in
Believing.   R.R.R. p. 233.

15   ## 89. *The Heavenly Aeneas*

The Prince in the Poet wrapt about with a Thick and Darke
Ayre, entred into Carthage, passed thorow the Court into the
presence of the Queene, there stood in the midst of them un-
perceived, while they speak of Him, as absent, Lament him as
20 lost; till the ⟨A⟩ire purified it selfe into a Clearnesse. So the Great
Prince of Peace and Spirits, as He comes forth, casts a Cloud
about Him; so He comes on upon us; so He encompasseth us,
is still in Motion. Yet still we speak of him, as far above and
beyond the Starry Sky, and of His Comming, as at a Great Dis-
25 tance. But, Behold! He is already in the midst of us; He breaks
forth on our Right hand, and on our Left, like a Flame, round
about us, and we perceive Him not.   C.C.C. p. 18.

90. *A Glorious Resurrection*

Jesus Christ sends forth His Angels to gather His Saints from
30 the four Winds, at the Resurrection. When the Body of a Saint
crumbles and scatters into Dust; Every Dust lies gatherd up into
the Bosome of some Holy Angel. There all the Single Dusts are
comprehended in one Form of a Glorious Body. In This Form the
Angel brings them forth at the Call of Christ: This is the Resur-
35 rection of the Body. This is as true of each Piece of Life and Death
in our Persons or Affaires while yet we are on Earth. When our

Happinesse, Hopes, and Hearts are ground into the smallest Dust; They then lie Compact and compleat in their Angelicall Chamber; on a sudden, as at the Blast of an Angels Trumpet, or Glance of an Angels Eye, can Jesus Christ give our Dead Hopes a Glorious Resurrection out of their Dust. *C.C.C.* pp. 55, 56. 5

91. *In a Clear Evening*

He, that in a clear Evening fixeth his eye on the Firmament above him, beholdeth by degrees innumerable Stars, with springing lights sparkling forth upon him. If God lift up a little of his Vail, and by the least glimpses of his naked Face enlighten and 10 attract the eye of our Soul to a fixed view of Himself, with what Divine Raptures do we see the eternal Truths of things, in their sweetest Lights, springing and sparkling upon us, besetting us round in that Firmament of the Divine Essence, as a Crown of incorruptible Glory? *D.F.W.* p. 44. 15

92. *One Hour's Prayer*

While the Soul is wholly intent upon the Glory of God in Prayer, many sweet Appearances, high Truths shew themselves clearly to the Soul, which were before utterly unthought of, or very difficult. They now appear, as in their Element, like Stars to 20 him that looks stedfastly on a clear Skie in an Evening. They come forth as out of their Bride-Chamber, ready Trim'd, prepar'd for the Soul, in sweet and clear Notions. Often they come thick and swarming about the Soul, from the midst of this Glory; like Bees out of a Hive. A Man frequently learns *more* and *better*, at 25 *one Hour's Prayer*; *than in the Study of many days.*

A.G.M. pp. 161, 162.

93. *As the Evening-Star*

The Knowledge of God brings all the Fulness of God into our Spirits. As the Evening-Star leads forth all the rest of the Stars 30 into the open Sky; so the Knowledge of God, as it proceeds itself, leads on every Kind, every Degree of Divine Grace and Glory.

A.G.M. p. 187.

94. *The Gentle Rain from Heaven*

Eternal Life is the whole Work of God upon the Souls of the Elect from the Beginning to the End; the Divine Life begun in Grace on Earth, compleated in Glory in Heaven. I have formerly
5 said, that Knowledge maketh the Spirit One with that which is Known. How should this endear the Knowledge of our Blessed Lord, and quicken us to follow hard after it; The true Knowledge of our Beloved maketh us One Spirit with Him, and transformeth us into His Image, which is the whole Armour of God put on at
10 once; the compleat frame and fabrick of all Grace rising up at once in the Heart? All Graces are One in the Person of *Christ*. By taking him in, and being made One with Him, we take in All Grace, and are molded into All Grace, in One, according to the measure of the Revelation of our Lord *Jesus* in us. The want of
15 having this Pattern upon the Mount, *Jesus* in His Heavenly Form in the Eye of *our* Spirits, is the great reason why the Tabernacle of God goeth up so imperfectly, and brokenly in us. One Saint is careful of his way, but goeth sadly on; another is chearful, but careless. One is sweet and slight, another serious and soure,
20 censorious. One is zealous and ignorant; another high in his Light, and loose in his Life. Particular rules and precepts, are like a Watering-pot, which a man carrieth up and down in his hand, watering his flowers and plants singly and slightly. While one is watered the other withereth. The Discovery of our Saviour in His
25 Spiritual Person to the Eye of our Spirits is, as the gentle Rain from Heaven, which at once watereth thy whole Garden, and descendeth to the Root of every Truth, Grace, and comfort in thee. *Grow*, saith St. *Peter, in Grace, and in the Knowledge of Jesus Christ. 2. Pet. 1. 1.* Grace indifferently, universally in the whole
30 Nature, and Kind is inseparable from the Knowledge of *Jesus Christ.* These two mutually breed, and feed each other. All Grace in the entire Frame and Harmony is the similitude, the Image of *Christ's Person*, as it is in Glory, formed in us. As *Christ* riseth and shineth forth upon us, this Image springeth up, groweth clearer
35 and fairer. As this Image cometh to perfection; so *Jesus Christ* is seen more perfectly in it, as in a Glass. If you be compleat Christians, grow at once proportionably in all Grace, in Light, in Life, in Love; study the Heavenly Person of your Bridegroom, grow in the Knowledge of him. As the Eye of the Husband
40 should be the Looking-glass of the Wife, by which she adorneth herself: so let this glorious Person of thy Beloved be that Spiritual

Glass, in which thou O Queen, O Believing, and loving Soul
dressest thy self.   R. R. R. pp. 241, 242.

95. *O Believer O Heavenly Prince*

When a Prince goeth his progress, his Gests are set down before he leaveth his Court; which way, and how far he shall Travel 5
every day; where he shall lodge at night. His Servants with
Furniture, and Provisions from his Court wait upon him all
along.

A Promise is a Declaration, and Obligation of Divine Love,
which it maketh of itself, which it layeth upon itself, free, and 10
immutable.

Whoever thou art, that hearest this, believe in the Promise.
Believe freely, in a free Promise. This Faith will make thee the
Prince, of which I speak. Thou art now a Prince come forth from
Heaven to take thy Progress thorow this world, and so return 15
home to Heaven again. All thy Gests by day, and Rests by night
are set down Eternally in Heaven in the Book of Love there,
which is the Heart of God, and from thence in a Promise, which
is Eternal Love, or the Heart of God transcribed, to be read by
thee. The day of a Saint is the Light shining from the Face of 20
God. The night is the drawing in, and darkning of this Light.
All thy motions by day with every Circumstance, O Believer, O
Heavenly Prince, are described exactly in the draught of Divine
Love, the Promise. Thou goest, as it is written of thee there.

The Holy Angels, thine own Servants from thy Court in Heaven 25
attend thee in all thy way with Heavenly Provisions, and Minister
unto thee, as is appointed there. Thy resting-place every Night
is ordered in the Promise. The Blessed Angels go before thee.
They take up thy lodging for thee. They make it ready with
Heavenly Furniture. They make thy Bed for thee. They are a 30
Guard round about thee for the fear of the night. All things are
done, as was set down before in the Bosom of Eternal Love
opened in the Promise. Thus the Gospel is all a Promise. The
Promises are Love shining forth by its own Brightnesses, and
Beams. Love is that name of God, which is an Ointment poured 35
forth. Love is the Divine Nature freely flowing, and diffusing
itself, like Live-Honey. As a Bottom of Silk is unwound, and
wrought out into divers beautiful Figures in a Garment of Needle-
work: such is thy Life, thy whole Story, O Saint, Divine Love spun
forth from the glorious Heart of God, as Silk from the curious 40

Worm, is wound up into a Bottom in the Promise. This rich
Bottom worketh out itself into all thy motions, and rests, into
all thy Changes, and Chances thorow thy whole course, as into
so many exact, and shining Figures of Eternal Glories. Thus
5 Love maketh itself the entire History of thy Life; of that History,
and Life it maketh for thee a Garment to wear in Heaven, becoming the Bride of the great King.   R. R. R. pp. 352, 353.

96. *A Paradise Within*

The Lord Jesus lay in the Womb, was laid an Infant in the
10 Manger, slept as a man, had all the Light of Heaven, Visible, or
invisible withdrawn from him, being deserted by the God-head
itself in respect to any sensible presence, assistance, or enjoyment
of it, died on the Cross, was shut up a dead Corps in the Grave.
Yet in the Womb, in the Manger, in his sleep, in his Desertion,
15 on the Cross, in the Grave, had he Heaven, and Paradise with
their divinest sweetnesses, and fulnesses in himself, he himself
was after the sweetest, fullest, and Divinest manner in Paradise,
and Heaven, For he himself in his own Person is the Light, the
Life, and Truth of both. All this was unchangeably true of him
20 even in his Flesh, and in his natural man, when to him in his
Flesh, and in his natural man nothing of this appeared, or seemed
to be at all. Thus may it be with thee, O doubting, and mourning
Christian, who weepest for that life of the Spirit, which hath
Heaven, and Paradise in it by having Jesus Christ risen from the
25 dead in it. Thou refusest to be comforted, because these are not,
or rather appear not in thee. But consider this, and be comforted.
Cast thy eye upon thy Pattern the Lord Jesus, and then say;
Christ with Heaven and Paradise may be in me. I may be in
Heaven, and in Paradise by being in Christ, though this appear
30 not to me. Christ may be in me, I may be in Christ in the Womb,
or in the Manger, in a deep sleep, or a desertion upon the Cross,
or in the Grave. But in Truth by all these, Heaven and Paradise
with all their Divine store, and furniture, rise up in me so much
the more Gloriously, by how much the more Christ is formed in
35 me, and I am conformed to Christ.   R. R. R. pp. 505, 506.

97. *Silver Trumpets*

The Bridegroom chargeth the Virgins of *Jerusalem*, by the Roes, and Hinds of the Field, that they stir not up, nor awake his Love, until She please. *Cant.* 2. 7. The Angels of Heaven, which are the Invisible Ministers, by whom all things move in the whole 5 Order of Second Causes; are here understood according to the sense of some learned Divines, By the Virgins of *Jerusalem*. The Roes, and hinds of the Field are the Pleasant Loves, and Lovelinesses of the Eternal Spirit in the Heavenly Person of *Christ*. The Law of the Eternal Beauties, and Loves of the Divine Nature 10 lieth upon all things, upon all the Ministers, and Armies of God; that the Spouse of Christ be never laid to sleep, or awakened; but according to its own good pleasure, as it is One Spirit with the Lord Jesus by a knot of Everlasting Love, as a Queen at the Right hand of her King, set down in Heavenly Places with him, 15 upon the same Throne. When the Divine Principle, which is the *Bride*, and the *Spiritual Man* in a Saint retireth itself, and goeth to its rest: in this Night the Wild Beasts, Bruitish Lusts, Raging Passions come forth to prey upon the Natural Man covering it with filth, & wounds. But, when the Day spring ariseth from on 20 high when the season cometh for this Man, this Heavenly Seed, & Bride to awake, to stir up her self, and come forth again; in this New Morning the Beasts return to their Den; Lusts, and Passions sink down into their own Principle, the Bottomless Pit, out of which they arose. But the Musick, to which the Spiritual Spouse 25 moveth in these Retirements, and Returns, is the Love of the Spiritual Bridegroom, like the Silver Trumpets of the Sanctuary in the Wilderness to the Children of *Israel*, sounding a Retreat, and a Rest, or a March, and a Progress. R. R. R. pp. 407, 408.

98. *Thou hast All* 30

Thou hast all in Heaven. A Believer is ever in Heaven, and hath Heaven in himself. For that Spirit, which is his Principle is the highest Heaven. The Joys of the Gospel are compared often to a Feast, to a Wedding-Dinner at the Marriage of a Kings Son. Now there go to make up a Feast, not only costly, and curious 35 fare, but all things suitable, Stately, and rich Rooms, Musick, Perfumes, excellent company, all the Furniture, and Entertainment great, beautiful, and dilighting. Thus thy Sufferings only

change the Scene. What thou hadst before on Earth; now thou
hast in Heaven, in the glorious Fellowship of all Angels, and
Triumphant Spirits, with the Ointments of the Holy Ghost, the
Melodies, and Harmonies of Divine Love sounding thorow all
5 the Beauties of the Divine Nature, in the purest Light guilding
all; Joys, and Immortal Pleasures like Doves with Silver Wings,
and Golden Feather⟨s⟩ flying about every where, being nothing
but the Spirit of all Grace, Joy, and Glory in various Forms.

R. R. R. p. 200.

10   99. *An Immortall and Divine State*

The Druides were the Priests of the ancient Gaules, in the
Countreys of France, & Britaine. They had their name from a
Greeke word, which signifieth properly an Oake, & generally all
Trees. The Heathen consecrated Groves to their Gods, & to the
15 worship of them. These Priests led their Life in the fields, &
woods, among which they had a peculiar Veneration for the
Oake. We reade Oakes in Greeke, sacred to the chiefe God Jupiter;
famous for his Oracles, & Holy Doves which gave Oracles there.
So Abrahams Oake of Mamre was famous for his Residence,
20 Sacrifice & Converse with God in Visions, & Apparitions of
Angells, under the forme of men. Thus Jesus inviteth His Love
into the ffieldes, that there He might give her of His Loves. He
saith, He raised Her up under the Apple trees. At the ffeast of
Tabernacles the Jews dwelt in Booths made of green boughs. All
25 these Honours put upon ffieldes, Woods, & Trees seeme to be a
Commemoration of Paradise with a secret, sacred, & sweet Impression of it on the Mindes of men, arising from the Holy Story
spread obscurely, & confusedly from the beginning of the world
through the nations, or from that Sympathy, wch seemes to be in
30 nature between a Divine State of things, & the ffieldes, or groves;
ffor so wee generally find the nativenes, the Springing Life, the
ffreshnes, & flourishing Lustre⟨,⟩ the Solemnity, the Quiet, the
Purity, the Sweetnes, the Liberty, the Pleasures, the Mixtures of
Light, & Shade, the Opennes of the Light, the Depth of the Shade,
35 the Murmurings of windes, the Clearnes, & Course of Rivers, all
conspire together to awaken in the Soule a certaine sense, &
Image of an Immortall, & Divine State, & to raise the Soule to
desyring of it, & aspiring to it.

Preface to Dialogues "Of Divine Friendship". MS. VI, f. 2.

100. *Thou indeed art in Heaven*

The chief Object and Pleasure of the Natural Eye is the Glorious Body of the Sun in its Purity, at its Height. The second is the Skie, Air, the Earth, the Seas, as they are enlightned and gui⟨l⟩ded with the Sun-Beams. This is the first supream Object and Delight of the 5 Spiritual Eye, of Divine Love, Christ in Glory, the Face of God shining forth in the full strength of its most ravishing Beauties, without any Veil or Cloud upon them. The Pleasure next to this, is to see all Things every where in the Sunshine of the Godhead, as the Beams from the most high and sacred Beauties in the Face 10 of God, full upon them. How will every Bush of Thorns shine in this Light? How will every heap of Dust sparkle, as a heap of Diamonds, as a knot of Angels, yea a Constellation, a Combination, a shining and singing Harmony of Divine Attributes, Divine Excellencies? What a Heavenly Heat or Flame, rather of Divine 15 Love and Joy will each thing thus seen, raise in thee?

The great Men in *Rome* had of old Galleries, in which the Walls on each Side were cover'd under and between the Light with Polish'd Stones, Clear and Transparent as our Looking-Glasses: In these they saw, as they walk'd, the entire Images of themselves 20 and of their Company.

O what a Heaven doth he continually walk in, to whom all Things round about him are hung with these Curtains of *Solomon*, the living Brightnesses of a Divine Light; the Flower of Light springing from the Face of God? In what lovely Images doth this 25 Light, as the Looking-Glass of Eternal Truth and Love, present him to himself, his Company, all Things round about him, to him? In the 68th Psalm, v. 17. *The Chariots of the Lord* are said to be *Thousands of Thousands, and God himself in the midst of them, as on Mount* Sinai. While thou first fastnest the Eye of thy Spirit on the 30 Majesty of God, and then beholdest all Things, as they appear in the Light of the Divine Presence; thou indeed art in Heaven: All Things are as the Angels of God, as Divine Emanations, Divine Figures, and Divine Splendors circling thee in on every side, and God himself as a Fountain of Glories in the midst of them.   35

A. G. M. p. 341.

101. *A New World of Glories*

All Things, as they are Known in Christ, are a Treasure. That which is born of the Spirit, is Spirit; John 3. 6. That which is seen in this Spirit of Immortality and Glory is an Immortal, and Glorious
5 Spirit. This is the true multiplying, magnifying, and glorifying Glass. Each Dust is here known in the bright Form of a Beautiful Star; each Star is discovered here to be an Heaven of Stars, a new world of Glories. Every thing as it appeareth in *Christ*, is something of *Christ*. *Christ altogether is lovely; Can.* 5. 16. It is in the
10 Original; *Every thing of him is desirablenesses*. The least Point, that a Spiritual Eye can touch upon in the *Person of Christ*, is a fresh spring, a full Sea, a great, and bottomless deep of all Beauties, Excellencies, and Joys that may render any thing perfectly, universally desirable.

R.R.R. p. 240.

15 ## 102. *In the Holy of Holies*

In the Holy of Holies was placed a Mercy-Seat all of Beaten Gold, the Throne of Grace, the Throne of Love. Out of this Throne of one piece with it, rose up two Cherubims of Beaten Gold. They stretched forth their Wings, they set their faces one to
20 the other. They together looked down to the Mercy-Seat. This is the Heavenly Figure of your Christ, and you, O ye Children of Love, in your Love-Union, and Spiritual Communion. God in *Christ*, Christ in the Glory of the Father is the Golden Mercy-Seat, the Throne of Love. The Saints are the Cherubims, the
25 Children of Love rising up from the Throne of Love, of one piece of Gold, of one Love-Spirit with it. With their Faces, their Divine part they look one to another, and maintain a mutual society. They spread their Hearts, their Spiritual understandings, their Spiritual affections to each other, and so meet, so embrace.
30 With united Spirits they look down to the Throne of Love in the midst of them, out of which they grow up together, from which they continually draw fresh Beams, fresh Love, Life, and Joy.

O Saints, O Holy Souls be rooted in Love, grow up out of this Throne of Love, Shine forth with Faces of Love, spread forth
35 wings of Love. Be in all things one piece, one pure Gold of Divine Love with the Throne of Love, the Divine Nature. For God is Love.

R.R.R. p. 381.

103. *The Blessed Work of Death*

O Saints! why do you fear for your Bodies hidden Conspiracies, or open force, diseases, the fury of the Elements, the malice of Men, or Devils? These Bodies of yours are the Temples of the Holy Ghost. Here are the Holy Assemblies of all the Heavenly 5 Company in the unity of the Spirit, whose Temples your Bodies are. Of these it is Prophesied, to these it is promised, that God will create upon them a cloud, and a smoak by day, the shining of a flaming fire by night. Upon these the Glory is a defence, or a covering. God himself with all his holy Ones, his Angels, his 10 Watchmen, his ministring of this Divine Cloud, Flame, and Glory. From off these Temples of your Bodies this Glory never removes. From within these Temples of your Bodies the Heavenly Company never departs; for as much as the union in the Spirit of Grace under the Gospel is Eternal.   15

Thus the Bodies also of Believers in this Life are the Temples of the Holy Ghost. All things in them here are divine Figures of a divine Glory. They are filled and covered with the Glory itself. They are the seats of the freest Communion with this Glory, being the Temples of the God of Gods, and so the Pallaces of the 20 King of Kings. All this is true of them here, as they stand in a Spiritual Principle, and in union with Christ by the new birth.

But this Life is a mixt State. We stand partly in a Spiritual, partly in a Fleshly Principle. These Temples of our Bodies are covered with a corrupt Flesh, that we can hardly discern their 25 Spiritual Beauties. They are too frequently in too great a part filled with a smoak of Hell, the smoak of the Spirit of this world, that a Believer can rarely enter into this Temple of his Body to behold, and converse with the Glory there.

This is the precious, the blessed work of Death in a Believer. 30 It breaketh the union, it maketh a separation not between Christ, and a Believer, not between the Soul, and Body of a Believer, as they are joyned together in Christ by the band, and unity of the Eternal Spirit, and make one Spiritual Man, or Person in Christ; but between the precious, and the vile, between the Carnal and 35 Spiritual Principle of a Saint both in Soul and Body.

Now in the moment of Death the Soul, and Body of a Saint come forth immediately, clear, and shining Temples of the Spirit; the smoak, and clouds of the Fleshly Principles, and of this worldly Image being for ever driven away from within them, and 40 from without.   R.R.R. p. 463.

104.　*A Fair Summer-Morning*

The Sweet Colours of a fair Summer-Morning in the sky are so made, that they fade not, but go on changing to fair and fresher Colours still, until they all vanish into Pure Light. For These
5 Colours are the Light of the Approaching Sun figuring itself in divers degrees into Different Forms of Beauty; till at last it Break up into the Full Glory of unmixt Light by the immediate Presence of the Sun appearing with the unclouded Brightness of his heavenly Body.
10　　In like manner all the Excellencies, Entertainments, and Joys of a Saint, in his Immortal, and Mortal Part; The Immortal, and Mortal Parts themselves of a Saint thorowout are so framed by the Father of Lights, and Loves; that they can never fade, nor pass away; but in the moment of Death itself, are cloathed upon
15 from above with a Brighter, a Diviner Form, and are swallowed up into the Abysses, the Incomprehensiblenesses of Eternity.

　　　　　　　　　　　　　　　　　R. R. R. p. 428.

105.　*Filling Time with Eternity*

The Person of Christ hath passed thorow all Changes after an Un-
20 *changeable manner*, *St. Paul* teacheth us that the Lord *Jesus* hath descended to the *Nethermost parts of the Earth, and ascended above all Heavens to this end, that He might fill All*, Eph. *c.* 4. *v.*⟨10⟩. O that I had the tongue of the Learned, the Learned with the Learning of the Holy! that I could speak to you with Words taught by the
25 Holy Ghost! O that you had hearts to take in and understand more, than I can express! *Jesus Christ* our forerunner is gone into every Form of things from the Height of the God-Head above to the lowest Deeps of the Creature to this end, that He may fill every Form of Things with the Unchangeable Fulness of His own
30 Person, in which All Fulness dwelleth together in a Spiritual and Divine Body. He hath by this mean filled every point of time with Eternity: every spot of Earth with Heaven, every Change on Earth, in Time, with the Unchangeableness of Heaven, and Eternity. St. *Paul* said to his Friends: *This I know, that Bonds await me*
35 *in every place. But my life is not dear to me for the Testimony of Jesus.*
A Believer in a contrary sense may say, This I know, that my *Jesus* in the fulness of Unchangeable Loves, Beauties, and Joys, waiteth for me in every Change; as a Spiritual Bridegroom in a

Spiritual Bed of Loves, which is ever green, which hath a
Perpetual Calm upon it, and a Perpetual Spring. Nothing therefore is dreadful, or melancholy to me for the unchanged Pleasantness of my *Jesus.*   R. R. R. p. 278.

106. *Clear Crystal*   5

There is an Art by Fire to make Glass of Ashes. The Holy
Ghost is that Fire, which first reduceth this Creation, as into Ashes;
then out of these Ashes raiseth a new Heaven and Earth: The
same in a new Form of Gold for Glory, pouring forth Divine
Beams; of Crystal for transparency, taking in the Divine Light. 10
Then shall the glorify'd Person of him, who is the righteousness
of God; then shall the Person of the Spirit, with all his Riches and
Beauties, dwell unveil'd in this Natural Image thus Spiritualiz'd;
as the Sun-Beams dwell in every Part and Point of clear Crystal.
                                                    A. G. M. p. 406. 15

107. *Every thing Beautiful in his Time*

Every thing is beautiful in his Time. The Time of every thing is
Divinely set; by a Divine Pattern, in a Divine Proportion; by a
Divine Power. Thus each thing is cloathed with a double Beauty.
1. The Divine Harmony of the Universal Image in Nature, re- 20
sulting from, and resting upon each particular fitly set with a
sacred proportion, and contrivance in its own Time, and in his
Time, that is, by a Divine Hand in a Divine Time. 2. An exact,
and ravishing Harmony with the Eternal Image of the supream
Glories in God. As line for line, feature for feature, colour for 25
colour, motion for motion from a Face in a Glass answer to the
Beautiful Face, which beholdeth itself in the Glass; so is God, and
this world; the Face in the water, and the living Face; Beauty
itself, by looking upon the water, at once Figuring itself upon it,
and beholding itself in it; all being reflections of its own Glories. 30
Obj. But you will say, we see not now this resemblance of the
Divine Glory in the face of the Creature.
Ans. What God doth, he doth for ever. v. 14. As *Jesus* said to
Peter of washing his Feet: *What I do, thou knowest not now : but thou
shalt know hereafter;* that may be applied here. The work of God 35
in this World, and Time, is for Heaven, and Eternity, to be understood, and enjoyed there. When we shall come into the presence

of the Life, and the Original, then shall we look again with
another manner of Eye upon the Picture, and have an unexpressible pleasure to behold one in the other. As the Tabernacle, when
its season was past, was taken into the Temple. So when
5 Time, and this world are past away, Time, and this world from
the Beginning to the End shall be taken up into their first Patterns,
into Eternity. God shall call every thing to the least dust, or
moment by its name, and no one shall be wanting. There shalt
thou see the Beauty of the whole, and every part in the light,
10 and life of its Glorious Original. Then shalt thou know, what God
hath done from the Beginning of the world to the End. Thou
shalt now possess, and enjoy all with unexpressible pleasures,
when thou shalt thus meet them again in a new Light, to be for
ever with thee.   R. R. R. pp. 285, 286.

15   108. *Thy Will be done*

Thy Will be done on Earth, as in Heaven. When God shall answer
this *Petition,* the *Godhead* shall not swallow up the *Creature*; nor
Heaven, Earth. But the *Creature* and the *Earth,* shall have together
with a full *Community* in Glory; as Distinct a Property, and Unity
20 in themselves, as *God* and *Heaven.*

Heaven and *Earth* shall be in those Days, as *Husband* and *Wife,*
tho'*one Principle, Nature* and *Shape*; yet *two Sexes, one* the Image of
the *other*: And *two Persons, each* having the *entire Principle, Nature,*
and *Shape, Distinctly,* and *Compleatly* in itself.

25   But who shall live, when God doth this, when he answers this
Prayer? Thy Will be done on Earth, as it is in Heaven. Perhaps there
are those now living, and present, who shall not Die, till they see
this Petition perform'd upon this *visible Frame.*

                                         A. G. M. pp. 164, 165.

30   109. *The Work of Christ*

The Glory of God encompasseth the World, as the Sky doth
the Earth. As the Earth Eclipseth the greatest part of the Sky: So
the World, Dark, Gross and Envious, interposeth itself between
the chiefest Parts of Divine Glory, and our Spirits. Christ subdues
35 the World to himself. He takes away the dark Grossness from it,
works it to a Spirituality, a Transparency, like a Crystal Glass, that
the Beams of God may fill every Point of it, and the Person of God

be seen thro' every Part. Thus God is All in every Eye, All in
every Object.   *A.G.M.* p. 309.

110. *A Golden Bridge*

To forgive much. This is the Divine way of making our Brethren
Captives in a noble War of Love, and Binding them to us in 5
Golden Chains of Affection; *To forgive much.* It is said, that we
should make a Golden Bridg for a flying Enemy. By retaining our
Anger we force our Brethren to retain their Enmity: So we bring
upon our selves the Danger of a Desperate Enemy. But by
pardoning freely, speedily, sweetly, we make a Golden Bridg for 10
our Brethren to pass over from their Enmity to Love. When we
have an offending Brother at our Mercy, let us think we hear
Jesus Christ from Heaven pleading for him, as *Paul* did for *Onesimus*
to *Philemon*: *Receive him, that is, my Bowels; once unprofitable, but now
by mine and thy pardoning of him made profitable, and faithful to thee and* 15
to me.   *T.W.U.* p. 26.

111. *Contrary Opinions*

All our Notions and Opinions can be but broken Things; we can
have in them but Pieces, but Bits of Spiritual Truth, and but little,
very little of Spiritual Glory. It is impossible for us to have a full 20
View of the whole Face of Truth; Truth is Heavenly and Divine,
great as God is: Is it impossible to represent God fully by any one
Piece of Created Excellency? So impossible is it to represent
Spiritual Truth in our Understandings, fully by any Opinion of
ours. Our Souls are Spiritual Things, and therefore when its 25
represented by the Body, 'tis represented by several Pieces, by
several Members, because no one Bodily Thing can give you a
full Representation of the Soul. Truth is a Spiritual Thing, and
Divine; The Opinions and Notions, in which we see it, are all
Earthly Things, and Natural Things: And therefore it's impossible 30
for any one Notion or Opinion to give you the full Truth; but
we have that little Truth, which we have in a Thousand broken
Notions. Take heed then of overvaluing any Notions of thine;
or undervaluing a Notion of Truth, which another Man hath, and
thou hast not. Thou hast but one Piece of Truth in thy Notions; 35
perhaps the other Man hath the other Piece in his Notions. But
then again, the same Truth may appear under contrary Notions,

and in contrary Opinions. This is the Glory of Spiritual Things, that they can cloth themselves with all manner of Earthly Shapes. It is the Greatness and Majesty of Jesus Christ, that he passes thro' all Forms and all Conditions; and yet still is the same in the midst
5 of them all. Is there any thing more contrary than a Cross and a Throne? And yet you may see the same Jesus in both.

A.G.M. p. 410.

NOTES

1. p. 121, l. 5. *Moses: Deut.* xxxii, 4.

p. 121, l. 7. *St. Paul: 2 Cor.* xii, 2.

p. 121, l. 23. *Leo Hebraeus:* Latin form of Leone Hebreo, the *nom de plume* of Don Judah Abranavel (*c.* 1460–1530), Jewish physician and philosopher who lived in Naples at the beginning of the sixteenth century. Leone Hebreo's *Dialoghi di Amore,* first published at Rome in 1535, was a work that enjoyed considerable popularity. It passed through many editions in Italy and was translated into Latin, French and Spanish. The Dialogues are a series of discussions of the nature of love between Philo, the Lover, and Sophia or Wisdom.

p. 122, l. 1. *Campanella:* Tommaso Campanella, the famous Neapolitan friar and philosopher (1586–1639), one of Sterry's favourite authors. The allusion here is apparently to the following passage in Campanella's *De Sensu Rerum et Magia,* Frankfurt, 1620, Cap. xxv, p. 145: "Particulares causae...potius organa et modificationes primarum causarum sunt quam causae;...". Cf. also *Thomae Campanellae Universalis Philosophiae...Partes Tres,* Paris, 1638, Pars II, lib. II, pp. 94–6.

p. 122, l. 13. *the Comœdian:* cf. Plautus, *Poenulus,* 627, 628:
"Viam qui nescit, qua deveniat ad mare,
    eum oportet amnem quaerere comitem sibi."

p. 122, l. 29. *first and great Command: Matt.* xxii, 37–40.

p. 123, l. 13. *Plato:* I have been unable to find any place in which Plato says this. Sterry's references to Plato are commonly vague and inaccurate, cf. note to p. 135, l. 13. It is possible that this passage is based on memories of *Phaedrus,* 244, 245, where Socrates expounds to Phaedrus the *four* kinds of "divine madness", those of the prophet, the initiate into the mysteries, the poet and the lover.

p. 124, l. 7. *a Pope:* Probably Gregory the Great (St Gregory), Pope from A.D. 590 to 604.

p. 124, l. 30. *when his Helmet shall be taken off:* Probably a reminiscence of the passage in Spenser's *Faerie Queene* (IV, vi, 19), where the combat between Arthegall and Britomart (disguised as a knight) is described. A "wicked stroke" from Arthegall's sword cleaves her helmet so that her

"angels face unseen afore
Like to the ruddie morne, appeard in sight".

Overcome by astonishment at this radiant vision, Arthegall falls "humbly downe upon his knee"

"And of his wonder made religion,
Weening some heauenly goddesse he did see".

1. p. 125, l. 13. *An hundred Mouths:* Cf. Homer, *Iliad*, II, 489; Virgil, *Aeneid*, VI, 625–7.

p. 125, l. 24. *Anti⟨dote⟩:* The original text has "antitode", obviously a printer's error.

p. 125, l. 26. *Horace:* Horace, *Odes*, I, 3. 8.

p. 126, l. 30. *gaul:* Old spelling of "gall".

p. 126, l. 40. ⟨και⟩ροῖς: 1675 reads χαροῖς, probably the error of a transcriber or compositor.

p. 127, l. 5. *Zipporah:* Ex. iv, 25, 26.

p. 127, l. 12. *Forgiving one another:* Eph. iv, 32.

p. 128, l. 10. *St. Paul saith:* Rom. vii, 11.

p. 128, l. 14. *Cupid:* Aeneid, I, 657–722.

p. 128, l. 26. *the Athenians:* Acts xvii, 23.

p. 129, l. 4. *St. James*... πικρὸς ʒῆλος: *James* iii, 14, "εἰ δε ʒῆλον πικρὸν ἔχετε", κ.τ.λ. "bitter envying" is the translation of the Authorized Version.

p. 129, l. 12. *Scabbard⟨,⟩:* 1675 reads "scabbard:", obviously a printer's error.

p. 129, l. 30. *Corazin and Bethsaida:* Luke x, 13.

p. 130, l. 16. *If I give all my Goods:* 1 Cor. xiii, 3.

p. 130, l. 36. στέγει: Sterry is right with regard to the literal meaning of this word: "to cover closely, to protect by covering". Here, however, it seems to mean "by covering to ward off, bear up, endure". Abbott Smith, *Manual Lexicon of the New Testament*.

p. 131, l. 9. *Solomon:* Prov. xvii, 9.

p. 131, l. 11. *He putteth the highest comeliness:* 1 Cor. xii, 23.

p. 131, l. 23. *All things are yours:* Cf. 2 Cor. v, 17–20.

1. p. 132, l. 3. *The Master of the Sentences:* The name given to Peter Lombard (d. 1164), scholastic philosopher, author of four books of *Sententiae*, one of the most widely read epitomes of medieval teaching. Sterry seems to be referring to *lib.* 1, *Distinctio* xvii: "idem Spiritus Sanctus est amor sive charitas qua nos diligimus Deum et proximum".

p. 132, l. 9. *Can the same Fountain: James* iii, 11.

p. 132, l. 38. *St. Paul distinguisheth: Rom.* v. 7.

p. 133, l. 2. *He that loveth:* 1 *John* ii. 10.

p. 134, l. 37. *the Revelations: Rev.* xviii, 1. The plural, "Revelations", is common in the seventeenth century.

p. 135, l. 12. *an Angel standing in the Sun: Rev.* xix, 17. Sterry may have been thinking also of Milton's great description of Uriel (*Par. Lost*, iii, 622–8).

p. 135, l. 13. *Plato:* This passage seems to combine memories of *Republic*, 517 c and *Phaedo*, 110. In the first of these passages the Platonic Socrates compares the Idea of the Good to the Sun as the source of all brightness and beauty; in the second he describes the earth as it would appear from a distance as a coloured ball and goes on to speak of a mythical country where the colours are finer and brighter than those of this world.

p. 136, l. 5. *Æeneas:* Virgil, *Aeneid*, vi, 190–204.

p. 136, l. 21. *Thomas Aquinas:* The famous scholastic philosopher (1226–74). In his *Summa Theologica*, St Thomas defines "voluntas" as "appetitus rationalis", and "appetitus" as "inclinatio appetentis in aliquid" (*Summ. Theol.* ii, viii).

p. 136, l. 23. *St. Augustine: De Civ. Dei*, xi, xxviii: "Nam velut amores corporum momenta sunt ponderum, sive deorsum gravitate, sive sursum levitate nitantur. Ita enim corpus pondere, sicut animus amore fertur, quocunque fertur".

p. 137, l. 14. *the Soul in its essence and faculties, are really one:* If Sterry had revised the MS. of the *Discourse* for the press himself, he would probably have corrected this ungrammatical sentence. His meaning seems to be that the essence and faculties of the soul are really one.

p. 138, l. 33. *Helena⟨,⟩:* 1675 has a full stop.

p. 139, l. 1. *the Canticles: Song of Solomon* vii, 1.

p. 140, l. 27. *All Philosophy:* Cf. Aristotle, *Met.* xi, 1059 a.

1. p. 140, l. 35. *Homer:* Cf. *Iliad,* xv, 18–24.

p. 141, l. 24. *Persons engaged on both sides:* There were eminent Puritans who were probably friends of Sterry defending both the Calvinist and Arminian teachings on the subjects of Free Will and Predestination. John Goodwin and Milton may have been among the Arminians to whom he refers, while the majority of his colleagues among the Independents such as John Owen, Thomas Goodwin and many others together with all the Presbyterians were on the side of Calvin and Predestination.

p. 142, l. 9. *St. Paul saith: Rom.* xi, 12, 15.

p. 143, l. 11. *the Marquess de Rente:* More correctly Marquis de Renti, Gaston Jean-Baptiste de Renti (1611–49), a saintly French Catholic nobleman. His life was written by the Père de St Jure, and translated into English under the title of *The Holy Life of Mon^r De Renty a late Nobleman of France...faithfully translated into English, by E. S. Gent...London,* 1658. Sterry seems to be referring to an extract from one of the Marquis's letters given on p. 70 of this work, describing his reception at Dijon in 1643. It is characteristic of Sterry's tolerant attitude that he refers in this way to a French Catholic, who founded a religious order, and was moreover particularly renowned for the help which he gave to poor English Catholics exiled in France.

p. 143, l. 16. *golden sentence:* 1 *Cor.* xvi, 14.

2. p. 145, l. 17. *Socrates in Plato:* Sterry is referring to the famous passage in the *Symposium* of Plato (210, 211), where the ascent of the soul from external beauty to the beauty of the mind and thence to the Absolute Beauty (τὸ καλόν...εἰλικρινές, καθαρόν, ἄμικτον) is described. The passage is placed by Socrates in the mouth of Diotima, the prophetess, when he is relating his conversation with her to his friends. The notion of the ascent of the soul through the imperfect beauties of sense to spiritual beauty was one of Plato's most important legacies to the Renascence. It was a favourite theme with the Italian Platonists, such as Ficino, and Pico della Mirandola, etc., with whose works Sterry was well acquainted.

p. 145, l. 26. *golden wings:* In the myth related by Socrates in the *Phaedrus* of Plato the soul is represented as a charioteer in a chariot drawn by winged horses. He also speaks of the soul itself as acquiring wings when it soars towards the Divine, and as losing them when it sinks earthward. The wings of the soul are said to grow when the lover looks on beauty (*Phaedrus*, 246, 251).

3. p. 146, l. 6. Both this passage and the preceding one probably owe much to Nicholas of Cusa (1400–64), an author whose works Sterry seems to have studied carefully (see p. 89). In his principal work, *De Docta Ignorantia*, Nicholas shows that God or the Maximum is absolute Being (I, 6), and also the absolute Unity, because he is eternal: "si enim plura essent aeterna: tunc, quoniam omnem pluralitatem praecederet unitas, aliquid esset prius naturâ aeternitate, quod est impossibile". Further (I, 21, 22), he maintains that God is an infinite circle whose centre, diameter and circumference are one. Donne writes in one of his sermons that "One of the most convenient Hieroglyphicks of God is a Circle, and a Circle is endlesse" (*Eighty Sermons*, London, 1640, p. 13).

5. p. 146, l. 33. *not a solitary Unity:* Cf. Donne's description of "the *sociablenesse*, the *communicablenesse* of God" (*Fifty Sermons*, London, 1649, p. 280).

6. p. 147, l. 8. *The Divinity and Poetry of the Heathen:* In the *Symposium* of Plato, Phaedrus begins his speech in praise of Love by declaring that Love is the eldest of the gods. He quotes in support of his opinion passages from Hesiod and Parmenides. Agathon, on the other hand, contends that Love is the youngest of the gods and the possessor of eternal youth. See *Symposium*, 187b and 195c.

8. p. 148, l. 11. *contemplation of Himself:* Cf. Aristotle, *Nic. Eth.* x, viii.

p. 148, l. 11. *Beatifical Vision:* Cf. Nicholas of Cusa, *De Visione Dei*, Cap. ix: "Visus tuus, Domine, est essentia tua".

p. 148, l. 37. *the first seat of all Images of things:* Cf. Pico della Mirandola, *A Platonick Discourse upon Love*, translated by Thomas Stanley in *Poems by Thomas Stanley*, London, 1651, I, v: "Though God produced onely one creature, yet he produced all, because in it he produced the Ideas and forms of all, and that in their most perfect being, that is the Ideal, for which Reason they call this Minde, the Intelligible World".

p. 149, l. 5. *The universal Idea:* Cf. Nicholas of Cusa, *De Doct. Ign.* II, 6: "universale enim penitus absolutum deus est".

14. p. 150, l. 27. *full ripeness:* The text of 1675 has "fulness". The reading "full ripeness" is given in the list of errata at the end of the volume.

15. p. 151, l. 15. *Vandike:* Sir Anthony Van Dyck (1599–1641), the Flemish painter, who spent much of his life in England and was knighted by Charles I. As a young man Sterry may well have seen him at work in his house at Blackfriars.

p. 151, l. 15. *Titian:* Tiziano Vecelli (*c.* 1489–1576), the famous Venetian painter, whose works were greatly admired in England, and were well represented in the royal and other collections.

p. 151, l. 18. *The Plague:* Sterry is probably referring to the description of diseases among cattle and of a great plague in Italy at the end of Virgil's Third Georgic (see especially ll. 478–566).

16. p. 151, l. 35. *Nothing is mean and vile:* Cf. Campanella, *Atheismus Triumphatus,* 1631, VI, p. 32: "Res nulla vilis est, si mala non est: res omnes a deo factae valde bonae".

p. 152, l. 1. *Every thing...hath the Throne of Being:* Nicholas of Cusa in his *De Docta Ignorantia* (II, 5) quotes the saying of Anaxagoras that "all things are in all things" and comments upon it at length. Cf. also the great line of William Blake:

"There is a Throne in every Man, it is the Throne of God".

(*Jerusalem,* II, Nonesuch ed. p. 614.)

17. p. 152, l. 28. *Plotinus:* Cf. Plotinus, *Enneads,* II, 9. 2, 3, 4.

p. 152, l. 32. *upon it⟨;⟩ from his Face....* The text of the 1675 edition has a comma after it; a semicolon is obviously needed.

p. 153, l. 2. *World; as:* The text has a full stop after "world". It is corrected in the list of errata to a semicolon.

19. p. 153, l. 28. *two Lillies or Roses joyned upon one stalk:* Perhaps a reminiscence of Shakespeare's lines in *Richard III* (IV, iii, 12, 13):

"Their lips were four red roses on a stalk,
Which in their summer beauty kiss'd each other".

Sterry possessed Shakespeare's works. See p. 57 and cf. note to no. 94.

20. p. 154, l. 1. The use of the sun as a symbol of the deity was traditional among Platonists. Sterry would be well acquainted with the passage in Plato's *Republic* (508, 509), where the Sun is used as the symbol of the Idea of the Good.

p. 154, l. 4. *Plutarch:* In his *De Placitis Philosophorum,* Plutarch relates various opinions of early philosophers about the sun. Sterry seems to be referring to the account which he gives of the view of Empedocles, whom he declares to have believed that there are two suns, one the "archetype" or original of the other. According to Empedocles the sun that we see is only a reflection of the true "archetypal" sun.

21. p. 154, l. 14. The transcript of this piece is not in Peter Sterry's own hand. The sources are probably *Ezek.* i, x, and Plato, *Phaedrus,* 246. I have included it not because of its literary merit, which is slight, but because of its interest as an experiment. See p. 85.

p. 154, l. 25. *Every:* The MS. has Eevery, obviously a slip of the amanuensis.

23. p. 156, l. 17. *In a Book:* This passage may be suggested by Campanella's sonnet beginning:

"Il mondo è il libro dove il Senno eterno
Scrisse i propri concetti,...".

(Poesie, ed. Gentile, p. 16.)

Cf. also the sonnet of William Drummond of Hawthornden (1585–1649) in his *Floures of Sion* (1630) of which the following are the opening lines:

"Of this faire Volumne which wee Worlde doe name,
   If wee the sheetes and leaues could turne with care,
Of Him who it correctes, and did it frame,
   Wee cleare might read the Art and Wisedome rare".

(Works, ed. Kastner, Manchester, 1913, II, 8.)

24. p. 156, l. 32. *He breathed into his Nosthrils: Gen.* ii. 7.

p. 156, l. 36. *draws back to their Head again:* Cf. Virgil, *Georg.* IV, 221–6.

26. p. 157, l. 20. *Plato:* Cf. Plato, *Laws,* 892–7, and also *Epistle* II, 312d, e.

27. p. 159, l. 9. ⟨*both*⟩ *our Souls, and Bodies:* The text of 1683 has "our Souls, and both Bodies", obviously a misprint.

29. p. 160, l. 14. *Malachy:* Cf. *Mal.* iii, 1.

30. p. 160, l. 29. From a Catechism in two parts "writ", according to the editor of *The Appearance of God to Man in the Gospel,*

"for the Instruction of young Persons sometimes under his Tuition". This extract is from the Second Part of the Catechism, which is said by the same writer to open "the coming in of Sin, in too elevated a manner for such Readers [i.e. children]". There is a transcript of it in manuscript books no. (4) (see Bibliography), concluding with the words "Scriptum a me Matthaeo Hutton Anno: Dom: 1680".

p. 161, l. 25. *In the midst of Man stood this Paradise; in the midst of this Paradise Man walk'd:* Cf. Milton, *Paradise Lost,* xii, 585-7 (Michael's words to Adam):

"then wilt thou not be loath
To leave this Paradise, but shalt possess
A Paradise within thee, happier farr".

and also A. Marvell, *The Garden,* 63, 64:

"Two Paradises 'twere in one
To live in Paradise alone".

32. p. 161, l. 33. From the very interesting essay "Of a Spirit" which contains the pith of Sterry's idealistic philosophy. The essay is also transcribed in MS. book no. (4), where the following variants in this passage occur:

p. 161, l. 35, for "Varietie", "Varieties".

p. 162, l. 2, for "tasts", "feeles"; "tasteth", "feeleth".

p. 162, l. 5, for "itselfe": "itselfe," (this is probably the better reading).

p. 162, l. 9, for "this world": "ye World".

p. 162, l. 9, for "the body": "this body".

p. 162, l. 15, for "superior, and true Glories": "superior Glories".

p. 162, l. 10. *Narcissus:* Plotinus has a somewhat similar image in his description of the delusion and fall of the soul through its infatuation with objects of sense: 'Ανθρώπων δὲ ψυχαὶ εἴδωλα αὐτῶν ἰδοῦσαι, οἷον Διόνυσον ἐν κατόπτρῳ, ἐκεῖ ἐγένοντο ἄνωθεν ὁρμηθεῖσαι. *Enn.* IV, 3. 12. See also the fine poem by Robert Bridges, where the myth of Narcissus is used as an image of the delusion of the spirit of man (*October,* London, 1920, p. 8).

33. p. 162, l. 18. *The Philosopher:* "The Philosopher" in the seventeenth century usually means Aristotle, but I cannot find anything like this quotation in Aristotle's works, and scholars

whom I have consulted have been equally unsuccessful. Mr J. B. Leishman has drawn my attention to the following passage in the *Paradiso* (XXVIII, 106–8), where Dante is clearly referring to the same doctrine:

"E dèi saper che tutti hanno diletto,
Quanto la sua veduta si profonda
Nel vero in che si queta ogni intelletto".

36. p. 163, l. 12. *The Jews:* Mr H. Loewe has kindly given me the following note: "Targum to Micah, iv, 8. 'But thou Messiah of Israel, who art hidden on account of the sins of the congregation of Zion, to thee is the kingdom destined to come and there will return also the former sovereignty to the kingdom of the congregation of Jerusalem'. Kimhi and ibn Ezra point out that the version of the Targum is based on the possible meaning of עֹפֶל Ophel = hidden. Parallels to this use exist.

Pesiqta Rabbathi, ch. xxxv, ed. Friedmann, f. 161 a. foll. on *Isa.* lx, 1, 2. The following extract is shortened: "Arise, shine for thy light hath come...". "In thy light shall we see light (Ps. xxxvi, 10). What is the light that Israel awaits? The light of the Messiah. God saw the light that it was good. God foresaw the Messiah before the Creation and hid the Messiah till his generation should come beneath the throne of glory. Satan said to God, 'Whose is the light that is hidden beneath Thy throne?' God said 'It belongs to him who is destined to confute thee....' Satan then acknowledges the Messiah....God then makes conditions with the Messiah and says, 'Those who are hidden with thee, their sins are destined to put on thee an iron yoke and they will make thee as a calf whose eyes are dim and they will torture thy spirit in the yoke. And through the sins of these thy tongue will cleave to thy palate. Wilt thou accept this?' Messiah then asks how long this will endure. Messiah accepts on condition that Israel, past, present and future shall be redeemed with him."

37. p. 163, l. 29. *They that travel:* For this image Sterry is probably indebted to Leone Hebreo (Don Judah Abranavel), the Italian-Jewish Platonist (see note to no. 1, p. 121, l. 23). Cf. Leone's *Dialoghi Di Amore*, Venice, 1552, I, 22: "nõ e dubbio, che in quella parte meridionale circa del polo si trovano molte altro stelle in alcune figure à noi altri incognite, p esser sẽpre sotto il nostro hemisperio, del qual siamo stati migliara d'anni ignorãti, bẽche al presẽte se n' habbia qualche notitia, p la nuova navigatiõe de Portughesi, e Spagnuoli,...".

39. p. 164, l. 11. *estrangeth himself:* Cf. the words spoken by God in *Paradise Lost,* VII, 170–2:

> "I uncircumscrib'd my self retire,
> And put not forth my goodness, which is free
> To act or not,...".

See also the parallels from the *Zohar* quoted by Saurat in his *Milton, Man and Thinker,* London, 1924, p. 287.

40. p. 165, l. 14. *Aristotle in his Discourse of Poetry:* Cf. Aristotle, *Poetics,* XI, XIV, XVI.

42. p. 166, l. 9. *Love-play:* The experience of the love-play or game of love is described by many mystical writers. It usually consists of a combination of opposites (pain and pleasure, harmony and discord, etc.). To English readers it is probably known chiefly from Crashaw's lines based on the words of St Teresa:

> "O how oft shalt thou complaine
> Of a sweet and subtile paine?
> Of intollerable joyes?
> Of a death in which who dyes
> Loves his death, and dyes againe,
> And would for ever so be slaine!"

(*In memory of the Vertuous and Learned Lady Madre de Teresa, Poems,* ed. Martin, Oxford, 1927, p. 134.)

Cf. also the passages quoted in Evelyn Underhill's *Mysticism,* London, 1930, p. 228.

43. p. 167, l. 12. *how clear:* "how" is omitted in text, but inserted in the list of errata.

p. 167, l. 42. *[new] married anew:* There is no correction in the list of errata, but "new" is crossed out in the editor's copy, apparently by a seventeenth-century hand which has carefully written in all the corrections in the list at the end of the volume. The passage certainly reads better when this word is deleted.

49. p. 170, l. 32. From Sterry's sermon, *England's Deliverance from the Northern Presbytery,* preached after Cromwell's victory over the Scottish Presbyterians at Dunbar (see pp. 23–6). "our *first enemies*" are the Roman Catholics; "our *last enemies*" are the Presbyterian Scots.

51. p. 172, l. 27. *Cresus:* This story is told by Herodotus in his *History* (I, 86). Croesus, the last king of Lydia, was defeated by the Persians. A Persian soldier was about to seize him, when his son, who had hitherto been dumb, in an agony of fear and grief, cried, "Man, do not kill Croesus".

54. p. 173, l. 27. Transcript in the hand of an amanuensis. I have omitted two sentences after "Rosebush" which introduce a different image from that of the rose-bush and add nothing to the sense.

p. 173, l. 32. *sowne in the Grave:* The story of the rose-bush growing from the grave is a very ancient one that appears in many forms in European literature. Cf. the following lines in the ballad of *Earl Brand*:

> "Lord William was buried in St Mary's kirk,
>   Lady Margret in Mary's Quire;
> Out o' the lady's grave grew a bonny red rose
>   And out o' the knight's a briar".

(Child's *English and Scottish Ballads*, ed. Kittredge, p. 23.)

55. p. 174, l. 6. *A Poet in a clear night:* Sterry is probably thinking of the story of the death of the early Greek poet Ibycus told by Plutarch in his *Moralia* (De Subtili Loquacitate). Erasmus in his *Adagia* (ed. Geneva, 1606, p. 1853) tells the story and gives some other sources, including a Greek epigram by Antipater. It was used by Schiller in his ballad, *Die Kraniche von Ibykus*. Sterry treats the legend in a characteristically free and imaginative way. In the epigram of Antipater Ibycus calls on a flock of cranes that is passing overhead to be witnesses of the murder. Later the robbers betray themselves by alluding to the crime when they see a flock of cranes passing. Sterry leaves out the cranes and the "poetic justice" and makes his dying poet appeal to the starry heavens.

56. p. 174, l. 22. *Æneas in Virgil:* Virgil, *Aeneid*, VI, 260. See Mackail's note *ad loc.:* "The naked sword was part of the ritual. Ghosts were supposed to shrink from cold steel". Cf. also Andrew Marvell, *An Horatian Ode upon Cromwel's Return from Ireland*, ll. 113–18:

> "But thou the Wars and Fortunes son
> March indefatigably on;
>   And for the last effect
>   Still keep thy Sword erect:
> Besides the force it has to fright
> The Spirits of the shady Night...".

Margoliouth in his note on this passage in the Oxford edition refers to the belief that "the cross hilt of the sword would avert the spirits". Perhaps Marvell, like Sterry, was also alluding to this passage in the *Aeneid*.

57. p. 175, l. 8. From a transcript in Sterry's own hand. The page numbers given are the correct page numbers of the manuscript book. The numbers in brackets are the page numbers according to the incorrect pagination. See account of this MS. in the Bibliography, p. 223. I have followed the same system of reference in other extracts from this MS. Cf. no. 64.

p. 175, l. 10. *Jacob: Gen.* xxxii, 24–8.

58. p. 175, l. 16. From a transcript in the hand of an amanuensis.

60. p. 176, l. 22. *The Pythagoreans:* Cf. Iamblichus, *Vita Pythagorae*, I, xv, pp. 69–71 (ed. 1598); Porphyry, *Vita Pythagorae*, §§ 30, 32.

64. p. 178, l. 6. Transcript in Sterry's own hand. For a reproduction of part of the original MS. see frontispiece.

65. p. 178, l. 31. Transcript in the hand of an amanuensis.

p. 178, l. 32. *Brutus wooden staffe:* According to Livy, Lucius Junius Brutus in his youth accompanied his cousins, the two sons of King Tarquin, to Delphi to consult the oracle of Apollo. Brutus, who pretended to be half-witted in order to escape the fate of his brothers whom Tarquin had murdered, brought as a gift to the god a golden staff enclosed in one made of cornel wood "per ambages effigiem ingenii sui" (Livy, I, 56).

76. p. 182, l. 26. Cf. Whichcote *Sermons* (Glasgow, 1751), I, 300: "The sun itself, that enlightens the world, and scatters away all stench, putrefaction and corruption, is yet but darkness, and a cloud in compare with the motion of the mind and understanding...".

77. p. 183, l. 5. Cf. Traherne, *Meditations*, I, 17: "He is not an Object of Terror, but Delight, to know Him therefore as he is, is to frame the most beautiful idea in all Worlds. He delighteth in our happiness more than we: and is of all other the most lovely object".

79. p. 184, l. 2. *St. Paul:* I *Cor.* xii. 26.

80, 81. p. 184, ll. 11, 17. Cf. Whichcote, *op. cit.* III, 102: "The Mind diverted from God, wanders in darkness and confusion, but being directed to him, soon finds its way, and doth receive from him in a way that is abstracted from the noise of the world, and withdrawn from the call of the body; having shut the doors of our senses, to recommend ourselves to the divine light, which readily enters into the eye of the mind that is prepared to receive it".

86. p. 187, l. 14. *Numbers: Num.* xxi, 17, 18.

89. p. 188, l. 15. Cf. *Aeneid,* I, 410–588 and *Isaiah* liv. See p. 83.

p. 188, l. 20. ⟨*A*⟩*ire:* The reading of the text is "Fire", but the F is almost certainly a printer's error for A. In a copy of the sermon belonging to Sir Wasey Sterry it is corrected to A in an old hand. The Latin is "Scindit se nubes et in aethera purgat apertum".

90. p. 188, l. 28. See p. 84.

94. p. 190, l. 25. *the gentle Rain from Heaven:* Almost certainly a reminiscence of the second line of Portia's famous speech on mercy (*Merchant of Venice,* IV, i, 185). Cf. note to no. 19.

97. p. 193, l. 27. *Silver Trumpets: Num.* x, 1–10.

99. p. 194, l. 11. From the short prose preface to the dialogues in verse headed "Of Divine Friendship" in MS. book (6). The handwriting is probably that of Frances, Sterry's daughter, whose name appears at the beginning of the book. The contents were probably dictated by Sterry, who appears to have used his children as amanuenses.

p. 194, l. 17. *We reade Oakes in Greeke:* probably a mistake of the amanuensis for "We reade of Oakes in Greece".

100. p. 195, l. 1. This passage is, perhaps, Sterry's finest description of that state of illuminated vision which appears to have been one of his most vivid spiritual experiences. It may be compared with the third meditation of the third century in Traherne's *Centuries of Meditations.* The state of illuminated vision is not, however, connected specially by Sterry with childhood, as it is by Traherne and Vaughan (cf. Vaughan's *The Retreate*).

p. 195, l. 4. *gui*⟨*l*⟩*ded:* The reading of the text of 1683 is "guided", surely a mistake for "guilded".

101. p. 196, ll. 7, 8. *a new world of Glories:* Newman has nearly the same phrase in a noble passage in his *Parochial Sermons:* "This earth which now buds forth in leaves and blossoms, will one day burst forth into a new world of light and glory" (*Parochial Sermons,* no. xiii, "The Invisible World", London, 1839, p. 238).

106. p. 199, l. 5. Cf. Sir Thomas Browne, *Relig. Med.* 1, 50: "Philosophers that opinioned the worlds destruction by fire, did never dream of annihilation, which is beyond the power of sublunary causes; for the last action of that element is but vitrification, or a reduction of a body into glass; and therefore some of our Chymicks facetiously affirm, that at the last fire all shall be christallized and reverberated into glass, which is the utmost action of that element".

107. p. 199, l. 17. *Every thing is beautiful in his Time: Eccles.* iii, 11.

111. p. 201, l. 17. Compare with this passage the description in *Areopagitica* of the dismemberment of Truth and of the search for her limbs: "We have not yet found them all, Lords and Commons, nor ever shall doe till her Masters second comming...".

APPENDIX I

TWO POEMS BY PETER STERRY

I*

[Translation of Boethius, *De Consolatione Philosophiae*, III, ix]

O thou, who by the golden linked Chain
Of reason's Musick, with an even strain
Conductest all from thy bright Throne on high,
Father of shady Earth, and shining Skie.
By Undiscovered Tracts, Time's stream and spring,
Thou from Eternity's vast Sea doest bring.
Motion, and change ever unknown to thee,
From thee deriv'd, and by thee guided be.
This work of floating matter, which we see,
By inbred form of good, from envy free,
By sweetest force of Native Loves rich seeds,
Without external cause from thee proceeds.
In Loves eternal Garden, as its flowers,
Flourish in their first forms, and fullest powers
All Beauties. These are the life, the living Law,
From which thou dost all forms of Being draw.
As light to dazled eyes, all things below
From these pure Suns, in fading circles flow.
A World all fair, from thee supreamly fair,
Shines in thy mind, above controul or care.
In an harmonious Image thou the same,
By perfect parts dost to perfection frame.
By potent Charms of sacred numbers bound,
The waving Elements keep their set round.
Fire, Aire, Earth, Water in mysterious Dances
Move to thy Musick through all times and chances.

* This poem is the most famous of Boethius's works in verse. It is described by the latest editor of the *De Consolatione* (Mr H. F. Stewart in the Loeb edition) as "a masterly abridgement of the first part of the Timaeus". Sterry's version is very free. Dr Johnson quotes the opening lines of Boethius's poem as the motto to no. 7 of *The Rambler* and gives a verse translation of his own which may be compared with Sterry's.

Mixt into various figures with sweet grace,
In each form undivided they embrace.
Earth sinks not, nor doth fire to Heav'n fly,
Frosts, Flames, Droughts, Floods, meet in an Vnity.
The three-fold Natures golden Knot, mid-band,
The Soul thou tyest in one, by Love's Bright hand.
Then it by thee, unloosned, spread doth lie.
In Limbs well suited to a sympathy
Of motion, and distinct melody,
Diffus'd through things below, or those on high.
This is the Spring, and Circle ampler far,
And purer, than the Christal Heavens are;
The universal Beauties charming face,
Where sweetly spring and dance each lovely grace.
Within it self divided this great Soul
Into a double Globe it self doth roul.
One hidden from us by excess of Light,
One with shades sweetly temper'd to our sight.
As thorough these it moves, it still returns
Into it self, still with Love's fire it burns.
By force of this it still doth circle round
Th' eternal minds great deep⟨,⟩ Heav'n thus doth found,
And in like figure of those unseen Lights,
Doth turn about these Glories in our sights.
Brought forth from causes like Souls, and less lives,
Thy will aloft in airy Chariots drives,
And sows in Heaven, in Earth, which by Love's Law
Turn'd back to thee, thou to thy self dost draw
By the innate returning flame.
Grant Father, to our minds thy glorious Mount
To climb, to view of good the sacred Fount:
In thine own Light, which doth within us shine,
To fix the clear eyes of our Souls on thine.
Cast down the mists, and weight of earthly mold.
The joyous splendors of thy face unfold.
Thou art to holy minds the golden Calm,
The sweet repose, the grief-appeasing Balm.
To see Thee our Beginning, is our End,
Guide, Chariot, Way, our Home, to which we tend.

D.F.W. pp. 85–7.

II

Rough draft of Lyric in Manuscript Book no. VII.*
(N.B. Words enclosed in round brackets are crossed out in the
   original.)

1

Sweete Light, ye spring of things f̄r unseen height,
Thou dost thy selfe in golden laugh[t]er spread
Thorow vast spaces filld with pure delight
With various glorys crowning thy bright head
With shining days with sparkling shades of night
With crownes of starres, posies o[f] flowers dight
Thou richly varid glorys & vast space
Dost in ye christall of thy lovely face
To
(In) mortall eyes, im̄ortall soules in one unite.

2

Vitall center brides
The starres, wch with theyr twinkling beames allure
Our eyes, & hearts unto those joyes above,
The flow(e)rs, wch spring on earth so sweete, so pure;
Tending to Heav'n, sprung from an heav'nly Love
                     bright
All these in theyr (owne) spheares shine fixt, & sure;
Springs of sweete life making theyr owne bright days,
Spirits appearing in (they) rich, circling rays,
The Unitys of golden Light from death secure.

3

sparkling
set full with starres of gold
The Chrystall Heavens, (wch golden starres infold)
        at
And them (with) theyr transparent breasts doe feede,
The Earth, wch doth in her rich bosome hold
The flowers, wch she in her rich womb doth breede;
All orbes, wch theyr owne starres, & flow'rs infold;
Sweet prospects, wch Heav'ns, Earth in one compose,
Where shines at once ye Sun, & Sun-like rose,
All are fayre Unitys in fayrer orbes inrol'd.

* The first stanza is in the hand of an amanuensis; the rest is in Sterry's
own hand.

4

                                                        comprise
Soules, wch in one rich glance rich thought (containe)
All prospects within themselves, rich, & cleare:
    2   1 flaming wings ore-saile y^e
Angells (w^{ch}) whose (compasse farre transcends y) skys
Whose vast, whose unknowne treasures sweet, & deare
Are Lights, & Loves in an immortall spheare;
Angells, & Soules, your spacious, golden Rounds
Your inmost vitall center holds, & clasps, & bounds;
          glorious   sweete
Your (blisseful) Unitys by your (owne) Lights appeare.

5

Great God, Light's spacious, & all-shining field,
W^{ch} flow'rs perfum'd with sweetes divine doest bring,
W^{ch} starres with glory-beames all crown'd doest yield,
Where Soules, as thine own Sister-Brides doe spring,
Angells grow up with them, & to them sing,
All things One Beauty make in thy bright eye;
All in One Love within thy bosome ly;
Thy glorious Unity shuts up ye golden ring.

6

Thou first, & Last of things in all ye Same;
Nothing before, beyond doth thee confine;
Nothing within divides thine unmixt flame;
With endles glories ever new you shine
Yet ever One thine high, adored Name;
A boundless Deepe of softest, sweetest Light,
Where thy golden births bathe in sweete delight,
Thy pure blissfull Unity all Things proclaime.

APPENDIX II

RICHARD BAXTER AND PETER STERRY

Richard Baxter was so impressed by Peter Sterry's book, *A Discourse of the Freedom of the Will*, which he appears to have read soon after it was published, that he devotes a special section to it at the end of the Second Part of his *Catholick Theolcgie* (London, 1675). The opening words of this earliest critical account of Sterry are quoted as an epigraph to the present volume. Baxter is obviously greatly attracted by Sterry's character, and by the spirit of his writings, and sincerely regrets that at one time he thought rather hardly of him and his followers. This admission and apology do great credit to Baxter, and they also show that even grave divines were misled by malicious gossip about the "sectaries". But although Baxter admired Sterry as a man he thoroughly disliked his philosophy, and compares it not only to the teaching of "Dr Twisse, Rutherford and Hobbes" but also to the doctrine of *Benedictus Spinoza*, of whose works he must have been one of the first English readers, and whom, of course, he regards as a dangerous infidel. He admits, however, that he was so carried away by the beauty of Sterry's style that his temptation to accept the doctrine of determinism was very strong.

He summarizes Sterry's doctrine in two and a half folio pages, on the whole very fairly, though he finds it difficult to do so, because of the author's metaphorical style. He criticizes it on the ground that it seems "to reconcile Philosophy (or Gentilism) and Christianity", to identify Christ with "*An universall Intelligence* or *soul of the world*", and to make "sin, death, hell; and holiness, life, Glory...but as Winter and Summer, Night and Day" and to regard the wicked as Origen regarded them to be "but in a state of revolution" and to suppose that they "shall come about again into a state of hope".

He also attempts a long refutation of Sterry's doctrine of determinism, and considers the root of his error to be his "overlooking and undervalueing Gods Design in *Making* and *Governing* free Intellectual agents, by his Sapiential Moral Directive way". He confesses, however, that "we differ but in this, *Whether God get not all that glory that Mr. St. floridly describeth, notwithstanding sin*, *or on supposition of it as barely permitted (negatively, but with a decree or volition of all the good consequents occasioned by it,) rather than by sin it self, as a willed, designed effect of his own necessitating Negations, and in the positive part of the acts as circumstantiated, of his own determining premotion".* After reading that sentence we may perhaps be permitted to long for what Baxter calls the "florid disguise and paint" of Sterry's beautiful prose. Finally he judges Sterry's religion to be not so good as Dr Twisse's, Rutherford's, Bradwardine's or Alvarez's, "nor yet so bad as *Hobbes's* or *Spinoza's*", but on a level with that of "the old *Platonick* or *Stoick* Philosophers", though he hastens to explain that he does not refer to Sterry's life, "for I hear he was an excellent person", but to the doctrine that "his Book (though obscurely) intimateth".

BIBLIOGRAPHY

I. MANUSCRIPTS

[The Property of Mrs E. Poolman of Melbourne, Australia]

I. *Foolscap.* $11\frac{1}{2}" \times 7\frac{1}{2}"$. Binding: old sheepskin considerably worn and cracked. 170 leaves.

Pages numbered up to 181 at one end and 92 at the other.

Writing at both ends in at least three different seventeenth-century hands, one of which can be identified as Peter Sterry's own by comparison with the letter to Cromwell at the Society of Antiquaries,[1] and a note at the Public Record Office. Inscribed at one end, "R. J. Webb, Tunbridge Wells, 1869", and the other, "R. J. Webb, Tunbridge Wells, Vol. 1". Contents include transcripts of forty-nine letters, mostly from Peter Sterry to members of his family, and certain friends and disciples, among whom is a Mr Robert Liddell. One letter is from N.S. (presumably Nathaniel Sterry) addressed to "Dear Coz" (i.e. Peter Sterry junior). There are also a number of miscellaneous pieces in verse and prose, including some religious and mystical discourses, two of which, entitled "Of ye Sun" and "The Consort of Musick", are included in the list of the contents of the projected Second Part of the Volume of 1710 (see p. 65). The pieces in verse include a paraphrase of the Canticles in heroic couplets, which is also included in the list of 1710, and which we learn from the Preface to that volume was composed by Sterry as an amusement during his last illness. In view of Sterry's association with Milton, it is interesting to find a transcript of the first seven lines of "At a Solemn Musick".

II. *Stout octavo* bound in old calf. $8" \times 6\frac{1}{4}"$. 254 leaves. Inscribed "R. J. Webb, Tunbridge Wells, Vol. 1, 1869" and "Joseph Lee Sterry 15 Aug. 1678". At one end transcripts of letters in seventeenth-century hands occupy 170 pages. At the other end unimportant notes in an eighteenth-century hand on "Mrs. Kindersleys letters wrote from the East Indies in 1767". Pages are numbered up to 178 at one end and 4 at the other. There is a mistake in numbering after p. 31. The next page is numbered 38 and is followed by 39 and so forth.

[1] See p. 22.

The letters in seventeenth-century hands include forty-one from Peter Sterry to his son, Peter Sterry the younger, and one to his brother (probably Nathaniel). These transcripts are in two hands, one of which is Peter Sterry's own. See Frontispiece for reproduction of a page in Sterry's own hand from this book.

III. *Stout octavo* similar to II. $8'' \times 6\frac{1}{4}''$. 173 leaves.

Pages numbered at one end up to 257, at the other up to 33.

Writing at both ends in two seventeenth-century hands which are not Sterry's own. Inscribed at one end, "R. J. Webb, Tunbridge Wells. Vol. 2"; at the other, "Peter Sterry". Contents: a number of philosophical and mystical prose essays, including a kind of general introduction to philosophy and logic, part of which is repeated in a Latin version, "Of yᵉ Nature of A Spirit", "Certaine Propositions", "The State of Wicked Men after this Life", "An Eternity of Duration that hath a beginning and not an End", Notes on "The Dogmatick Idea of Jansenisme", "The Chariot", "Of Vertue", "Of a Plant", and a sermon on *Ecclesiastes*, vii, 16. The last-named is printed in *The Appearance of God to Man in the Gospel*, p. 406.

All the other pieces, except the notes on Jansenism and the introduction to philosophy and logic, are included in the list of 1710.

IV. *An octavo* similar to the foregoing, but slightly smaller. $7\frac{1}{2}'' \times 6''$. 276 leaves.

Pages lettered A to Z at one end as for an index, then after a blank leaf, leaves numbered up to 24. At the other end after 49 unnumbered leaves, pages numbered up to 84 in ink and from 85 to 157 in pencil.

Inscribed at one end, "R. J. Webb, Tunbridge Wells. Vol. 3" and "Frances Webbs Book 1696"; at the other, "Frances Sterrys Booke ye 2ᵈ of January Anno Dom 1669". Writing at both ends in at least three different seventeenth-century hands, none of which is probably Peter Sterry's. Contents include what appear to be a child's exercises consisting of anecdotes from classical mythology, history, etc., written in an unformed hand on ruled lines and probably dictation lessons given by Peter Sterry to his daughter. A copy of the essay called in III "Of yᵉ Nature of a Spirit", and here divided into two parts called "Of a spirit" and "Of the Nature of a Unity"; a fragment of a sort of mystical romance partly in dialogue, which seems to refer to the death of a son of Sterry's daughter Gratiana; a copy of the Catechism printed in *The Appearance of God to Man in the Gospel* followed by the words "Scriptum a me Matthaeo Hutton, Anno Dom. 1680"; transcripts of twenty-three letters, nineteen of which are from Peter Sterry to his son Peter, and were apparently transcribed by Matthew Hutton, as they are in the same hand as the Catechism; two are to "M^r L" and "Mr R. L." (perhaps Robert Liddell) from Peter Sterry, one to a "Dear honoured Madam", one to a lady called "Calianthe", one to a person called "Sylvander", and one beginning "My dearest love", probably to Mrs Sterry.

V. *A thinner octavo* bound in tooled leather. $7\frac{1}{2}''\times 5\frac{3}{4}''$. 98 leaves. Pages numbered up to 182.

Inscribed "R. J. Webb. Tunbridge Wells. Vol. 4." and "The Gift of Mr Joseph Collins to me Frances Webb 1697." Writing at one end only occupying the whole book, except the last five leaves. Contents: apparently a selection from Sterry's sermons headed "Some Discourses of P. S. Drawne into Paragraphs into two Parts", occupying pp. 1–181 in a very neat script hand. On p. 182 four short religious meditations in Frances Sterry's hand (*i.e.* the same hand as that of the inscription). The extracts from Sterry's sermons are not striking passages judged either by literary or religious standards, and the punctuation, grammar and spelling are weak. It is therefore pretty safe to conclude that this selection was not made under his own supervision, and was probably the work of Mr Collins, who may have been an uncritical admirer.

VI. *A thin octavo*. Plain leather binding. $7\frac{1}{2}''\times 5\frac{1}{2}''$. 146 leaves. Pages numbered up to 142.

Inscribed "R. J. Webb, Tunbridge Wells. Vol. 5" and "Frances Sterry the younger her booke". Writing nearly continuous throughout in a neat seventeenth-century hand, not Peter Sterry's. Contents include a series of poems in dialogue, *Of Divine Friendship*, with an introduction in prose, probably identical with *A Divine Dialoue* [sic], which appears last in the list of Contents of the Second Part of the volume of 1710; a number of prose pieces, some of which are copies of those which appear in I. The longest and most elaborate is a sort of mystical poem called *The Palace of the Sun* in five chapters. The volume concludes with a long discourse called "The State of a Saints Soule & Body in Death", which is printed in *The Rise, Race and Royalty of the Kingdom of God*, p. 434.

VII. *A thin octavo* similar to (VI). $7\frac{1}{8}'' \times 6''$. 191 leaves.
Pages numbered at one end only up to 15.
Inscribed "R. J. Webb. Tunbridge Wells. Vol. 6. 1869."
Writing at both ends in three seventeenth-century hands, one of which is Peter Sterry's. Contents: commonplace book, extracts from various authors, mostly classical, in translation or original, short notes and reflections, rough draft of the verse paraphrase of the Canticles which appears in I. Memorandum of books "at Chelsey Apr. 21. 1663", two short poems, two letters addressed to "Deare ff" and "Deare Scipio" respectively, the latter being a duplicate of part of a letter in I.

II. PRINTED BOOKS

(1) THE | SPIRITS | CONVICTION | OF SINNE. | OPENED | In a Sermon before the Honorable | HOUSE OF COMMONS, | Assembled in Parliament upon the solemne | day of their Monethly Fast, | *Novemb.* 26. 1645. | By PETER STERRY, sometimes Fellow | of *Emanuel Colledge* in *Cambridge.* | AND NOW | Preacher of the Gospel in LONDON. | (rule) | *Published by Order of the House of Commons* | (rule) | LONDON, | Printed by *Matth. Simmons,* for *Henry Overton,* and *Benjamin* | *Allen,* and are to be sold at their shops in | Popeshead Alley, 1645. (The whole surrounded by ornamental border.)

> 4° Sigg. A–F2 in fours. pp. (8)+36.
> Collation: (A) blank + (A)v. Order to print sermon + (A2)
> Title + (A2)v. blank + A3–(A)4v. Epistle Dedicatory +B–(F2)v. The Sermon.
> Running Title: *A Sermon Preached at the Monethly Fast, before the Honorable House of Commons.* (Between double rule.)
> (Brit. Mus. E. 310 (4).)

Entry in Stationers' Register: s.d. The First Day of January 1645 i.e. 1645/6.

(page 4)

| Master Overton and Ben Allen | Entred...by Order of the Comons' house of Parliam^t p^{r}ched at the late solemne fast called *The spiritts convincing of sinne* by Peter Sterrey.   vjd |

(A Transcript of the Registers of the Worshipful Company of Stationers 1640–1708 A.D., London, 1913, I, 209.)

(1a) Another Issue of the same with different Title Page: THE SPIRIT | CONVINCING | OF SINNE. | OPENED | In a Sermon before the HONORABLE House of | COMMONS, | Assembled in PARLIAMENT upon the Sol-|lemne day of their Monethly Fast, *Novemb.* 26. 1645. | By PETER STERRY, *sometimes Fellow* | of *Emanuel Colledge* in Cambridge | AND NOW | Preacher of the Gospel in London. | (rule) | *Published by Order of the House of Commons.* | (rule) | LONDON, | Printed by *Matth. Simmons,* for *Henry Overton* and *Benjamin* | *Allen,* and are to be sold at their shops in | Popes-head Alley, 1645. (The whole surrounded by ornamental Border.)

4° Sigg. A–H in fours. pp. (8)–36.
Collation and Running Title as in no. (1).
(Brit. Mus. 694. e. 3 (12).)

(1b) A Reprint of the same:

FOURTEEN | SERMONS | ON | VARIOUS SUBJECTS | CHIEFLY BY | CELEBRATED DIVINES OF THE SIXTEENTH CENTURY | REPRINTED, | BEING VERY SCARCE AND OF HIGH EXCELLENCE, | TO LEAD THE MIND TO | TRUTH, FAITH, AND LOVE; | THAT IS TO VITAL RELIGION | (short rule) | " Every person has a soul, a precious soul to look after; which, without know|ledge, and real and powerful know-ledge, is like to be miserable to all eter|nity; and if it be so, he will find that he himself is most to blame: he therefore | should get knowledge and preserve it, whatever it may cost him." p. 118 | (short rule) | LONDON: | SOLD BY HOLDSWORTH AND BALL, | 18, ST PAUL'S CHURCH YARD. | 1831. | J. Haddon. Printer   Castle Street Finsbury.

12° Sigg. A–S 4 in twelves. pp. xvi + 392.
Collation: (A) blank–(A) v. Notice concerning publication +
   (A 2) Title + (A 2) v. blank + A 3, A 4, Contents + (A 5)–(A 8)
   To the Reader. (Preface unsigned, dated Southampton,
   1831.) + B–S 4 v. The Sermons.
No running title. Page numbers in top centre of pages.
   Sterry's Sermon, *The Spirit Convincing of Sinn,* the fourteenth
   and last of the Collection occupying pp. 363–392. The
   Original Dedication is given in a footnote on pp. 363–365.
   (Brit. Mus. 4461. b. 33.)

(2) THE | CLOUDS | IN WHICH | CHRIST COMES. | OPENED | In a Sermon before the Honourable | House of COMMONS, assembled | in Parliament, upon the Solemne Day of their | Monthly Fast,

Octob. 27. 1647. | (rule) | By Peter Sterry, *Sometimes Fellow* | *of* Emanuel Colledge *in* Cambridge: | AND | Now Preacher of the Gospel in LONDON. | (rule) | *Published by Order of that House* | (double rule) | LONDON, | Printed for R. *Dawlman,* and are to be sold at the signe of | the Crowne and Bible at *Dowgate,* neere | *Canning-street.* 1648.

4° Sigg. A–H4 in fours. Pp. (8)+56.

Collation: (A) Title + (A) v. Order to print sermon+A 2–(A 4) Epistle Dedicatory+(A 4) v. Errata+B–(H 4) v. The Sermon.

Running Title: *A Sermon preached at a Late Fast &c Before the Honourable House of Commons.* (Between double rule.)

(Brit. Mus. E. 411 (27).)

Entry in Stationers' Register: s.d. The 30th of December, 1647.

(Page 111)

Master Dawlman	Entred…by order of the house of Comons, Two sermons (vizt) one called, *the cloud in wch Christ comes* &c, being a fast sermon preached the 27th of October last; the other called, *England saved,* &c preached the 5th of November last both of them by Phillip Sterrey… xijd

(A Transcript etc. I, 283.)

The Sermon called *England Saved* seems to have been printed, as under the date of 18th October, 1659, it appears in a list of printed sermons "entred…by vertue of an assignment or Bill of Sale, under ye hand and seal of Richard Dawlman Esqre admi. of the goods & chattels of his late Father."

(A Transcript etc. II, 239, 240.)

(2a) A Reprint of the same:

The Porch. | ISSUED EVERY TWO MONTHS | (rule) | No. 3 Vol. II November, 1914 | (rule) | Contents: THE CLOUDS IN WHICH CHRIST COMES | OPENED | In a SERMON before the Honourable House | of Commons upon the Solemne Day of their | Monthly Fast, October 27, 1647. | By PETER STERRY | (rule) | Single Copies 6d. net. post free 7d. | Annual Subscription 3/6 post free. | (short rule) | Issued from the Scriptorium, at 21, Cecil Court, Charing Cross Road, London, W.C. | where Books are to be bought and sold.

8° Sigg. A–D4 in eights. pp. 54.

Collation: Title on paper cover + Advertisements on verso

of cover + (A 1) Reprint of original title page +(A 1)v.
blank + (A 2)–(D 3)v. The Sermon + (D 4) blank + back
cover with advts. on recto and verso.
(Brit. Mus. PP. 636. Cig.)

(3) THE TEACHINGS | OF | CHRIST IN THE SOULE | OPENED In a
SERMON before the Right Honble | House of PEERS, in Covent-
garden-|Church upon the Solemne Day of their Monthly Fast,
March 29, 1648. | (rule) | By PETER STERRY, M.A. Sometimes |
Fellow of Emmanuel Colledge in Cambridge: | AND | Now Preacher
of the Gospel in LONDON. | (rule) | Published by Order of that
House | (rule) | (ornament) | (rule) | LONDON, | Printed for
R. Dawlman, and are to be sold at the signe of | the Crowne and
Bible at Dowgate, neer | Canning-street. 1648.

4° Sigg. A–H 3 in fours. pp. (8)–54.
Collation: (A) Title + (A) v. blank + (A 2) blank + (A 2) v. Order
to print sermon + A 3, A 4 Epistle Dedicatory +B–H 3 v. The
Sermon.
Running Title: A Sermon preached at the monthly Fast, Before
the Right Honourable House of Lords. (Between double
rule.)
(Brit. Mus. E. 433 (30).)

(4) THE | COMMINGS FORTH OF CHRIST | In the Power of his
Death. | OPENED | In a Sermon Preached before the | High Court
of Parliament, on Thursday the first | of Novemb. 1649. being a
publike Thanksgiving | for the Victories obtained by the Parlia-
ments Forces | in IRELAND, especially for the taking of Droghedah,
since which Wexford also was taken. | (rule) | By PETER STERRY,
Sometimes Fellow | of Emanuel Colledge: | AND | Now Preacher of
the Gospel in London. | (rule) | LONDON, Printed by Charles
Sumptner, for Thomas Brewster, and Gregory Moule, and are to be
sold at the three Bibles | in the Poultrey, under Mildreds Church.
1650.

(The whole surrounded by double rule.)
4° Sigg. A, a, aa, B–H 2 in fours. pp. (24)+51.
Collation: (A) blank + (A) v. Order to print Sermon + (A 2)
Title–(A 2) v. blank–A 3, (A 4), a, a 2, a 3, (a 4), aa, aa 2, aa 3,
(aa 4) Epistle Dedicatory + B–(H 2) The Sermon + (H 2) v.
Errata.
Running Title: A Sermon preached before the High Court of
Parliament. (Between double rule.)
(Brit. Mus. 4461. cc. 2.)

(5) *ENGLAND'S* | DELIVERANCE | From the | Northern Presbytery, | COMPARED With its Deliverance from the Roman Papacy: | OR A Thanksgiving SERMON | PREACHED | On Nov. 5. 1651 at St *Margarets Westminster,* | Before the *Supreme* Authority of this Nation, | The High Court of PARLIAMENT. | (rule) | By PETER STERRY, once Fellow | of *Emmanuel* Colledg in *Cambridg,* now Preacher | to the Right Honble the Councel of State, sitting at WHITE-HALL. | (rule) | LONDON | Printed by *Peter Cole,* and are to be sold at signe of the | *Printing Presse* neer the Royal Exchange. 1652.

> (The whole surrounded by ornamental border.)
> 4° Sigg. A–G4 in fours. pp. (8)–46–(2).
> Collation: (A) blank + (A)v. Order to Print Sermon + (A3) Title–(A3)v. blank + (A4), (A5) Epistle Dedicatory + B– (G3)v. The Sermon + (G4) Advt. of Books Printed for Peter Cole etc.
> Running Title: *A Thanksgiving* Sermon *Preached before the Parliement,* Nov. 5. 1651. (Between double rule.)
> > (Brit. Mus. E. 4645 (2).)

Entry in Stationers' Register: s.d. 20th of January 1651. (Page 232)
Peter Cole Entred...by authority of Par^t, a *sermon preached at Margarets, Westminster, Nov. 5th 1651. Englands deliverance from the Northern Presbytery, compared with its deliverance from the Roman Papacy: By* Peter Perry... vjd
> (A Transcript etc. 1, 389.)

(5 a) Another Issue of the same:

ENGLAND'S | DELIVERANCE | From the | Northern Presbytery | compared with its Deliverance from the | Roman Papacy: | (rule) | By PETER STERRY, | Once Fellow of Emmanuel Colledge in | Cambridge, now Preacher to the | Right Honorable Councell of State, sitting at WHITE-HALL. | (rule) (ornament) | Printed at Leith by Evan Tyler, 1652. (The whole surrounded by ornamental border.)

> 4° Sigg. A–F3 in fours. pp. (8) + 46.
> Collation (A) Blank + (A2) Title–A3, (A4) Epistle Dedicatory + B–F3 v. The Sermon.
> No running Title. Page numbers in brackets in top centre of pages.
> > (Cambridge University Library, Syn. 7. 45.)

(6) THE NAKED WOMAN, | OR A RARE EPISTLE | SENT TO | Mr. PETER STERRY | Minister at WHITEHALL; | Desiring him to shew the Causes or Reasons | of his silence, in that he neither by his Ministerial, | Office, charged the Magistrates that were present to redresse, nor so much as shewd any signe of grief or | detestation, as became a sincere Christian; | Against that most strange and shamefull late Act of an | impudent woman, in the midst of his sermon on a | Lords day at Whitehall Chapell concerning the Resur|rection, before the chief States of this Nation. | A satisfactory Answer he returned; which with a loving accep|tation thereof, are here also printed; very worthy the observation | of all both sexes and degrees of People in these Nations. | (rule) | Prov. 7, 25, 26, 27. *Let not thine heart decline unto her wayes, go not forth astray in her paths, for | she hath cast down many wounded, yea many strong men have been | slain by her :: her house is the way to Hell, going down to the chambers of death.* | (rule) | LONDON | Printed for E. *Blackmore*, at the Angel in *Pauls* Church-yard, | 1652 (Novemb. 23 in seventeenth century MS. in Brit. Mus. copy).

    4° Sigg. A–C4 in fours. pp. (4) + 19.

    Collation: (A) Title + (A)v. blank + A2 The Prologue to the impartial Reader + A3–C2 The Epistle sd. David Brown + C2v., C3 The Answer sd. Peter Sterry + C3v., (C4) The Epilogue sd. David Brown.

    No running Title. Page numbers in brackets in top centre of pages.

(Brit. Mus. E. 681. 20.)

(7) THE | WAY of GOD | WITH HIS | PEOPLE | IN THESE | NATIONS. | *Opened in* | A Thanksgiving Sermon, preached | on the 5ᵗʰ of *November*, 1656. be-|fore the Right Honorable, the | High Court of Parliament. | (rule) | By PETER STERRY. | (rule) | LONDON: | Printed by *Peter Cole*, Book-seller and Printer; and are to | be sold at his Shop at the sign of the Printing Press in | Cornhil, neer the Royal Exchange. 1657. (The whole surrounded by ornamental border.)

    4° Sigg. C–I2 in fours. pp. (6) + 49 + (2).

    Collation: Three unsigned leaves, the first with advts. of several Books Printed by Peter Cole etc. on recto and verso, the second with Title on recto, and verso blank, the third with Epistle Dedicatory on recto and Order to print Sermon on verso + C–I The Sermon + I1v., (I2) list of Books printed by Peter Cole.

Running Title: *A Sermon preached before the Right Honorable House of* Parliament, *on* November 5; 1656. (Between double rule.)

(Copy belonging to Sir Wasey Sterry.)

(8) THE | TRUE WAY | Of Uniting the | People of God | In These | NATIONS. | Opened in a Sermon Preached in | the Chappel at White-Hall, | *Jan.* 1. 1659. | (rule) | *By* PETER STERRY. | (rule) | LONDON: | Printed by *Peter Cole,* | Printer and Book-seller, at the | sign of the Printing-press in Cornhill neer the | Royal Exchange. 1660. (The whole surrounded by double rule.)

4° Sigg. B–F3 in fours. pp. (6) + 27 + (3).

Collation: Unsigned leaf with Title on recto and verso blank + B–B2 To the Christian Reader + C–(F2) The Sermon + (F2)v., (F3) list of Books printed for Peter Cole, etc.

Running Title: *A Sermon Preached in* White-Hall *Chappel, On the Lords day in the After noon* Jan. 1. 1659. (Between double rule.)

(Copy belonging to Sir Wasey Sterry.)

(9) A | DISCOURSE OF THE FREEDOM | OF THE WILL. | (rule) | By PETER STERRY, | Sometimes Fellow of *Emmanuel* Colledge in *Cambridge.* | (rule) | HEB. 13. 2. *Be not forgetful to entertain* STRANGERS: *for thereby* | *some have entertained* ANGELS *unawares.* | (rule) | LONDON: | Printed for *John Starkey,* at the *Miter* near *Temple-*|*Bar,* in *Fleetstreet.* 1675. (The whole surrounded by double rule.)

Folio. Sigg. a–d3, B–z4, Aa–Ii4 in fours. pp. (34) + 245 + (3).

Collation: Two unsigned Leaves, the first with Title on recto, and verso blank, the second with "The *Stationer* to the *Reader*" on recto and verso blank + a–d3 The Preface to the Reader + B–(s3) The Discourse Part I + (s3)v. + cc2 The Discourse Part II + cc2v.–(113) An Enlargement etc. + (113)v. blank + (114) Errata.

Running Title: *A Discourse of the Freedome of the Will.* (Between double rule.) "Part I" on the inside top corner of each page down to p. 133. "Part II" in same position from p. 134 to p. 208.

(Brit. Mus. 695. i. 7.)

Entry in Term Catalogues: s.d. *Novemb.* 25, 1674.

A Discourse of the Freedom of the Will. By Peter Sterry, some-time Fellow of *Emmanuel Colledge* in *Cambridge.* In Folio. Price bound, 10s. Printed for John Starkey at the Miter in *Fleet street*, near Temple Bar.

(Term Catalogues, ed. Arber, London 1903, I, 184.)

(9a) Another issue of the same:

A | DISCOURSE | OF THE | FREEDOM | OF THE | WILL. | (rule) | By PETER STERRY, | Sometimes Fellow of *Emanuel* Colledge in *Cambridge.* | (rule) | HEB. 13. 2. | *Be not forgetful to entertain* STRANGERS : *For thereby some have entertained ANGELS unawares.* | (rule) | LONDON : | Printed for *John Starkey*, at the *Miter* near | *Temple-Bar*, in *Fleet-street*. 1675. (The whole surrounded by double rule.)

Folio. Sigg. a–d3, B–Z, Aa–ii. pp. (32)+242.

Collation: Unsigned leaf with Title on recto and verso blank + a–d3 v. The Preface to the Reader + A–S3 The Discourse Part I + s3 v.–cc2 v. The Discourse Part II +cc2 v.–iii v.

An enlargement etc.

Running Title as in No. 9.

Differs from the foregoing in the following respects: (1) slightly different Title. (2) No Stationer's Preface. (3) No errata at the end. (4) 242 pp. of text instead of 245. Text however is the same, contents of pp. 241–245 of no. 9 being printed in small type on pp. 241 and 242 of no. 9a.

(Copy belonging to Mrs E. Poolman:

This copy contains the following inscriptions in four different hands. (1) "Sarah Gavy", (2) "Bull's Library Bath", (3) "Purchas'd by R^d Webb of Manchester Square in Novr 1805 ", (4) "R. J. Webb. Tunbridge Wells 1869."

From a label on the cover it appears that the book once formed part of Bull's circulating library, a well known institution in Bath at the end of the eighteenth century (see Madame D'Arblay's Diary, ed. Dobson, I, 243, and note). It is rather surprising to find that the Discourse must have found readers in eighteenth-century Bath.)

(10) THE | Rise, Race, and Royalty | OF THE | 𝕂ingdom of 𝔾od | IN THE | Soul of MAN. | OPENED | In several Sermons upon *Matthew* 18. 3 | AS ALSO | The Loveliness & Love of Christ | Set forth | In several other Sermons upon *Psal.* 45. *v.* 1, 2. | Together with | An Account of the State of a Saint's Soul and Body | in Death. | (rule) | By PETER STERRY, sometimes Fellow of *Emanuel*

Colledge | in *Cambridge,* and Late Preacher of the Gospel in *London.* | (rule) | Matthew 11. 19. *But Wisdom is justified of her Children.* | (rule) | LONDON, | Printed for *Thomas Cockerill,* at the Three Leggs over against the | *Stocks-Market* in the Poultry. 1683. (The whole surrounded by double rule.)

    8° Sigg. A–A 3, b–d 2, B–Z, Aa–zz, Aaa–Uuu 2 in fours. pp. (26) + 515 + (1).

    Collation: (A) Title + (A)v. blank + A2–(A 3) + b–d 2 The Publisher to the Reader sd. J. White + B–Z, Aa–Bb 2 Sermons on Matth. XVIII. 3 + Bb 2 v.–Kkk 1 v. Sermons on Psal. XLV. + Kkk 1 v.–Uuu 2 The State of a Saint's Soul and Body in Death + Uuu 2 v. Errata.

    No running Title. Page numbers in brackets at top centre of pages.

    (Brit. Mus. 4473. g. 22. Copy inscribed " Johan: Byrom T.C.C. Augt. 18. 1711 ".)

    (11) The Appearance of | GOD to MAN | In the GOSPEL, | AND THE | *GOSPEL CHANGE.* | Together with | Several other Discourses from Scripture. | To which is added an | Explication of the TRINITY; | And a Short Catechism. | (rule) | Being the Second Posthumous VOLUME. | (rule) | The Second PART will contain | Miscellany TRACTS on several Subjects, | handled Metaphysically. | To which may be added, A Paraphrase of the *Canticles* in Verse. | TOGETHER With many Excellent LETTERS to Friends. | (rule) | Taken from the Original Manuscripts, left by P. S. | Late of *Emanuel* College *Cambridge,* and Minister of | the Gospel in *London.* | (rule) | 1 Thess. 20, 21. *Despise not Prophecyings, Prove all things.* | (rule) | LONDON: Printed in the Year, 1710. (The whole surrounded by double rule.)

    8° Sigg. A–Z, Aa–zz, Aaa–ppp 4 in fours. pp. (8) + 480.

    Collation: (A) Title + (A)v. blank + A 2–(A 3) v. The Publisher to the Reader + (A 4) Contents of First Part and of the projected Second Part + (A 4)v. The same continued and Errata + B1–L 2 v. A Discourse upon 2 Cor. III. 18 + (L 3)–(cc 4) A Discourse of Prayer + (cc 4)–(Ff 3) Of Free-Grace + (Ff 4)–L 2 v. The Mission of Christ + Ll 2 v.–(ss 3) The Comforts of a Christian + (ss 3)–(xx 4)v. Directions to a Life in Heaven + yy 1–Ddd 2 The Manner of Christ's Second Coming + Ddd 2–(Ggg 4)v. Sermons on various texts + Hhh 1–(Hhh 3) Five Questions Answer'd + (Hhh 3)v. –Mmm 2 An Explication of the Trinity + Mmm 2 v.–

ooo 1 v. A Catechism in Two Parts + ooo 2–ppp 4 v. Five Letters.

No running title. Page numbers in brackets in top centre of pages.

(Brit. Mus. 4379. e. 19.)

(12) PRAYERS | SELECTED FROM THE | NEW TESTAMENT; | KEMPIS OF THE IMITATION | OF CHRIST; | DR. J. EVERARD; | WILLIAM LAW; | And, chiefly | PETER STERRY. | Printed M.DCC.LXXXV.
8º Sigg. A–B 8 in eights. pp. 31.

Collation: (A) Title–(A) v. blank + A 2–(B 8) Prayers.

No running title. Page numbers in brackets in top centre of pages.

(Brit. Mus. 3457. g. 42.)

INDEX

Abercrombie, Prof. Lascelles, xiii, 67
Abranavel, Don Judah, *see* Leone Hebreo
Achilles Tatius, 62
Acts of the Apostles, 204
Adamas, 56
Adam Kadmon, 98 n.
Addington, 58
Adonais, 95
Aeneas, 54, 77, 83, 136, 174, 205
Aeneid, 8, 77, 204, 205, 215
Aetna, 176
Agathon, 207
Alvarez, 222
Aminta, 62
Anaxagoras, 208
Anchises, 174
Anima Poetae, 70
Antipater, 213
Apollo, 214
Apollonius Rhodius, 62
Aquinas, St Thomas, *see* Thomas Aquinas, St
Areopagitica, 13, 216
Argenis, 62
Aristotle, 67, 110, 205, 207, 210, 212
Arius, 88
Arnold, Matthew, 6, 63, 68, 69, 109
Arthegall, 203, 204
Ascanius, 128
Asheworth, Mrs Frances, 11, 12; *see also* Sterry, Mrs Frances
Athanasius, 62
Athenae Oxonienses, 13 n., 14 n., 28, 38
Athenians, 128, 204
Augustine, St, 136, 205
Augustus, 151
Averroës, 88

Bacon, 57, 58, 62
Baillie, Robert, 14, 36, 38, 40
Baker MSS., 5 n. 10 n.
Baker, Thomas, 10
Barclay, 62
Barrow, Henry, 7
Bastwick, 10

Baxter, Richard, vi, 3, 16, 18, 87, 89, 221, 222
Bedford, Lord, 15
Behmen, J., *see* Böhme
Benivieni, 66
Berkhamsted, 59
Berry, Mr John, 59
Bible, The, 7, 67, 83
Bishops' War, 10
Blake, W., 5, 88, 97, 98, 208
Blyenbergh, 107 n.
Bodleian Library, 58
Boethius, 67, 217
Böhme, Jacob, 57, 58, 62, 89, 113
Bolton, Robert, 54
Bradley, F. H., 88 n., 96
Bradshaw, 40
Brettergh, Mr, 22
Bridge, 14
Bridges, Robert, 210
Britomart, 203
Brooke, Lady, 13, 15
Brooke, Lord, 11–13, 41
Brown, David, 26, 27, 231
Browne, Sir Thomas, 68, 117 n., 216
Browne, William, 73
Brutus, 53, 178, 214
Bulkely, Mr, 30
Bull's Library, 233
Bunyan, 6, 63, 108, 109
Burnet, Bishop, 5 n., 9, 35
Burroughs, 14
Burton, Robert, 83
Burton, William, 10
Bushell, Mr Edward, 59, 60
Butler, Samuel, 36
By-Ends, Mr, 63
Byrom, John, 4, 234

Calvin, 66
Calvinists, 105
Cambridge Platonists, 3, 9
Camden, 62
Campanella, Tommaso, 67, 109, 122, 203, 208, 209